Drinking in America

Drinking in America

A History

The Revised and Expanded Edition

by Mark Edward Lender
James Kirby Martin

THE FREE PRESS
A Division of Macmillan, Inc.
NEW YORK

Collier Macmillan Publishers
LONDON

The Free Press
A Division of Macmillan, Inc.
866 Third Avenue, New York, N.Y. 10022

Collier Macmillan Canada, Inc.

Printed in the United States of America

printing number

1 2 3 4 5 6 7 8 9 10

Library of Congress Cataloging-in-Publication Data

Lender, Mark E.
  Drinking in America

  Bibliography: p.
  Includes index.
  1. Alcoholism—United States—History.   I. Martin,
James Kirby   II. Title.
HV5292.L4   1987   394.1′3′0973   86–32885
ISBN 0–02–918570–X

With love,
  for Jonathan,
  David, and
  Paul Lender,
  brothers and friends

Contents

Preface to the Revised and Expanded Edition

We were very gratified by the favorable reception accorded *Drinking in America* after it first appeared in 1982, and we are very pleased to have this opportunity to present a revised, updated edition. Indeed, much has happened during the 1980s in the way of shifting American attitudes and practices relating to the use of alcohol. For the first time since the end of National Prohibition, consumption rates have taken a downward turn. In addition, a small number of well-organized lobbying groups, determined to control the many societal problems associated with alcohol, have sprung into existence. These groups have been intensely vociferous in pursuit of their objectives—and they have been effective. They have helped to mold a new public consciousness about the consequences of abusing alcohol in our highly complex society. Countless Americans have supported their programs, yet others have begun to wonder whether we are entering a new era of repression, perhaps pointing toward something so extreme as a return to National Prohibition.

One purpose of this updated edition, besides making minor revisions in the first four chapters (taking the story through prohibition), has been to incorporate information about these most recent trends and groups into our narrative. Thus our readers will find new materials in Chapter Five, which investigates the theme of the ambivalence that Americans have felt toward beverage alcohol in modern times. It is our conviction that recent patterns, whether viewed as a "neotemperance" crusade, as "neoinhibitionism," or as something less extreme, may best be appreciated in historical perspective. And it remains our hope that *Drinking in America* offers that kind of meaningful context.

We are indebted to scholars and friends alike who have made many suggestions for improving the book. Besides again thanking those who were so helpful with the first edition (as listed in the original preface), we would like to acknowledge the special assistance of historian Robert S. Bader. Joyce Seltzer of The Free Press has been a special friend of this study and has provided invaluable guidance and aid, as have our families. And as before, we alone remain responsible for factual or interpretive errors.

Mark Edward Lender
Kean College

James Kirby Martin
University of Houston

Preface to the First Edition

There has always been drinking in America. From the earliest days of colonial settlement to the present, Americans have incorporated beverage alcohol—in one form or another—into their daily lives. At different periods, they have allowed their attitudes toward alcohol to become the basis of heated social and political debates. Yet historians have seldom addressed drinking in depth, and in trying to understand the subject within the broader setting of the national experience, students have faced at least two serious difficulties. First, many studies of drinking have tended toward the antiquarian, giving us only glimpses of alcohol use in local settings or limited periods. Other works—usually not by historians—simply have ransacked history, pulling out isolated alcohol-related phenomena to explain or compare to aspects of modern alcohol problems. Second, even studies that have looked at drinking in more than cursory fashion all too often have fallen into the prohibition trap. That is, the story of the temperance movement, and its related controversies, usually has overshadowed the history of drinking itself whenever an author has tried to deal with both in the same inquiry. In either case, alcohol use, and its relationships with other facets of society, generally have not been treated in any interpretive framework, and we have been left to reintegrate the history of drinking behavior into the mainstream of social history as best we can.

In the 1970s, however, a number of authors—historians and sociologists mostly, but others as well—offered a variety of new perspectives on American drinking. In general, recent treatments have focused on drinking behavior either as a reflection of other aspects of the sociocultural process or as a contributing factor in the formation of a broad range of popular attitudes on the nature of the social order. These investigations have only begun the process of relating drinking—at least in any detailed and interpretive way—to the central flow of historical writing, but they have already produced some informative and even novel conclusions.

What we have done in *Drinking in America* is to bring original research together with the best of the new historical and social science investigations and to put forth our own interpretation of what drinking (or, for that matter, *not* drinking) has meant to passing generations of Americans. It has meant quite a bit: Drinking behavior and popular reactions to it have both mirrored and shaped national responses to any number of social issues. The temperance crusade, in particular, was more of a functional social response to alcohol use and some of its related activities than most historians have allowed. And the ideas that defined the specific nature of the response stemmed directly from the republican ideology of the American Revolutionary period. Thus, from the very birth of the republic, drinking has been measured against an extremely exacting standard of personal and social conduct—a circumstance with profound implications for the next two centuries of the American experience.

The focus on republicanism—and its legacy over the years—makes our interpretation secular. This, too, is something of a departure from historical tradition, especially when we consider the temperance response to drinking-related problems. Most studies have emphasized either the evangelical or the conservative religious roots of the dry crusade. And while we have no quarrel with this (by now, well-documented) view, we think that the secular origins of the liquor question warrant further exploration. *Drinking in America* is intended as a step in that direction.

A note is in order on illustrations. This volume includes 55 pictures, many of which are reprinted here for the first time. These reprints represent an integral part of the narrative. Points raised in the text are frequently amplified in the captions and by the illustrations themselves. Indeed, it is difficult to understand the activities of the liquor industry or the temperance movement without reference to graphic materials. We wish to thank the following both for their help in assembling the illustrations and for permission to publish them in this book: the *Journal of Studies on Alcohol,* the Rutgers University Center of Alcohol Studies, the Library of Congress, the National Archives, and the Woman's Christian Temperance Union. Other picture sources are credited in the text.

In our efforts to produce this history of drinking in America, we have enjoyed invaluable and generous help from many friends and colleagues. Professor Leonard U. Blumberg of Temple University read the initial manuscript with particular care. He saved us from many a slip and offered critical suggestions that greatly improved the text. Professors Suzanne Lebsock and Gerald Grob, both at Douglass College, Rutgers University, and David Musto, at Yale University, also read drafts and provided helpful advice. Their combined perspectives on women's history, nineteenth- and twentieth-century reform, and the history of medicine were invaluable. Jill Schumann, a predoctoral fellow at the Rutgers Center of Alcohol Studies, prevented some serious errors in our discussion of American Indians. Karen Stubaus, who is now completing a comparative study of drinking law and practice in seventeenth-century Massachusetts and Virginia, read the manuscript as well — and kindly allowed us to use some of her research findings on early Virginia. Tim Coffey, former editor of the *Journal of Studies on Alcohol,* Professor Gail Gleason Milgram, and Penny Page, all of the Rutgers Center of Alcohol Studies, always offered helpful advice. Jane Armstrong, librarian at the center, not only assisted us regularly but also suffered gracefully as two historians pillaged her otherwise tightly run library. When Penny Page took over in the library, she gave us the same generous aid. Carol Miller, Gail Heseltine, Rose Ullrich, Dot Kelleher, Anne Smith, Sujini Murthy, Mary Louise Grzes, and Mary Kapuscienski typed portions of the manuscript, for which we are grateful. Lucille Hynda, business manager at the center, greatly facilitated travel and research arrangements. We owe much to all these people, and they have our thanks. At the same time, we keep for ourselves all blame for any errors in fact or interpretation.

Mark Edward Lender
Kean College

James Kirby Martin
University of Houston

List of Illustrations

Chapter 1

Holiday drinking in New Amsterdam

Concern of nineteenth-century temperance advocates with the drinking habits of the Founding Fathers

The Old Tun Tavern, Philadelphia

"Black drink," an emetic of local ingredients, used by some Indian tribes of eastern North America

The maypole, liquor, and Indians

The slave trade, as depicted in a nineteenth-century print

Benjamin Rush (1745/46–1813), temperance advocate

Rush's "Moral and Physical Thermometer" of Temperance and Intemperance

Chapter 2

Neal Dow (1804–1897), the "Father of the Maine Law"

Twentieth-century stereotype of the "drunken Indian"

The County Election, by George Caleb Bingham (1851–1852), showing drinking as a part of the electoral procedure

The inauguration gala of Andrew Jackson, 1829

The "log cabin campaign," 1840

An antebellum brewery and beer garden in Fort Wayne, Indiana

Attention-getting Pennsylvania advertisement showing innovations in cider mills; "apple bees," popular autumnal get-togethers

The Drunkard's Progress from the First Glass to the Grave, by N. Currier (1846)

A Sons of Temperance membership certificate

A scene from an early edition of Timothy Shay Arthur's *Ten Nights In a Bar-Room*

The sixth in a series of eight prints, *The Bottle*, by George Cruikshank (1847)

Drinking in America

CHAPTER ONE

The "Good Creature of God": Drinking in Early America

---

*Drink is in itself a good creature of God,
and to be received with thankfulness,
but the abuse of drink is from Satan,
the wine is from God, but the Drunkard
is from the Devil.*

—Increase Mather,
Wo to Drunkards (1673)

Plymouth, 1621

The coast of Massachusetts can be bitterly cold in February, and so it was in February 1621. The scene was bleak and forbidding. Back from the water's edge a few half-finished structures, the foundations of the Pilgrim colony of Plymouth, endured the lashings of wind and rain; offshore, the lonely *Mayflower* tossed at its anchor on a frigid ocean. It was not a happy ship. Some of the colonists lived aboard while work parties toiled ashore to erect permanent shelter, and life on the crowded decks had become unbearable. A raging "General Sickness"— no doubt a combination of exposure, scurvy, pneumonia, and other maladies—made death a common occurrence. To make matters worse, passengers and crew were almost out of beer. In fact, the Pilgrims had tasted the last of their own beer the previous December; since then, only the generosity of the *Mayflower's* captain had allowed them an occasional sample of the crew's stores. But now that supply was perilously low, and a crisis seemed inevitable.

Even in the midst of their other difficulties, no one took the beer situation lightly. It was an age that considered alcohol safer than water, and the souls on the *Mayflower* were not the last to face a liquor shortage with trepidation. Water had a bad reputation in seventeenth-century Europe, where much of it was polluted, and many colonists expected a similar situation in America. There was genuine surprise upon finding the stuff potable. Besides, the wisdom of the day held that alcohol was essential for good health: A stiff drink warmed a person on cold nights and kept off chills and fevers; a few glasses made hard work easier to bear, aided digestion, and in general helped sustain the constitution. Abstinence invited trouble, and some people considered nondrinkers "crank-brained." There was also a practical consideration: Liquor kept well at sea, whereas water fouled in its wooden barrels. This was an important point for colonials, who both mistrusted water and could not anticipate a quick resupply of alcohol from Europe.

Like the Pilgrims, then, other settlers also brought generous supplies of liquor with them. The *Arbella*, which carried the Puritans to Boston in 1630, set sail with three times as much beer as water, along with ten thousand gallons of wine. Most settlers also brought along a ration of distilled spirits, which kept even longer than beer. So liquor was more than a luxury in the colonial mind; it was a necessity to be kept close at hand.

The *Mayflower*'s crew belonged to this tradition. Moreover, the sailors knew that if they continued to share their meager beer supplies with this band of religious dissenters, there would probably be no alcohol left for the voyage home. They were not prepared to take that risk, and matters came to a head. William Bradford, the faithful diarist of Plymouth and for years its able governor, recorded the scene. The settlers "were hasted ashore and made to drink water," he lamented, "that the seamen might have the more beer." Bradford's pleas from the shore for just a "can" of beer brought refusal. If he "were their own father," one sailor responded, "he should have none." It was an inauspicious beginning to the new venture. (Most versions of the Pilgrim story pass over the beer crisis in favor of the traditional tales of Plymouth Rock and the first Thanksgiving. The modern brewing industry has overlooked an advertising bonanza.) The suffering on the beach finally became too much for the *Mayflower*'s captain; he sent word that there would be "beer for them that had need for it," particularly the sick, even if it meant his drinking water on the way back to England. His humanitarian gesture assured the Pilgrims that as they faced the "starving time" of Plymouth's first winter, they would have an occasional taste of the Old World.

But the basic problem remained. The last major source of beer disappeared with the *Mayflower*, and over the rest of the winter alcohol became scarce indeed—nonexistent for many. There was a small supply of gin and other spirits, but not enough to go around, and most of the settlers quickly learned to drink water. The logic that dictated liquor rations aboard ship, however, remained compelling in Pilgrim eyes and prompted efforts to secure a reliable flow of alcohol for Plymouth. This real concern ultimately was shared by all the early colonists.

It was clear from the start that the only sure solution lay in local production. Relying exclusively on imports was impractical on a number of counts. England was a long way off, and in the early colonial period contacts with home were irregular at best. Shipping costs were also high, a problem compounded as second- and third-generation settlers moved inland, away from the coastal ports. Besides, the colonial population—even that of tiny Plymouth—quickly grew too large to supply through ordinary shipping channels. In the early 1620s there were only two or three thousand people scattered throughout Virginia and New England. With the Great Migration of the 1630s and forties, the American population rapidly climbed upward (as many as seventy thousand people left England for the New World; many went to the

West Indian islands). There were enough settlers to found all the original English North American colonies, with the exception of Georgia, by the 1670s; by 1700 America boasted nearly 250,000 native-born colonists and immigrants (including the residents of New Netherland and New Sweden, which settlements the English had by then absorbed). In the thirteen colonies that revolted, the population had soared to 2.5 million by 1775. Farther north, there were several thousand French in Canada (which Britain would annex in 1763 after the French and Indian War). So while European liquor was a frequent export to the New World, there was never enough shipped to satisfy burgeoning colonial demand—which in turn meant that if the settlers insisted on drinking something more salubrious than water, they were going to have to produce most of it themselves.

And they did. Initially duplicating traditional European beverages, the early colonists ultimately introduced a host of new drinks using American ingredients and methods. Equally important, they also developed a range of drinking patterns and attitudes to match, all of which reflected the environment and resources of their New World homes. This took time, of course, and new habits emerged in different places on different schedules. Yet they did emerge—and over the years between the founding of Plymouth and the close of the eighteenth century, the colonists integrated alcohol into their evolving American culture in ways that were distinctively their own. In fact, this formative period saw what amounted to the Americanization of European drinking practices.

Bad Beer and "Hot Waters": The First American Beverages

In the early settlements, colonial tastes generally mirrored those back home in Europe. Beverage preferences were as much a part of the immigrants' cultural baggage as were their styles of dress, architecture, and art. Thus, the English provinces that ultimately dominated eastern North America imported the traditional homeland affection for beer. From a strictly practical standpoint, this was a touch irrational. If the colonials wanted alcohol for health reasons, beer was the least convenient drink to ship: It spoiled faster than gin or brandy and had a considerably lower alcohol content. But in matters close to the heart, rationality has more than once given way to sentiment and tradition, and so it was with beer. Englishmen—which the new Americans fully considered themselves until the Revolution—dearly loved their beer. By the time the *Mayflower* sailed, the most popular brew was a dark, hearty drink, about 6 percent alcohol, that was made from barley malt and flavored with hops (this potion evolved into modern porter and stout). The beers carried to America, then, were hardly similar to the pale brews preferred in the United States today, but they were the most popular beverages in the colonies in the years following the arrival of the first settlers.

Local brewing began almost as soon as the colonists were safely ashore. Colonial wives incorporated brewing into their household routines, and beer became a dietary staple. "Common brewers," who sold wholesale and retail, appeared in short order as well, and many tavern owners also produced their own supplies. In addition, the evolution of commercial ties with the Old World generally made some imported beer available to those who could afford it. But while it was soon apparent that nobody was going to die of thirst, quality control was a persistent problem. Although brewers used traditional ingredients when they could, hops and malt from the parent state were not always available, especially inland. Accordingly, the provincials used whatever domestic substitutes they had on hand to fill the gap, even if this meant doing considerable violence to English recipes. A verse from the 1630s applauded this early ingenuity:

> If barley be wanting to make into malt,
> We must be content and think it no fault,
> For we can make liquor to sweeten our lips,
> Of pumpkins, and parsnips, and walnut-tree chips.

One suspects that the beers produced from such recipes were little better than the poetry. Certainly, however, the new American beer rapidly became a highly diverse creature. Tastes varied sufficiently to provoke an official response by the mid-1600s, as local governments, concerned over uniform quality, stepped in more than once to regulate the ingredients of commercial brews. Most beer, however, was made at home, and no government could dictate a housewife's recipe.

Nor did official scrutiny discourage some truly searching experiments to replicate the original English product. In 1662, for instance, John Winthrop, Jr., governor of Connecticut and son of Governor John Winthrop of Massachusetts, brewed a palatable beer from Indian corn. This novel contribution ultimately got the younger Winthrop elected to the Royal Society of London—perhaps the highest honor the age could bestow on those who advanced the frontiers of science. Much later, Thomas Jefferson did a bit of brewing at Monticello, and Benjamin Franklin employed his famous ingenuity to come up with a passable spruce beer. At Mount Vernon, George Washington drank a molasses based home brew. As the frontier line of settlement advanced in the seventeenth and eighteenth centuries, there were doubtless unsung practitioners of the brewer's art whose various concoctions have not come down to posterity. At any rate, the colonists expended real effort in order to satisfy their preferences for a beverage with a hint of Old World flavor.

But if brewing got off to a healthy start in the colonies, beer did not retain the popularity it continued to enjoy in England. While colonial attempts to replicate English beer demonstrated something of the power of tradition, exact reproductions of the old tastes were not the rule, and local substitutes were often of uneven consistency. This by no means killed loyalties to malt liquors, but it did leave considerable room for the emergence of other products. Most of these also had roots in England.

Wine had a certain popularity. Shakespeare's Falstaff had reveled in "sack" — sherry — and the emerging colonial gentry of the eighteenth century shared his appreciation. Other European wines had some popularity as well, but they were almost exclusively a delight of the well-to-do: For unlike the Spanish and French, who planted vines in their New World possessions, the English had no early viticulture to speak of, and the wines served in New England and Virginian homes were imported at considerable expense. It was not that vines would not grow — New York and other Eastern states produce some fine wines today — but most Anglo-Americans were too busy drinking beer to make a large domestic wine industry pay. In Virginia a promising attempt to establish vineyards quickly ended when the growers, a group of French Huguenots, found a greater demand for tobacco and tore out their vines. So wine never seriously challenged colonial beer, certainly not among the masses.

Hard liquor was a different matter. The most prevalent form of spirits in the first settlements was "aqua vitae," a general term for distilled beverages, but which usually meant brandy. Popular throughout Europe, the colonists valued it for its high alcohol content, which enabled it to keep longer than beer. The same was true of "strong" or "hot waters" — grain whiskeys and other distilled drinks (although at times these terms were apparently used interchangeably with aqua vitae).

From the beginning, distilled spirits were potent enough to raise concerns over misuse. Aboard the *Arbella* Puritan elders noted that some of the youth were prone "to drink hot waters very immoderately." But spirits had real advantages in the colonial view. Those who moved inland, for example, could carry a potent beverage with relative efficiency; one cask of hard liquor could have as much absolute alcohol as ten casks of beer and would keep as long as the travelers refrained from drinking it up. The premium placed on distilled beverages also allowed them to be used as wages in the early years. In fact, when the town fathers of Boston moved to halt the practice in the 1640s — it seemed to them that workers became somewhat less productive after a few sips of their "wages" — one group of laborers responded with what may have been America's first strike. The authorities backed down and restored their liquor. So while strong drink was not as popular as beer in the first decades of American settlement, many colonists liked it better than did their Old World brethren.

Some of this so-called strong water was probably gin, which, like beer, had deep roots in English culture. Unlike beer, however, gin had a dubious reputation. Introduced in the 1530s by soldiers returning to England from the Low Countries, gin — grain spirits flavored with the juniper berry — was produced cheaply and easily and became highly popular among the urban poor (a profitable mass market for distillers, who could sell gin at prices lower than those of good beer). Gin drinking grew to an alarming extent and, in the view of many Englishmen, was thoroughly out of control by the 1730s. The "gin epidemic" ravaged the poorer districts at least until 1751, when a vexed government stepped in and placed controls on sales. By then, however, the problem, immortalized in Hogarth's *Beer Street–Gin Lane* series of prints, had caught the public imagination. Gin itself was never again wholly respectable with the middle and upper classes. The drink retained a number of faithful imbibers throughout England, but it never caught on in the colonies: The early colonists drank some, and so did the Dutch in New Amsterdam and elsewhere, but seventeenth-century America lacked a large urban population, the traditional stronghold of gin. (This spirit remained a relative pariah until the twentieth century, when combined with vermouth and optional olives or onions it came into its own as the martini.)

As the colonists turned to distilling hard liquor, they proved as adaptable as they had been in their search for beer. In fact, it was technically easier to use local ingredients — grains or fruits — in producing

Holiday drinking in the Dutch colonial town of New Amsterdam (New York) in the mid-1600s.

quality spirits than it was in getting a consistently good beer. In addition to making home brew, many colonial households began to operate backyard stills called "limbecs." This not only assured a supply of distilled liquors but also generally diffused the skills necessary in production. And as the colonials started to standardize their distilling operations and to introduce their own beverages, a preference for hard liquor developed.

The movement toward strong waters in domestic production was evident by the late 1600s, as witnessed in the rise of respectable regional liquors, some of which later became popular throughout much of North America. In New England, pears emerged from the vat as "perry," while settlers in the territory that ultimately became Vermont distilled honey into a mead so good, as local tradition had it, that drinkers could hear the buzzing of the bees (indeed, after a quart or so one could probably hear all sorts of buzzing). In the Back Country, which ran down the eastern slopes of the Appalachians from New England to Georgia, grains like corn and rye (as well as potatoes and berries) offered a "buzz" of their own (these grain liquors assumed a central role in shaping American drinking patterns in the eighteenth century — a story to which we will return).

Even the apple provided a major impetus in distilling. The fruit was not native to North America, but European seeds did well in the hospitable climate, and orchards flourished. Hard cider, naturally fermented to about 7 percent alcohol content, became especially popular in the Northern provinces (although Tennessee took a liking to it later on as well), where the drink ultimately rivaled beer in popularity. By the early 1700s, and probably before, Anglo-Americans were distilling their cider into a potent applejack. Applejack found a particularly loyal following in the Middle Atlantic colonies, and the best came from New Jersey. "Jersey Lightning" was stuff fit for the serious drinker: Too much could bring on "apple palsey," although one aged connoisseur recalled that he downed a quart a day over the years "without the slightest inconvenience."

In the South, particularly in Virginia and Georgia, the peach — introduced into Florida by the Spanish and spreading north over the decades — also became a distilling staple. Peach brandies emerged as great favorites, and a bit of this popularity still lingers.

"Wo to Drunkards": Early Use and Abuse

All these drinks had their partisans, and drinking constituted a central facet of colonial life. Indeed, two of the key characteristics of early drinking patterns were frequency and quantity. Simply stated, most settlers drank often and abundantly.

Most colonial drinking was utilitarian, with high alcohol consumption a normal part of personal and community habits. In colonial homes, beer and cider were the usual beverages at mealtime. In fact, alcohol was more common at the family table in the colonial era than in our own; even children shared the dinner beer. This practice of taking beer or cider at dinner made steady drinkers of most Americans, a pattern reinforced by activities outside the home. In New England, communal projects such as clearing the common fields or raising the town church seldom proceeded without a public cask of spirits to fortify the toiling citizenry. Private labor also called for a steady pull at the jug. Farmers typically took a generous liquor ration into the fields each morning, and if the farmer hired help, particularly at harvest, the practice of drinking on the job expanded. Employers in the seventeenth and eighteenth centuries regularly provided their hands with a (sometimes goodly) supply of libations, and over the years liquor remained an accustomed part of labor relations on the farm. (Later on, as New England and the Middle Atlantic states began to industrialize, liquor rations often entered the shops and factories.) While encouraging alcohol on the job seems more than a little foolhardy by modern standards, there was a clear rationale: Labor both on the farms and in the towns was back-breaking, and timely jolts of beer, cider, or spirits helped deaden the pain. And even if someone drank too much on occasion, safety or productivity was seldom jeopardized as seriously as would be the case in today's more interdependent workplace. At any rate, it is clear that normal daily alcohol use involved frequent drinking—and fairly heavy drinking as well for many colonials.

Drinking became institutionalized in other spheres, too. Both the Anglican and the Puritan church, for example, used communion wine. (The notion that Christ had broken bread with unfermented grape juice was a bit of nineteenth-century theological tinkering.) Some New England towns held "ordinaries," weekly community gatherings with compulsory attendance. The citizenry prayed, ate, drank, and caught up on local affairs; absentees were assessed a fine to be paid in liquor, donated to the common table the following week. In the South, politics and drink combined to give the regional vocabulary a new verb, "to treat." One did not seek office at any level without "treating" the electorate during the campaign—that is, without providing all and sundry with generous libations. Polling places themselves were rarely dry: There was only one poll per county and after making the long trek to do his citizen's duty, the voter expected some tangible reward. He usually got it. This meant that in order to qualify as a Founding Father, George Washington, John Marshall, Thomas Jefferson, and other Revolutionary leaders must have provided many a drink for the multitude.

Weddings, baptisms, holiday celebrations, ministerial ordinations, militia musters, and even funerals also were normally wet. In 1678, at the funeral of Mary Norton, wife of one of Puritan Boston's most celebrated clergymen, those who came to pay their last respects downed over fifty gallons of expensive wine. A few years later, the mourners at a minister's funeral in Ipswich, Massachusetts, enjoyed a full barrel of wine and two of cider. Daniel Dorchester, the great temperance historian of the late nineteenth century, took a dim view of such customs. "You may easily judge the drunkenness and riot," he noted soberly, "on occasions less solemn than the funerals of old and beloved ministers" — like ordinations, for instance. After Thomas Shepard was ordained

The drinking habits of the Founding Fathers attracted the attention of nineteenth-century temperance advocates, a concern demonstrated in these Currier and Ives prints. In the first engraving, from 1848, Washington bids farewell to his officers over a toast; a supply of liquor rests on the table. A reengraved version from 1876 reflects the influence of the temperance movement: A hat now graces the table and Washington no longer clasps a glass.

head of the church at Newtowne, Massachusetts, the celebration that followed would have made Dorchester cringe. Attended by local parishioners and civil and clerical dignitaries, the celebrants feasted for hours on course after course of food; while, as Samuel Eliot Morison described the scene, "the special brew of 'ordination beer' passed about freely in leather jacks, while the clergy and gentry put away choice Canary sack. Then a farewell was said to the guests, some of whom may have mounted their horses a bit unsteadily." Shepard's affair was not unusual, as similar scenes were fairly common at other church-related functions. Even before the 1650s, Virginia was obligated to reprimand a number of local ministers for "drunkenness and riotous conduct."

Liquor often had a hand in reducing militia drills to something less than demonstrations of martial prowess. While militia training—particularly in times of Indian or foreign conflict—was crucial, many training sessions were little more than social gatherings, with liquor a central aspect. An eighteenth-century Virginia militia commander recalled that "for several years" he frequently gave his men alcohol and that afterward "they would . . . come before his door and fire guns in token of their gratitude, and then he would give them punch 'til they dispersed." Crack regiments were not built in this fashion—but in this case at least muster-day morale was high. An entire sober drill was remarkable, and when Governor John Winthrop of Massachusetts saw one on Boston Common he was especially pleased.

Funerals, ordinations, and militia musters, however, did not fill the social calendar, and most drinking outside the home or work environment went on in taverns. Taverns, generally among the first structures erected in colonial communities, took root quickly in America. In Boston, there were only a few licensed establishments in the 1630s, but there were dozens by the 1680s. And judging from colonial records, Boston was typical: All the major population centers had numerous taverns, and smaller towns commonly had two or more. Indeed, concern for the accommodation of travelers was such in New England that if any village lacked an inn, authorities could direct the locality to see that one opened in the near future. Unlicensed establishments also flourished in many areas—including Puritan New England—drawing the attention of the law only if they became centers of more serious illegal activities.

Taverns filled a variety of practical social needs. In many areas, they were the most convenient retail outlets for liquor—and often the only place where travelers could find food and lodging. They provided

The Old Tun Tavern, Philadelphia. The Old Tun was considerably bigger and more elaborate than were small-town drinking establishments, but it was typical of colonial taverns in that it offered not only food and drink but also lodgings and a forum for public gatherings.

all localities with a forum for social intercourse, which often included political, religious, or other gatherings. Before and during the Revolution, for example, inns were favorite places for political discussions, and they served as rallying points for the militia and as recruiting stations for the Continental army. Innkeepers ideally reflected the high public status accorded their establishments, and in reality they often did. Publicans were commonly among a town's most prominent citizens and not infrequently were deacons. And if they were good hosts, they did their best to make patrons comfortable. While some taverns were only rude structures with plank bars — there were a lot of these in port towns like New York, Philadelphia, and Charleston and on the sparsely settled frontier — others were well-appointed, pleasant places to spend time. The Reverend Dorchester is again helpful at this point, describing a tavern scene common any time between the late seventeenth and the early nineteenth century — although we can doubt that he intended to make the picture as appealing as he did. In the winters, he noted, "the great fireplaces, with abundant fuel, huge backlogs and loggerhead, were kept at white heat," while all sorts of drinks "were dispensed to the motley assembly, who came together to hear the news, gossip and talk politics." The taverns were a vital early American institution — an institution highly regarded by most colonials and attended as faithfully as many churches.

One may safely assume, then, that abstemious colonials were few and far between. Counting the mealtime beer or cider at home and the convivial drafts at the tavern or at the funeral of a relative or neighbor, all this drinking added up. Under most modern definitions, the majority of Anglo–Americans easily would qualify as moderate or heavy drinkers. While precise consumption figures are lacking, informed estimates suggest that by the 1790s an average American over fifteen years old drank just under six gallons of absolute alcohol each year. That represented some thirty-four gallons of beer and cider (about 3.4 gallons of absolute alcohol), slightly over five gallons of distilled liquors (2.3 gallons of absolute alcohol), and under a gallon of wine (possibly .10 gallons absolute). Because this is an average figure, calculated from the entire drinking-age population (those over fifteen), including nondrinkers, the level of consumption probably was much higher for actual drinkers. But even six gallons is a formidable amount. The comparable modern average is less than 2.8 gallons per capita. To put it starkly, America's colonists were serious drinkers.

But America's colonists were not problem drinkers — at least not if social policy directed at alcohol abuse is any indication. Even with an annual per capita consumption level roughly double our own, the provincials heard little public outcry against alcoholism. Certainly there were no prerevolutionary equivalents of the temperance or prohibition movements. While few denied that intemperance was both physically and spiritually damaging, just as few thought it constituted a serious threat to social stability or individual rights. A general lack of anxiety over alcohol problems was one of the most significant features of drinking in the colonial era.

Why this was so has defied any single explanation. Possibly, a rough balance among cultural heritage, the beverage preferences of the first colonial generations, and the social norms of the day — norms that set the limits of acceptable drinking behavior — held extreme intemperance largely in check. That is, if the colonists drank a lot, their British drinking heritage stressed the use of less potent liquors: They drank more beer and cider than distilled spirits. This is not to say that alcoholism did not exist. People have developed problems from drinking only beer and wine (we note in this regard that in 1975 the average American consumed less absolute alcohol overall than the average colonial consumed through *only* beer and cider). So the potential for alcohol addiction was certainly present.

The social standards of the day had an important restraining effect on intemperance. As we have seen, much, if not most, colonial drinking was family and community oriented. And family and community conduct fell under the governance of social norms inherited, like drinking behavior, from England and the rest of Europe. These norms defined a largely traditional society whose members shared a common loyalty to and an identity with the community and its standards of individual conduct. People were taught to accept their stations in life without complaint and to defer in matters of leadership to society's "betters," whether seventeenth-century Puritan "saint" or eighteenth-century Southern planter "aristocrat." In sum, prerevolutionary America more often than not represented a traditional deferential society.

Most colonials willingly conformed to community values, and if some refused to do so voluntarily, the majority accepted the community's right to compel prescribed behavior. Thus, anything deemed inimical or offensive to the community, be it drunkenness, sexual promiscuity, or even Roman Catholicism, could be restrained for the good and safety of all. Viewed from an egalitarian perspective, the world was inflexible in many ways. Deference, however, characterized the age, although its strength varied in degree from region to region and was probably weakest on the frontier. And it had its advantages: If individual behavior was circumscribed, residents had the security of knowing where they stood in society, of enjoying its protection from internal and external threats (both spiritual and physical), and of knowing what their local communities and leaders permitted or expected of them.

Such was the context of early American drinking. The colonials had assimilated alcohol use, based on Old World patterns, into their community lifestyles. As long as mores remained intact, communities held drinking excesses largely in bounds. (Whether these norms could have restrained intemperance in a population favoring distilled beverages, however, is debatable.) Society would simply not allow things to get out of hand, even though it permitted plenty of drinking at the same time. Most people restricted their consumption primarily to the use of beer and cider; they very rarely became problem drinkers. Even if they had one or more too many on occasion (three or four times a year, for instance, at funerals or on militia drills days), they were not going to drink themselves into a state of alcoholism. Community values were generally strong enough to pull them back from the brink of chronic intemperance when individuals approached that state. Thomas Shepard, for example, whose ordination was so much fun, recalled that he had heard God's Word in his student days back in England but that he "fell from God to loose and lewd company to lust and pride and gaming and bowling and drinking . . . and I drank so much that I was dead drunk." Later, a sense of community propriety led him to ponder the errors of his way. He found himself lacking in acceptable standards of behavior, and pulled himself back on the straight and narrow. Shepard's experience was hardly unique, and it demonstrated something of the power of popularly-accepted social norms as a deterrent to chronic drinking problems in traditional communities.

If individual willpower wavered in observing these standards, however, families, friends, ministers, and civil magistrates were always there to guard against deviant behavior. The church played an especially powerful role in defending community values. The clergy saw drunkenness as an individual failing—Calvinists called it sin—and as such, an affront to the Almighty. Increase Mather, the great Puritan divine of early Boston, explained this point at length in *Wo to Drunkards* (1673). He lamented that human depravity was leading the young of New England toward sin and dissipation and warned that the "worse than brutish sin of drunkenness" could "become a prevailing iniquity all over the country." New Englanders had better mend their ways, Mather admonished, lest they not only speed personal doom but also invite God to afflict society with some evil for allowing such conduct to have flourished in the first place.

Nevertheless, when civil officials dealt with drinking problems, they usually had temporal concerns in mind rather than divine retribution. They saw the many ill effects of intemperance and quickly responded to contain them. The connection between drunkenness and crime was all too obvious. Local records abound with incidents such as one involving a Lynn, Massachusetts, man who had had too much to drink, broke into a home, and struck the inhabitant "on the head with a cudgel." In another case, a drunken argument resulted in the arrest of one William Pitts "for striking George Tucker with a pot and breaking his head." Fighting, swearing, and a host of other petty offenses clearly followed the bottle.

Each colony developed an extensive legal code to combat all aspects of liquor violations. These laws told tavern owners, for example, what they could sell, to whom, when, and even at what prices. Plymouth forbade sales to chronic drunkards, and Virginia, pursuing a similar goal, made any credit innkeepers extended topers unrecoverable by law. Authorities also frowned on breaches of the peace in the taverns. In an attempt to maintain decorum, Pennsylvania once outlawed the drinking of toasts. An even more serious expression of concern emanated from Boston in the 1670s, when the town exiled Alice Thomas after the courts had had her jailed, flogged, and fined for permitting conduct in her tavern so scandalous that it resulted in the first Massachusetts law against prostitution.

Strictures against individual tipplers could be severe. Drunkenness was a crime throughout the colonies, and the penalties against such behavior were potentially extreme. In order to emphasize community control, magistrates could (and did) set examples with jailings, fines, the stocks, and the lash. Recidivism brought heavier fines and longer imprisonments—or brutal corporal punishment. In Massachusetts, the unregenerate ways of one Robert Cole, perhaps a spiritual ancestor of Hawthorne's Hester Prynne, finally provoked the colony to disfranchise him and order him to wear a scarlet "D," for drunkard. Clearly, then, colonial statutes gave officials the power, if they chose to exercise it, to deal sternly with alcohol-related infractions.

Even drinking at home could become an official concern, especially in New England. The early Puritans stressed the importance of well-ordered families in maintaining stable, godly societies, and they were not about to let excessive drinking disrupt their world. Massachusetts expressly forbade drunkenness in homes in 1636 and again in 1654. But the law apparently had little impact, so in 1675 the Bay Colony established the post of tithingman. These officers, who as "sober and discreet men" were to oversee the conduct of ten or twelve families each, were to report on any liquor violations they found. Later, convinced that the roots of social vice lay in family sin, authorities directed the tithingmen to record infractions of all types. These men, however, were neither primitive secret police nor spies; rather, they did their jobs openly and were appointed to their positions at public meetings. Their neighbors knew who they were, and it is doubtful that they proved effective in checking drunkenness, which perhaps explains why the office was not long continued.

The tithingmen were probably unnecessary anyway. As we already noted, drinking seldom got out of hand. The long sermons and the stern laws did not reflect a wave of problem drinking; instead, they served to reinforce community norms, which were largely effective in restraining deviant behavior. Both civil and clerical leaders knew this and, secure in popular support, they were often sparing in applying legal and religious sanctions. As long as they could defend and demonstrate the authority of the community, and if the individual acknowledged his or her error (often as a public testament) and agreed to return to the fold, the colonials could be remarkably lenient with the occasional drunkard.

The Puritan churches were consistently forgiving. Local congregations, as the chief centers of community discipline, often displayed genuine concern for a member who had fallen into sin, even after the church had taken punitive action. The church could register its disapproval of a wayward son or daughter through admonitions, suspension, and, finally, excommunication. Thus was Joseph Davies suspended in Roxbury, Massachusetts, for "scandalous drunkenness" and John Mathews "cast out of ye church" for "notorious drunkenness." The Roxbury records, typical in this regard, noted such incidents infrequently. But they also reveal forgiveness. Davies and Mathews, "upon . . . repentence," were both restored to church membership. The congregation thus agreed that although intoxication was sinful, it did not represent an irredeemable fall from God's grace. The opposite was probably closer to the fact—sinners could repent and the fallen might again return to the fold.

The enforcement of civil laws against drunkenness also demonstrated collective concern for community harmony—a concern that frequently tempered justice with compassion. The case of Joseph Birch serves as a good illustration. Birch was the "local drunk" in Dorchester, Massachusetts. Though twice ordered in 1669 to find employment and "to put himself in an orderly way of living . . . , or else to expect that he will be presented to the Court for disorderly living," Birch over the years was repeatedly arrested for drunkenness and idleness. But only once was he punished: "He was ordered to pay his fine . . . or to sit in the stocks." Dorchester authorities thus were willing to give the man a chance to redeem himself. More than once he promised to mend his ways, and the selectmen took steps to help him. Once, after "abusing himself by drinking," he pled, "as formerly, that he hoped to reform and to that end he was granted liberty to cutt wood . . . to make

Coales for his calling." In spite of other drinking violations, he received at least one other opportunity to cut wood on public lands. We do not know if he stopped drinking. He is found on a list of "disparat debts" in 1680 (a debt he might have paid, since he was not on the following lists). The point here is that Puritan selectmen rarely applied the harsh letter of the law. Dorchester authorities looked closely at Birch's conduct and, instead of constant punishment, found understanding just as effective not only in helping him, but also in maintaining good order in the community. And the Birch case was not an isolated instance: Alice Thomas and Robert Cole were examples of others who had regained the good graces of local New England magistrates.

One would suspect that the Southern colonies, lacking in well-ordered communities by comparison to New England, were more given to individualistic behavior. However, the evidence on early drinking patterns in that region suggests a strong desire to control the drunkard and "unseasonable drinking." During the 1620s in Virginia, for example, the General Court (and later the county courts) focused squarely on excessive drinking as a threat to peace and harmony among the widely dispersed settlers. Indeed, the fact that settlements were not compact may have made the early Virginians as concerned as New Englanders about controlling deviant behavior.

A number of General Court cases are revealing. A decision in 1624, for instance, went against John Roe, James Hickmote, and Nathaniell Jeffreys for "having kept company in drinking, and committing of a riot." It was the rioting that bothered the court, and each man had to pay a heavy fine. In a case heard in 1625, Robert Fytts and John Radish faced not only the charge of drunkenness but also that of being so "disorderd in drink" that they were not "able to go home contrary to the proclamation made against drunkenness." Radish also had to stand up on the charge that he, at an "unseasonable time of the night," had taken Sir George Yeardley's servants to his house "and there gave them entertainment and made them drink." Fytts had to pay a stiff fine. Radish, who must have been the instigator of the reveling, also was fined. Finally, the court mandated that Radish "lie neck and heels or . . . make a good and sufficient pair of stocks" for punishing yet other disturbers of the peace.

Early Virginia cases demonstrate that magistrates did not worry about drinking but rather about drunkenness and its impact on community stability. The strange case of Thomas Godby serves to underscore this point. Godby and six others downed about five pints of claret after dinner at the house of William Parker. Godby had about four cups. He was "a little headed with drink" when a boat, manned by William Bently, became entangled on the shoals in front of Parker's house. Bently yelled ashore for assistance. Godby shouted back: "Do you think we have nothing to do but to fetch you out of the water?" Bently replied by calling Godby a cuckold. Godby slurred in return: "I were as good be a cuckold as a cuckold-maker." Now angry, Bently worked his vessel free of the rocks, made his way to shore, took hold of Godby, and gave him "a kick as he lay upon the ground." Godby never recovered. Some of his drinking compatriots carried him to a bed; the next morning they found him dead. The court eventually convicted Bently of manslaughter. The charge might have been heavier if Godby had not been drinking heavily, which, the court reasoned, had caused his needlessly provocative mood.

Some of the early cases link drunkenness and suspicions of sexual promiscuity. Goodwife Fisher came to the court's attention in 1626. One deponent claimed that he had seen Fisher walking with a man; he observed that she "did reel and stagger as she went." "It was a great shame to see a man drunk," another witness asserted, "but more shame to see a woman in that case." The court disagreed. With no evidence that Fisher had been doing anything more than drinking heavily, the magistrates took no action.

The same verdict greeted Alice Boise, who was openly accused of having had sex with Captain William Epes while drunk. Several male witnesses reported on an incident in early 1627 at the home of James Slight and Bridges Freeman. Boise, Epes, and half a dozen others apparently downed between two and three gallons of wine one evening. In his cups, Epes soon went to bed. The other revelers found makeshift accommodations, except for Boise, who "lay down upon the bed beside Captain Epes with her clothes on." Not long thereafter, one witness claimed that "there was so great a motion in that bed that [I] rose and said 'for shame do not do such things before so many people.'" Another deponent claimed that he "heard busseling . . . in the bed" at least three times that night. Finally, he "covered himself over head and ears" and was able to get to sleep. The court convicted no one of any crime: It must have been hard to tell whether the men were complaining because of lack of sleep, jealousy that Mrs. Boise preferred Captain Epes, or moral outrage. Furthermore, Mrs. Boise must have been a widow, since the Court did not charge her with violating the accepted canons of wedlock. In the end, the drinking bout and its aftermath had not threatened the public peace, and there was really no basis for judicial action in the name of community stability.

It is very important to recognize that colonial magistrates, in both the North and the South, rarely let concerns over excesses in drinking spill over into attacks on the consumption of alcoholic beverages in general. No one, at least no one willing to put themselves on the public record, considered a broad legal prohibition as necessary for communal harmony. That argument would have flown in the face of the entire European heritage. If people denounced cases of individual intemperance, they did not directly intimate that the fault lay in liquor itself; the problem was one of isolated deviants misusing what society viewed as a wholesome, healthful, and even necessary product.

The Exceptions: Indians and Blacks

While English colonists remained comfortable about alcohol for themselves, they did not see it as a "good creature" for some other groups. In fact, they could be very leery of liquor in the wrong hands. As we have seen, in closely supervised colonial communities, drinking sometimes was associated with social disorder and violence; and colonial leaders feared that drinking-related problems in groups potentially beyond community control could have serious implications.

In the port towns, for example, the authorities occasionally had trouble with sailors who did not share the common social concern over chronic intoxication. Plymouth once temporarily revoked all tavern licenses in Yarmouth when some mariners got particularly rowdy; the inns reopened after the seamen sailed away. There was also concern over the behavior of those who slipped beyond the control of established communities to the frontiers. But, most of all, white colonials worried about Indians and blacks—groups not only racially and culturally different but also frequently hostile. The colonists feared that alcohol consumption among these peoples could be dangerous to overall societal stability.

The Indians of eastern North America were unfamiliar with beverage alcohol before the invasion of the whites. Most tribes got their first taste from the explorers and adventurers who preceded the influx of settlers, just as they learned about other aspects of European culture from these initial harbingers of change. In some early cases, Indian

While some tribes in the Southwest and in Central America were familiar with beverage alcohol to an extent, the Indians in eastern North America were introduced to liquor by the European colonists. Some Eastern tribes, however, had their own "black drink" (shown here), an emetic of local ingredients, which was used on ceremonial occasions.

drinking did not seem to pose a problem. Some Indians appreciated the colonial beverages and did not drink to excess. Samoset, for instance, the tribesman who helped the Pilgrims survive their first winter, was particularly fond of beer. The first Thanksgiving saw red and white men happily downing gallons of liquor together. But the picture changed rapidly as the settlers became convinced that Indians, for reasons the Europeans could not explain, were especially prone to drunkenness. Alcohol seemed to hit Indians hard and fast, and they allegedly became unpredictable and even violent — at least it so seemed in the eyes of whites. The colonial view of Indian drinking, that red men could not hold their liquor, was in fact the beginning of a long-standing stereotype of the impact of alcohol on the tribes. Many early settlers believed Indians to be uncivilized — nothing more than "savages"; therefore, any sign of intemperate behavior served to confirm that image. Some modern anthropologists have termed the so-called Indian drinking problem the "firewater myth." This stereotype not only followed the white frontier line to the Pacific but in many respects has survived into the present.

Modern research has failed to explain the firewater myth. Some Indian groups today do have unusually high rates of alcoholism, while others do not. There is no positive evidence indicating a greater physiological propensity to alcoholism in Indians than in whites, nor is it absolutely clear how cultural conditioning factors may have distinguished Indian drinking reactions from those of other groups. Thus, it is difficult to say why the first reports of convivial Indian drinking in early Plymouth (and almost everywhere else) soon gave way to a litany of recorded abuses.

One possible explanation is that some tribes learned to drink from the wrong whites: fur traders, explorers, or fishing crews, all of whom drank hard and, frequently, in a fashion not condoned by the social norms in traditional, settled colonial communities. This model might have inclined the Indian — without prior experience with the effects of alchohol — toward problem drinking from the very beginning. But even if true in some instances, this represents at best only a partial explanation of the situation. Indeed, evidence suggests that both reactions to alcohol and drinking behavior varied markedly among tribal groups. At any rate, we know too little about the role of alcohol in initial white-red contacts to reach any solid conclusions. Nor can one be sure that the colonists were not exaggerating their accounts of Indian drunkenness. Perhaps they misunderstood Indian drinking behavior entirely, reading the worst into isolated abuses—it would not have been the only case of early whites completely misunderstanding because of their Old World cultural provincialism.

In any event, the settlers thought they had the evidence. They could recite incident after incident in which alcohol had served as an apparent catalyst for violence among individual Indians and whites. Frequently, the whites involved were traders or would-be land buyers who had deliberately besotted the tribesmen before talking business. Some settlers also went so far as to claim that atrocities committed by drunken warriors were the precipitating incidents in the early Indian wars. Because of their concerns over Indian violence, all the colonies enacted codes regulating the sale of liquor to the tribes. In 1682, for example, Pennsylvania ordered all sales halted on pain of a £5 fine, calling the practice "an heinous offence to God and a reproach to the blessed name of Christ and his holy religion." But most officials found outright bans both impractical and impracticable: Fines were too small to stop determined traders; besides, the tribes could either get enough liquor from illegal sources or take their lucrative fur trade to regions with less stringent laws, all to the economic loss of those areas with tougher legislation. Accordingly, provincial governments usually licensed agents to sell to the tribes under official supervision. But any Indian drinking, no matter how controlled, remained a perpetual source of uneasiness among whites.

On occasion, the colonists moved forcefully in situations they considered particularly serious. Even tiny Plymouth got bellicose at one point. In 1628, the settlement sent Captain Myles Standish and an army of eight men against the Merrymount colony of Thomas Morton, several miles north. Morton, an ex-lawyer turned renegade colonist— he recognized no authority save his own—had an unconcealed contempt for the godly mores of his Pilgrim neighbors. He maintained his colony as a fur trading center and also as America's first den of iniquity (or so the Plymouth magistracy believed). Morton liked Indians—especially Indian women—whom, in return for animal pelts, he liberally plied with all manner of alcohol. Setting up a maypole (a throwback to paganism in the eyes of William Bradford), Morton and his company took to "drinking and dancing about it many days together, inviting the Indian women for their consorts, dancing and frisking together like so many fairies, or furies, rather; and worse practices. As if they had anew revived . . . the feasts of the Roman goddess Flora, or the beastly

The maypole, liquor, and Indians. Scenes similar to this provoked the Plymouth raid against Thomas Morton's band at Merrymount.

practices of the mad Bacchanalians." In addition, Morton wrote mundane poetry in which he satirized the Pilgrims with as free a hand as he gave the Indians drink. Then he went too far; he gave his Indian friends guns. For most colonists, savages with alcohol were bad enough, but redmen with alcohol *and* guns were intolerable. "O, the horribleness of this villainy!" Bradford wailed, and, after obtaining the support of other settlements, he dispatched Captain Standish (Morton called him "Captain Shrimpe") to clean out Morton's nest. There could have been a nasty fight at Merrymount. When the "invasion force" arrived, Morton's men were under cover and well armed, but they were also so drunk that they could not handle their weapons. Morton was taken and shipped in chains back to England (where he was ultimately freed). Merrymount was finished, but its demise illustrated the gravity of the problem of Indian-colonist relations.

Although the authorities fined and jailed many colonists over the years for illegal beverage sales, in general white officials were very inconsistent in enforcing regulations. While they sought to restrain private liquor trade with the Indians, they were not above entering the traffic directly when it suited their purposes. Often they saw to it that treaty negotiations were soaking wet. For example, at the signing of the Treaty of Easton (Pennsylvania) in 1758, in which the Indians gave up claim to huge tracts of land, the colonial negotiators kept them supplied from beginning to end with as much as they could drink. Not infrequently, local governments openly told their licensed trading agents to get the Indians as drunk as possible in order to wring the most out of them, especially when dealing for furs or lands. It was a sordid business, but it paid handsomely.

The Indians themselves were not oblivious to what was happening. We are still unsure of what values different tribes placed on alcohol use — and it should be stressed that not all Indian drinking was problem drinking — as they assimilated liquor into their cultures. When problems arose, however, they were often quick to respond. As early as the mid-seventeenth century some tribal leaders denounced alcohol as one more white inspired plague, akin to disease and war, steadily tearing away at Indian cultural integrity. Those who sold liquor to the redmen were "blind," charged a New Jersey Lenape chief in 1677, and he blamed much of the misery of his people on the white man's alcohol. Having seen the impact of drink on the Indians living to their east, the Iroquois in western New York and the Shawnee and other tribes farther west labored to stem the tide of liquor before it overwhelmed them. In 1753, at the Treaty of Carlisle (Pennsylvania), a number of tribal sachems put their case before the colonial authorities. Liquor was destroying them, they said: "We beg you would prevent its coming in such quantities. We desire it may be forbidden and none sold in the Indian country." They charged that "the wicked whiskey-sellers" were deliberately besotting their people in order to cheat them in trade, and they "earnestly" beseeched colonial authorities to halt such sales lest the tribes "be inevitably ruined." While some whites were sympathetic to Indian appeals, they never did much that was effective in this regard. Indeed, by the early nineteenth century, there was so much tribal bitterness over alcohol that a number of Indian cultural-religious revival attempts — such as those led by Tenskwatawa ("the Prophet") of the Shawnee and the Seneca Handsome Lake — made abstinence a central tenet. These movements, however, were too localized and too short-lived to correct the situation and, while it is a gross oversimplification to conclude, as one temperance movement historian did, that drinking was the biggest "single cause" of the decline of Indian power, it is equally true that it played no small part in what was a tragic pattern of Indian cultural disintegration.

Colonial governments also kept a watchful eye on drinking among blacks. The floodgates of black slavery had opened in the English mainland colonies by the end of the seventeenth century. Drinking patterns, like most other aspects of slave life, were largely a matter of what white masters would allow. Like the Indians, blacks were perceived in terms of heathenism. Even more threatening, they lived among the whites, so that the consequences of violence were omnipresent and internal rather than sporadic and external (as in the case of the Indian nations). Furthermore, blacks played a functional role in providing back-breaking labor for whites, while Indians came to be viewed as a menace to be removed or exterminated.

But masters did permit a certain amount of controlled drinking among their chattel laborers—normally on special occasions. In the South, the end of harvest and the Christmas season generally saw holiday celebrations, with slave owners providing a day off for music, dancing, extra food, and drinking (largely of cheap distilled spirits). Some masters also used liquor to reward slaves for special service; still others, if they allowed their slaves time to work for themselves, let them purchase spirits with part of their wages (the extent of this practice remains unclear).

Unless a master specifically granted his slaves—or for that matter, his white indentured servants as well—permission to drink, the general rule was to keep the alcohol away. The demands of discipline in the slave and indentured labor forces necessitated such a policy. An imbibing slave did less work and was worth much less as a chattel. Thus, from the owner's point of view, keeping the slaves and servants sober was an exercise in protecting his investments and property while avoiding disruption of the labor force, particularly if drunken slaves fell to fighting among themselves. Overall, bonded laborers probably received just enough alcohol to keep them healthy—as defined by the wisdom of the day—but there were laws to prevent them from getting more than what was minimally medicinal. For example, lest either slaves or indentured servants spend time away from their masters in the taverns, local authorities carefully regulated the circumstances under which they could enter inns and, quite often, barred them altogether. Nor were these regulations confined to the South. A Connecticut statute of 1703, typical of New England policy, called for the flogging of slaves, indentured servants, and apprentices caught in taverns without their masters' permission. Other Northern statutes levied fines (some as high as £30) on whites selling liquor to any blacks, free or slave.

These laws reflected deep-seated white fears that blacks, like Indians, were especially prone to violence when intoxicated. Deathly afraid of slave insubordination or rebellion, colonial magistrates restricted drinking among blacks as concomitant parts of extensive slave codes—codes that by the early eighteenth century mandated harsh measures, including death, for any slave who threatened or harmed a white. In practice, however, these regulations were not always stringently enforced. This was certainly the case in the North, where there were vastly fewer blacks and the threat of slave insurrection seemed more remote. Even when slaves or servants got drunk after breaking into a master's liquor cabinet, which was apparently not that uncommon, there is little evidence that New England courts treated them much differently from drunken whites. And in the South, owners might also look the other way at the spree by slaves if it was neither violent nor disruptive. For instance, the well-known planter William Byrd of Virginia gave his slaves a day off in 1711 to get drunk—provided that they remained sober on Queen Anne's birthday.

Slaves in the colonial period did not leave behind written documentation of their feelings about drink. But their thoughts may have borne some resemblance to those of the black abolitionist Frederick Douglass, who grew up a slave in eastern Maryland during the early nineteenth century. Douglass pointed out that slave holidays represented "the most effective means in the hands of the slaveholder in keeping down the spirit of insurrection." "Their object seems to be," Douglass argued, "to disgust their slaves with freedom, by plunging them into the lowest depths of dissipation." The goal was to get "whole multitudes to drink to excess," thereby convincing them "that there was little to choose between liberty and slavery, . . . that we had almost as well be slaves to man as to rum." Douglass summarized his position this way: "So, when the holidays ended, we staggered up from the filth of our wallowing, took a long breath, and marched to the field,—feeling upon the whole, rather glad to go, from what our master had deceived us into a belief was freedom, back to the arms of slavery."

It cannot be precisely determined whether Douglass's comments were reflective of attitudes generally held by slaves or typical of views espoused by temperance and abolition reformers of the 1830s and forties. However, the essential issue is that special restrictions were placed on slave drinking as early as the end of the seventeenth century. They were yet another sign of evolving white dominance over other racial groups. They also represented further testimony that if alcohol was all right for the white community, others could only drink by permission. Social control and societal stability remained the preeminent values among free whites attempting to conquer the North American continent.

The slave trade, as depicted in a nineteenth-century print. While historians now doubt the existence of the "triangle trade," rum and other liquor did figure in the international commerce in human chattels.

The Rise of "the Demon": Early Distilling

By the late seventeenth century, a fundamental shift in colonial drinking preferences was well under way. As has been seen, new settlers had quickly turned to distilled spirits — mostly out of necessity. As this taste matured, it gradually led the colonists away from their traditional cultural allegiance to beer. The beverage that initially mounted the most direct challenge to beer was rum. The colonists had used rum in limited quantities since the mid-seventeenth century, and it had a reputation as potent stuff. Rum, a distillate of sugar refining by-products, principally molasses, usually has a strength of 100 to 200 proof (that is, anywhere from about a 50 percent to a pure alcohol content). First distilled from West Indian sugar cane in the 1640s, rum was soon produced throughout the Caribbean; from there it traveled to the Northern colonies, primarily as a trading product. Rum was cheap and had a pleasant taste, and Anglo-Americans warmed to it. They drank it straight, spiced it, poured it into punches, and learned to enjoy hot buttered rum and eggnog on cold evenings. While the nineteenth-century temperance movement would later denounce the beverage as the "hydra monster" and the "demon rum," strong liquor had clearly started to occupy a fond place in colonial hearts.

With the demand for rum growing, America's first commercial distillery opened in Boston in 1700. Using cheaply imported molasses, this operation turned a huge profit for its owners. Other distilleries soon sprang up throughout New England — Boston and Newport, Rhode Island, ultimately had some thirty apiece — and easily undersold their West Indian competition. Rum became a staple in the New England economy, and within a few years the region was exporting some 600,000 gallons annually. Although historians have long been aware that commerce in this beverage formed an integral part of the infamous "triangle trade," which supposedly saw merchantmen carrying sugar and molasses from the Caribbean to New England, rum from there to Africa, and slaves back to the West Indies, recent research has shown the triangle trade to have been largely a myth. Nevertheless, rum was one of New England's major trading commodities — a demonstration that colonial thirst could help sustain one of the era's major economic activities.

By the early 1700s, rum was effecting a revolution in provincial drinking habits. If we consider beer and cider separately, rum probably had become the single most popular beverage in the colonies and has generally received most of the credit for weaning the colonials, once and for all, from the tastes of the Old World. It would be easy to overstate this case, however. Distilled drinks, such as applejack and other fruit brandies, were already popular, as was cider, and many of the colonial beers were not good replicas of those brewed in England. So the triumph of cheap rum seems hardly surprising in retrospect, but it was important nevertheless: This trend indicated that the Anglo-Americans were evolving as a separate people, discarding some of their most familiar European cultural baggage. In fact, by the dawn of the eighteenth century (if not earlier), Americans were a people becoming confirmed in their love of hard liquor.

Rum found a major competitor as settlement spread to the frontiers. Both molasses and finished rum were too bulky and expensive to ship far inland, and as the eighteenth-century settlement line advanced, frontiersmen shifted their loyalties to grain whiskeys. Indeed, whiskey was particularly suited to the frontier. Grain was plentiful—much more was harvested than farmers could eat or sell as food—and a single bushel of surplus corn, for example, yielded three gallons of whiskey. This assured a plentiful liquor supply for Westerners and gave them a marketable commodity, which both kept longer and was easier to transport to market than grain. The advantages of whiskey were, therefore, such that it rapidly eclipsed rum as the staple drink in the Back Country. The arrival of the Scotch-Irish, who flocked to the frontier beginning in the 1730s, dealt rum a further blow. These immigrants had enjoyed reputations as whiskey lovers in their northern Irish homes, and they brought their distilling skills across the Atlantic with them. By the late 1700s they had given American grain spirits a new quality in taste.

The American Revolution also accelerated the shift from rum to whiskey. During the war years, the Royal Navy blockaded American ports, and both rum and molasses imports from the West Indies (much of which was British and thus enemy territory) became scarce. Domestic grain whiskey stepped in to fill the demand for spirits. And the demand, for both civilian and military purposes, was huge. Profits were handsome indeed, and so much grain ended up as whiskey that the Continental Congress, fearing food shortages, occasionally moved (although in vain) to limit distilling.

One of the biggest whiskey consumers was the Continental army, which attempted to provide a daily liquor ration of roughly four ounces. Spirits rations were normal in the armies and navies of the period; they were supposed to help keep the troops healthy in the face of extremely harsh service conditions. Thus, American colonial governments had given their men rum during the French and Indian wars, and during the War for Independence they tried to provide them with a gill (about 4 ounces) per day. But with rum relatively hard to come by in the Revolution, the soldiers usually got whiskey. They loved it, and the liquor ration proved a real morale builder, especially before battle. Alcohol even served as a reward on occasion: After losing the tough fight at Germantown in October 1777, the Continentals took a bit of comfort from an extra thirty casks of whiskey that Congress shipped them in recognition of their performance.

But army liquor also had its drawbacks. The troops, in addition to receiving alcohol rations, bought cheap whiskey from the sutlers who swarmed around military camps. Commanders were never able to deal effectively with the sutler problem, and drunkenness took its toll in inefficiency. Nor was such trouble confined to camp. During Washington's retreat across New Jersey in 1776, for example, one Continental patrol stumbled on a barrel of whiskey. Concerned that the booty not fall into enemy hands (or so the men said), they drank up the liquor on the spot. The result, an officer recalled, was a bad case of "barrel fever," with symptoms of black eyes and bloody noses. Later, in South Carolina during August 1780, a patriot force under Horatio Gates found itself out of rum on the eve of the Battle of Camden. Reasoning that the raw material of rum was better than nothing, the officers distributed a ration of molasses—the devastating cathartic effect of which promptly put scores of men sick in the bushes. Shortly thereafter, Gates lost much of his army and his reputation in a crushing defeat (although the general's ineptitude in making preparations for battle had more to do with this than the "demon molasses"). There were still other incidents: In 1781 at Eutaw Springs, a Continental force drove a strong opponent from its campground, stopped to loot and drink British rum, and became too drunk to hold off the redcoat counterattack. Armies were seldom paragons of sobriety, and the Revolutionary troops were no exception.

After the Revolution, American commerce was not fully restored with the West Indies (initially reflecting British policy), a condition aggravated by U.S. trade embargoes against Britain during the early 1800s. This, plus the fact that the Revolution had opened the floodgates to trans-Appalachian immigration, giving further impetus to grain distilling, additionally undercut the importance of rum. The nationally legislated end of the slave trade in 1808, and thus of the commerce in rum associated with it, also hurt. So by the end of the eighteenth century, rum had passed its zenith; whiskey was fast becoming the premier American beverage.

It must be noted that the distiller's art was a highly varied phenomenon. Some vats turned out perfectly awful stuff. "Red-eye" was the slang for much of it, probably after Proverbs XXIII: "Who hath redness of eyes? They that tarry long at the wine." On the other hand, there were excellent spirits whose partisans have become legion over the years.

In this latter category, the first distinctly American whiskey was rye. While we do not have the original recipe (if indeed there ever was a formal first one), this whiskey today is distilled from a combination of rye, corn, and barley malt, with at least 51 percent of the mixture rye. Who distilled the first batch is also obscure. One version gives credit to farmers in western Maryland and Pennsylvania—Scotch-Irish territory. On the other hand, a more pleasing account honors none other than George Washington. One of Washington's overseers, a Scot, supposedly persuaded him to plant some otherwise unprofitable land in rye for the express purpose of distilling. The resulting spirit is said to have made a fine impression on Mount Vernon's guests, including the Marquis de Lafayette. Rye whiskey then spread to Maryland, so this story concludes, when the overseer set up shop there after Washington's death. In any case, Maryland and Pennsylvania soon became national centers of rye production.

Corn also made fine whiskey. Frontier Kentucky made the best, although colonists since the earliest years at Jamestown had distilled limited amounts. Corn whiskey itself is about 80 percent corn, with a balance of rye and barley malt. Before use, the distillate is stored in oaken barrels to make a clear beverage, but corn whiskey has never been as popular as bourbon, a whiskey of 65 to 70 percent corn and a distinctive flavor and dark color imparted through aging in charred oak barrels. Bourbon was born in Kentucky, taking its name from Bourbon County, where it was first produced in 1789. Allegedly, the original distiller was the Reverend Elijah Craig, and Kentuckians quickly took a liking to his innovation. By the early nineteenth century, bourbon had become an important regional industry, and the renown of the liquor became such that, as much as any single beverage could, it assumed the mantle of the indigenous American national drink. Kentucky still retains a special place in America's heart for its bourbon.

The End of an Era

As the colonial period drew to a close, most Americans still held to the traditional view of drinking as a positive social and personal good. This favorable outlook survived even as the old European beverages declined in popularity and the new American drinks, largely distilled spirits, rose in appeal. Yet at the same time, there were a few dissenting voices.

The sticking point was hard liquor and, more specifically, the realization that its use was becoming so prevalent that (at least in the eyes of some observers) society was losing the ability to control drinking excesses. As the eighteenth century advanced, it became increasingly clear that the social norms that previously had controlled individual behavior with remarkable success were loosening. On the frontiers, for example, which were expanding steadily, the population was generally scattered, with few institutional controls to reinforce personal moral standards or to check deviant public conduct. Accounts of life along the shifting frontier line indicate that even before mid-century, drunkenness had resulted in few civil strictures. One surveying party in North Carolina reported finding rum everywhere in 1728 — people even cooked bacon in it. Visitors to the western areas of Virginia, New York, Pennsylvania, South Carolina, and some of the more remote parts of New England found intoxication quite common. The sight of down-and-outers sleeping off their whiskey became an accepted part of life.

Afraid of this set of circumstances in the 1730s, Governor James Oglethorpe and the London trustees of Georgia banned the use of hard drink in that new colony. They feared that liquor would breed lascivious behavior and result in civil disorder at the time when the province was getting on its feet. As an alternative, they encouraged the settlers to drink "English beer." Tastes among Georgia's first settlers, however, Americanized as quickly as those of the older colonists, and the 1735 law banning "Rum, Brandies, Spirits or Strong Waters" fell after seven years of unsuccessful implementation.

Fears for social stability found expression in the writings of elite leaders throughout the colonies. During the 1750s and sixties, a youthful John Adams of Massachusetts expressed concern over the abusive consumption of "spiritous liquors" and what he viewed as a related decline in the accepted set of community behavioral norms. Adams directed most of his ire at the taverns. They had started, he stated, as necessary places, but under the influence of hard liquor and a "prevailing depravity of manners throughout the land" they were fast becoming nothing more than dens of iniquity. The future president readily admitted that his concerns carried little weight. In fact, he thought that they were earning him the "reputation of a hypocrite and an ambitious demagogue."

If the public generally disregarded the thinking of men like Oglethorpe or Adams, concern over the social ill effects of strong drink soon became more clamorous. In 1774, Anthony Benezet, a Philadelphia Quaker with numerous philanthropic interests, published *The Mighty Destroyer Displayed* — the first full-scale assault on American drinking habits. Benezet argued that distilled liquor was not only unhealthy but also degrading and ultimately immoral for individuals and society. *The Mighty Destroyer* was widely read, although with undetermined effect. However, we know that by 1784 both the Quakers and the Methodists had urged their members to abstain from hard liquor and to take no part in its manufacture or sale. Like Benezet, they drew clear connections among drinking, personal moral decline and health complications, and social instability.

The bitterest denunciation of distilled spirits came in the immediate aftermath, and as part of the zeitgeist, of the Revolution. The Revolutionary period witnessed heightened concern that society's traditional values were being lost — that luxury and vice were threatening public virtue and liberty itself. A great many people traced these unwanted developments to American links with the British nation, which supposedly had grown increasingly decadent over the years, thus representing a corrupting influence on America. The result was what Revolutionary leaders often described as a rise in social dissipation and a decline in public spirit. The most zealous in this view were the ideological republicans — men like Thomas Jefferson, John Adams, and Patrick Henry — who finally came to agree that national salvation lay only in independence. They hoped that the Revolution would represent a cleansing process for Americans and that it would fire a rebirth of individual and public virtue.

"Virtue" was the catchword of republicanism. It dictated that citizens act, vote, and think not out of hopes for personal gain but out of a sense of public duty and concern for the general good. A nation founded on this premise had to maintain traditional concerns about order and stability, and republicans believed that true liberty could exist only in a society composed of such a virtuous people. Providence, they held, would certainly shepherd the fortunes of such a republic as long as it adhered to these principles.

Yet victory in the War for Independence failed to allay many republican fears. If republican forms of government had emerged on the state and national levels, the virtue of the citizenry—and thus of society in general—seemed less than ideal. Independence had clearly brought some unsettling changes: It had ushered in new leaders, hastened the decline of the established churches, stimulated Western migration, and allowed egalitarian ideals to challenge hierarchical social relationships as never before. Society as the colonials had known it was hardly falling apart, but the old deferential patterns—and voluntary compliance with them—were clearly giving way to a more individualistic, pluralist set of values. The doctrine of liberty espoused during the Revolution went a long way toward weakening communal responsibility for individual behavior in many areas. But while republicans cherished the ideals of the Revolution, no one (who was willing to admit it) wanted these ideals to proceed to anarchy or to a decline in general morality or civil order. And in this concern for social stability and virtue, few things seemed to have more disruptive potential than the intemperance that apparently was accompanying the startling rise in the use of distilled spirits.

Library of Congress

Benjamin Rush (1745/46–1813). Although he never advocated total abstinence, Rush was destined to be remembered as a dry champion by future generations of temperance workers. It is doubtful, however, that Rush himself ever envisioned any movement, based on his ideas, similar to the antiliquor crusade that arose shortly after his death.

This unsteadying fear lay behind America's classic early stricture of drunkenness: *An Inquiry into the Effects of Ardent Spirits on the Human Mind and Body* (1784), by Dr. Benjamin Rush of Philadelphia. Rush commanded attention. An ardent republican, he had been active in Revolutionary politics, signed the Declaration of Independence as a Pennsylvania delegate, and served for a time as Continental army surgeon general. Rush enjoyed a reputation after the war as perhaps the new nation's foremost physician. His interests ranged widely—his writings on mental illness earned him the title "Father of Psychiatry"— but most Americans of his time came to know him for his work on behalf of temperance. Rush had spoken out publicly against the use of hard liquor since at least 1772, but his masterpiece was the *Inquiry*.

The tract represented a radical challenge to previous thinking; it assaulted the old dictum that alcohol was a positive good. Rush had no quarrel with beers and wines, which he believed healthful when consumed in moderate amounts, but he correctly pointed out that Americans were now drinking primarily "ardent spirits," and, he argued, these did more than cause drunkenness. Consumed in quantity over the years, they could destroy a person's health and even cause death. More important was how alcohol went about its lethal business: For Rush was the first American to call chronic drunkenness a distinct disease, which gradually, but through progressively more serious stages, led drinkers to physical doom. In fact, he described an addiction process and specifically identified alcohol as the addictive agent. As Rush claimed, once an "appetite," or "craving," for spirits had become fixed in an individual, the victim was helpless to resist. In these cases, drunkenness was no longer a vice or personal failing, for the imbiber had no more control over his drinking—the alcohol now controlled him. In Rush's view, the old colonial idea that drunkenness was the fault of the drinker was valid only in the early stages of the disease, when a tippler might still pull back; once addicted, even a saint would have a hard time controlling himself.

The *Inquiry* was a powerful indictment, and it conveyed a sense of urgency. The threat of hard liquor, Rush believed, called for immediate action. As a doctor, he was genuinely concerned about personal health. Drinking habits as they were, many people *did* risk addiction and a host of related medical complications. Long-standing friendships with Anthony Benezet and early Methodist leaders had also convinced Rush of the moral and social threats posed by hard liquor. His republican ideology, moreover, had so affected his reactions to public behavior that he saw clearly in American drinking patterns what others had only hinted at and what we have traced in retrospect: The Americanization of drinking—that is, the movement from beer, cider, and other light alcoholic beverages to distilled spirits—had not resulted in new social controls to limit drinking excesses. Not only was there more drunkenness in the postrevolutionary era, but with the loosening of the old behavioral norms, more people seemed to care less about such behavior. The traditional consensus on how to handle drinking, or so it appeared to Rush, had broken down and nothing had taken its place. The prospect was societal anarchy and civil disaster.

As a good republican, he abhorred intemperance (and the strong drink that caused it). It was a personal and social vice, and it struck at the very heart of the Revolutionaries' vision of the ideal republican society. Allow drunkenness to flourish, Rush cautioned, with its attendant crime, degraded individuals, broken families, economic loss, and other disruptions, and the Revolution would have been fought in vain. "Our country," he warned, would soon "be governed by men chosen by intemperate and corrupted voters," rather than by citizens of virtue. "From such legislators the republic would soon be in danger," openly susceptible to demagoguery. Nor, of course, would the Almighty look favorably on a people who preferred to drink whiskey when they had the opportunity to build a golden edifice dedicated to liberty and a moral republican order. To avert such a calamity, Rush advocated not only personal abstinence from hard liquor but also a return to strict communal sanctions against drunkards. Drunkards, Rush pointed out, were the antithesis of virtuous citizens; they were incapable of managing their own affairs, could become mentally enfeebled, and certainly could not be responsible enough to vote. Better, Rush said, to lock them up in special asylums until they regained whatever faculties remained (he suggested the name "Sober House" for the asylum he envisioned for Philadelphia). He also urged that "good men of every class unite and besiege" their leaders with demands for fewer taverns and heavy taxes on "ardent spirits" as further ways to stem the tide of intemperance. So while Rush was no prohibitionist, he saw considerably more at stake in American drinking practices than did the vast majority of his countrymen.

But the Philadelphia doctor harbored few illusions. Americans loved their whiskey and anyone telling them to forego it would be waging an uphill battle. Still, stubborn and zealous as he was, Rush was willing to try: The very fate of the new republican nation—the great legacy of the Revolution—depended upon it. Before his death in 1813, Rush thus labored mightily to spread his gospel. He had thousands of reprints of the *Inquiry* distributed nationally, and in a later edition he attached a "Moral and Physical Thermometer" to illustrate the pro-

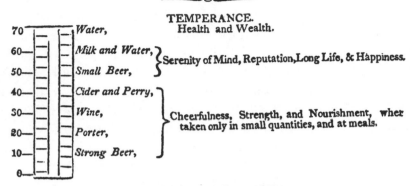

A MORAL AND PHYSICAL THERMOMETER.

A scale of the progress of Temperance and Intemperance.—Liquors with effects in their usual order.

TEMPERANCE.
Health and Wealth.

70 — Water,	
60 — Milk and Water,	Serenity of Mind, Reputation, Long Life, & Happiness.
50 — Small Beer,	
40 — Cider and Perry,	
30 — Wine,	Cheerfulness, Strength, and Nourishment, when taken only in small quantities, and at meals.
20 — Porter,	
10 — Strong Beer,	
0 —	

INTEMPERANCE.

		VICES.	DISEASES.	PUNISH-MENTS.
10	Punch,	Idleness, Gaming,	Sickness,	Debt.
20	Toddy and Egg Rum,	peevish-ness,	Tremors of the hands in the morning, puking,	Jail.
30	Grog—Brandy and Water,	quarrelling Fighting,	bloatedness, Inflamed eyes, red nose	Black eyes, and Rags,
40	Flip and Shrub,	Horse-Racing,	and face, Sore and swelled legs,	Hospital or Poor house.
50	Bitters infused in Spirits and Cordials.	Lying and Swearing,	jaundice, Pains in the hands, burn-	Bridewell.
60	Drams of Gin, Brandy, and Rum, in the morning,	Stealing & Swindling,	ing in the hands, and feet Dropsy, Epilepsy,	State prison
70	The same morning and ning. The same during day & night,	Perjury, Burglary, Murder,	Melancholy, palsy, apple-plexy, Madness, Despair,	do. for Life. Gallows.

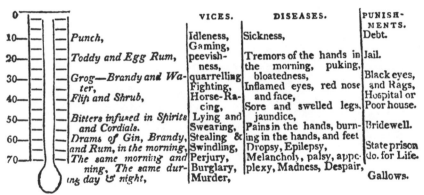

The "Moral and Physical Thermometer" of temperance and intemperance. Rush did not insist that particular levels of drinking corresponded precisely to the matching vices and medical and legal complications. Nevertheless, he did try to convey, in a way that a popular readership could understand, the progressive nature of alcohol addiction and its personal and social implications. In this regard, Rush's views come strikingly close to modern conceptions of alcoholism.

gressive nature of alcohol addiction, outlining the disease's social, medical, and moral complications. Rush wrote other tracts on temperance, and he made some headway in pressing his views on the Protestant churches. A minority of the American elite, certainly citizens of republican leanings themselves, adopted his position on strong drink and either banned it from their homes or limited its use. There was some comfort in knowing that men like James Madison had also denounced "the corrupting influence of spiritous liquors" as "inconsistent with the purity of moral and republican principles."

But the real impact of Rush's work was years ahead. He lamented that his generation would not see a change in popular drinking habits or attitudes and that it would probably be a hundred years before people really got upset about the social and medical consequences of drunkenness. Rush's attitudes on the entire subject of drinking marked him, at least in this regard, as a man of the future as well as of his own time. He lived at the end of an era with an overwhelmingly positive opinion of liquor — and hard liquor at that. Yet he had sown the seeds of reform movements to come. Rush did more than anyone else of his generation to point out the antirepublican implications inherent in the way Americans drank. The future welfare of the republic, Rush believed, depended heavily upon how vigorously succeeding generations would grapple with his message. As the nineteenth century dawned, he was to have at least a glimpse of what was to come.

CHAPTER TWO

Metamorphosis: From "Good Creature" to "Demon Rum," 1790-1860

'Mid pleasures and palaces, though we may roam,
Be it ever so humble, there's no place like home.
But there is the father lies drunk on the floor,
The table is empty, the wolf's at the door,
And mother sobs loud in her broken-back'd chair,
Her garments in tatters, her soul in despair.

Nobil Adkisson,
Ruined by Drink (c. 1860)

Portland, Maine, 1851

On June 2, 1851, the governor of Maine signed into law a bill prohibiting the sale of beverage alcohol in the state. In 1846 Maine had enacted a similar provision on a limited basis, but the earlier law had been "mild," as one temperance worker recalled, its negligible penalties "striking no terror to the hearts of the liquor dealers." Not so the 1851 version: This statute provided for the destruction of any liquor confiscated after the bill became law. The "Maine Law" was America's first statewide prohibition statute, and it represented the culmination of two generations of temperance agitation. To pass a law was one thing; however, to enforce it was another. In 1851 the burning question was whether the tough legislation would work. "All eyes were at once turned upon Maine," another antiliquor crusader remembered, "to see if she would execute her law." In reality, the immediate focus of attention was narrower than the state: "All eyes" were actually on one city — Portland.

There was good reason. The mayor of Portland was Neal Dow, renowned in his generation as the "Prophet of Prohibition" and, more to the point, as the "Father of the Maine Law." While other towns moved quickly to enforce the law — the mayor of Bangor opened Independence Day festivities by smashing ten kegs of confiscated booze — most of the nation expected the real test to come at the hands of Mayor Dow. He had already resolved to disappoint no one in this regard. As soon as the governor affixed his signature, Dow issued an ultimatum: Portland liquor dealers had sixty days to get their stocks out of town. After that, the city would seize and destroy all liquor. People were waiting for day sixty-one and Dow himself, who had dreamed for years of such a time, intended to enforce prohibition to the letter, even in the face of violent opposition.

Neal Dow was a formidable man. Possessed of immense self-confidence and burning drive, he had risen from relatively modest means to become one of Maine's leading businessmen. He had done well in tanning, banking, and timber. Dow was also a reformer — and a zealous one. Thoroughly committed to the rising industrial-commercial world that had nurtured him, he was convinced that this new society was the way of the future for America. Dow's view of the American future was an article of faith — a faith rooted deeply in the republicanism of the Revolutionary generation. Dow also saw the good society in holistic

Neal Dow (1804–1897). The "Father of the Maine Law" as a young man.

terms, and he linked spiritual, social, and political ideals in a single vision. Thus, the new era would be an immense benefit—it could demonstrate the abilities of a virtuous people to create a national order dedicated to justice, human dignity, and liberty. Progress and opportunity would abound within this context, sustained by citizens committed to shared values and common ideals. And if only America strove to fulfill its republican potential, Dow believed, then Providence would smile. In the thinking of the Maine crusader, God had offered the United States the chance both to provide bountifully for its own populace and to show humanity what a liberty-loving nation could accomplish in an autocratic world. In its essentials, then, Dow's world view echoed the old republicanism—drawn into the dawning industrial age of the mid-nineteenth century to be sure—but very much carved in the image of men like Benjamin Rush, who had earlier struggled to assure the survival of the republican experiment—both politically and *morally*. (We will therefore call Dow, and those of his mind, "neorepublicans.")

As a patriot and a Christian (the two were one in his mind), Dow felt called to oppose anything inimical to his vision of a virtuous United States. He was active on a number of reform fronts, but he was first and foremost a temperance man. Like Benjamin Rush, the mayor of Portland saw drunkenness as the nexus of a host of evils, none of which had a place in the good society. The list, like Rush's two generations before, was long, embracing civil disorder; immorality; the costs of courts, jails, and poorhouses; industrial accidents and inefficiency; and money wasted on liquor. Nor did he overlook the human side of the issue. Dow honestly thought that liquor was a prime disrupter of homes and a source of other domestic grief. Alcohol even damaged his own family: He once tried to dissuade a publican from selling to one of his wife's relatives; the taverner refused, the in-law went to a drunkard's grave, and Dow swore vengeance. Absolute prohibition of all beverage alcohol, he concluded, was the only cure for personal intemperance and its social ill effects. Toward that end he bent his considerable energies, sustained by the faith that he labored in a just cause.

Dow had no doubts that legal prohibition was a legitimate public policy goal. Society had to be protected. As in the colonial period, this was ample justification for the state to restrain the behavior of those who acted in a manner detrimental to the whole. Thus, the manufacture, distribution, and sale of beverage alcohol — known collectively as "the traffic" — had to be legally demolished in the cause of protecting the well-being of all citizens. To use other words, any rights belonging to the liquor business would have to yield to the higher needs of communal preservation and stability.

Armed with this doctrine, Dow canvassed the state throughout the mid-1840s — lecturing, buttonholing politicians, and helping establish local restrictions on liquor sales. In 1846 alone, he logged some four thousand miles and gathered over forty thousand signatures on a petition for state prohibition. Nevertheless, he suffered setbacks. The traffic took none of his efforts lying down, and the Maine government waffled on passing the measure he deemed essential. Dow was also threatened with personal violence. But, in 1851, he drafted yet another bill and presented it to the legislature: This was the Maine Law, the fruition of all his labors.

While fighting his temperance battles, Dow had other matters on his mind. His efforts had garnered him international attention (not all of it friendly), which later earned him a tidy sum on the lecture circuit.

Dow also used his newfound prominence to run for mayor of his native Portland in 1851, promising strict enforcement of the liquor law. His victory, after a raucous campaign, marked the start of a long and stormy political career. For the present, however, the coincidence of Dow's election with the advent of prohibition gave the zealous new mayor a chance to take a direct hand in the enforcement of the most important antiliquor measure yet on the books. He was overjoyed, and we can reasonably assume that he counted with glee every one of the sixty days he allowed "the traffic" to clear out of Portland. Then he made his move.

After the sixty-day grace period, Dow swooped down on a number of recalcitrant dealers and publicly dumped some $2,000 worth of liquor into the streets. This triumph — and sweet revenge for the past iniquities of the traffic — elicited not a murmur of opposition. "No resistance was made," one contemporary account noted. "The people stood quietly by and witnessed the whole in respectful silence."

If we believe the temperance commentators of the day, including Dow himself, wonderful things began to happen in Portland. With temptation out of the way, drunkards reformed, jails and poorhouses emptied, crime and poverty halved, and families stabilized and used their wages to purchase necessities rather than whiskey. These same reports also claimed that only hardened partisans of the traffic resented Dow's crusade. One old woman, watching as the confiscated alcohol met its demise, supposedly cried "that [had] this . . . been done twenty-five years ago; my husband would not have died a drunkard, and I should not have been [in the almshouse] with my children!" A lot of citizens of the 1850s apparently agreed with this favorable assessment. By 1855 twelve additional states and two Canadian provinces had enacted Maine Laws of their own. Other states had come close to doing so, and the general outlook for temperance appeared bright. Dow was a happy man, and he had a right to be. What he had done was impressive; even his enemies had to admit that much.

While impressive, however, Dow's crusade was also puzzling in the context of America's attitudes toward alcohol at the end of the eighteenth century — that is, just fifty years before. The traditional view of alcohol as a positive good, challenged only by Rush and a few others, obviously had collapsed between the Revolution and the Civil War. Instead, many Americans now classed drink as an unmitigated evil. For the first time, a coherent constituency labeled drinking a major social problem. To say the least, perceptions of drinking had changed both radically and rapidly—certainly faster than in the hundred years preceding Dr. Rush. Antiliquor sentiment had finally coalesced into a full-blown temperance movement, a reform effort that, by the late 1840s, made the "liquor question" one of the nation's most important political and social issues. Drinking, once such a socially uncomplicated matter, had become a thorny affair indeed. In considering the reasons *why*, we must return to the years following hard upon the close of the American Revolution.

Strong Drink, Strong Drinkers

As the nineteenth century dawned, the drinking habits that had so worried Dr. Rush continued unabated. Relatively heavy and frequent drinking, with the very American preference for hard liquor, had become common throughout the nation. In fact, the period from the 1790s to the early 1830s was probably the heaviest drinking era in the nation's history. Consumption estimates tell the story dramatically: From an annual average of 5.8 gallons of absolute alcohol per capita (for people aged fifteen or older) in 1790, mean absolute alcohol intake rose to 7.1 gallons a year by 1810 and, with minor fluctuations, remained at about that level until at least 1830. Of these amounts, as Samuel Dexter noted in 1814, "the quantity of ardent spirits . . . surpasses belief." And Dexter, who in 1814 was president of the Massachusetts Society for the Suppression of Intemperance—he had earlier served as treasury secretary and secretary of war—apparently knew what he was talking about, even if he was an interested source.

Dexter's data closely approximate modern consumption estimates (see the Appendix), which suggest that by 1800 (and possibly earlier) about half the absolute alcohol consumed was in the form of distilled liquor; this proportion was well over half after 1810. In 1830, for example, when average annual consumption was about 7.1 gallons (absolute), some 4.3 gallons were in hard liquor, while only 2.8 came from beer, cider, or wine. Again, however, as in dealing with the colonial drinking figures, it must be kept in mind that these were national averages, based on the entire population over fifteen years old. So, if, as Dexter insisted was necessary, we adjust our figures by excluding slaves and "others who, through disrelish, delicacy, or principle, drink little or none," average consumption levels for actual drinkers would have been much higher.

These figures seem almost too high. To drink enough whiskey, beer, or whatever to reach seven gallons of absolute alcohol in a year would be, for most people, a genuine feat, and we cannot be sure how accurate the estimates of nineteenth-century consumption really are. But at the same time, an extensive body of evidence (in the form of local histories, diaries, and travel reports) suggests that our best estimates are not far off the mark and that drinking had reached unparalleled levels. It seems clear that most Americans of the early nineteenth century drank pretty much as their Revolutionary period brethren had. They simply drank at an accelerated rate.

The question becomes why? For one reason, the old notion that alcohol was necessary for health remained firmly fixed. It was common to down a glass of whiskey or other spirits before breakfast, "and so conducive to health was this nostrum esteemed," noted a journalist in 1830, "that no sex, and scarcely any age, were deemed exempt from its application." Instead of taking coffee or tea breaks, Americans customarily stopped every morning and afternoon for eleven o'clock ("eleveners") and four o'clock drams. At the appointed hours, laborers in fields, offices, and shops halted and picked up the jug. Even school children took their sip of whiskey, the morning and afternoon glasses being considered "absolutely indispensable to man and boy."

Ardent spirits were a basic part of the diet—most people thought that whiskey was as essential as bread. In the evenings plenty of liquor was drunk during and after dinner to aid digestion and sleep; before retiring one took a "strengthening" nightcap, with one recipe calling for "whiskey, maple syrup, nutmeg, and boiling water, the whole dashed with rum." Taking a "healthful" dram, then, could have people drinking all day—a fact not unnoticed by many contemporary commentators. In "every corner," one Englishman recorded while traveling the Mississippi in the 1820s, "north or south, east or west, was the universal practice of sipping a little at a time, but frequently."

Social drinking, if anything, was even more prevalent in the nineteenth century than it had been in the colonial era. Even nondrinkers generally kept a supply of whiskey on hand for guests, and it was a rare occasion on which people got together without a bottle of spirits. "The friend who did not testify his welcome, and the employer who did not provide bountifully" in liquor "for his help, was held niggardly," one commentator noted. "The consequence was that, what the great majority indulged in without scruple, large numbers indulged in without restraint." According to a British observer, the Americans believed the British could settle nothing save over a good dinner; the Americans, he found, did nothing except over a drink. "If you meet you drink," he said, "if you part you drink; if you make an acquaintance you drink. They quarrel in their drink, and they make it up with a drink." And as in colonial times, the church by no means refrained from such goings-on. The Reverend Leonard Woods, one of New England's leading Congregational churchmen of the early nineteenth century, recalled that the ministers of the period could imbibe as well as anyone else. He remembered forty ministers "who were either drunkards, or so far addicted to drinking" as to limit their usefulness in the pulpit. He also wrote of an ordination celebration at which he had seen, to his mortification, "two aged ministers literally drunk, and a third indecently excited."

The story was much the same on the frontier, which by the first decades of the century was beginning to spill across the Mississippi River. There were, however, peculiarities in the drinking habits of some Western groups—patterns, fully evident by the 1830s and forties, that spread into the frontier areas of the later nineteenth century. Many of the earliest residents of both the trans-Appalachian and the trans-Mississippi West were uprooted individuals, drifters or people whose jobs kept them on the move and isolated for long periods: fur trapping "mountain men," cowboys, miners, and, to a lesser extent, federal troops. They lived hard, lonely lives, largely without families and without the social obligations or controls that constrained individual behavior in the East.

Thus, frontier drinking could be highly unrestrained and often was associated with gambling, fighting, and whoring. Drinking bouts tended to come after long dry spells; that is, after days or weeks—and in some cases months—in the mountains, on the trail, or in mining digs, where opportunities for drinking or other amusements were virtually nil. So at a mountain man's semiannual "rendezvous," a cowtown, or any other potential site of entertainment (which could have been only a sutler's wagon with a whiskey barrel), the impulse was to cut loose and make up for lost time. There was a tendency toward binge drinking, and many a trapper, miner, soldier, and cowboy blew their entire pay on a weekend debauch in towns with evocative names like Tombstone, Gomorrah, and Delirium Tremens. It was, in short, often a rude and individualistic group that pushed the frontier forward, often with personal and drinking behavior to match.

Some whites, for a variety of motives, encouraged binge drinking among the Western Indians. Not all tribes succumbed: They either shunned the white man's alcohol or learned to assimilate it without major cultural disruption. But others, like many of the Eastern Indians, fell afoul of fur traders and land speculators who employed established methods of getting Indians drunk before making deals with them. The shrewdest traders refused to negotiate with a sober Indian.

Library of Congress

The stereotype of the "drunken Indian," portrayed vividly in this twentieth-century drawing but shown by modern research to be inaccurate and misleading, survived in the popular mind for a long time. The context that encouraged acceptance of this view was contact between white traders and Indians in the late eighteenth and early nineteenth centuries. The traders plied the tribes with whiskey, hoping to take advantage of them in trade after alcohol had clouded the Indians' judgment.

They knew that, aside from trade with the whites, the tribes had little or no alcohol and that they usually drank all of what they received at one sitting (which practice the whites, of course, welcomed). This pattern frequently resulted in the violent intoxication of the tribesmen, making them prey to any manner of fraud. In exchange, the Indians did not even get good whiskey. Instead, traders generally substituted their own blends of "Indian whiskey," some of which, as the following example illustrates, were toxic:

> You take one barrel of Missouri River water, and two gallons of alcohol. Then you add two ounces of strychnine — because strychnine is the greatest stimulant in the world — and three plugs of tobacco to make them sick — any Indian wouldn't figure it was whiskey unless it made him sick — and five bars of soap to give it a head, and half a pound of red pepper, and then you put in some sagebrush and boil it until it's brown. Strain into a barrel, and you've got your Indian whiskey; that one bottle calls for one buffalo robe and when the Indian got drunk it was two robes.

Such vicious practices continued as long as the Indian trade lasted, and much of the consequent drinking among the tribes became part of Western folklore.

The drunken Indian became a stereotype, especially in fictional and romantic accounts of the period. In 1832, concerns over drinking-related violence, fused with humanitarian considerations, had prompted the national government under Andrew Jackson (an old Indian hater and baiter) to prohibit the flow of liquor into red territory. But as in the colonial past, traders largely ignored the ban, and many susceptible Indians epitomized the larger phenomenon of binge drinking in the West.

But in any given area, the wide-open phase of Western development generally passed soon enough. As the Indian nations were slaughtered or pushed aside, as the fur traders and the mountain men passed from the scene, and as the open range gave way to the fenced-in ranch, the trans-Mississippi West took on aspects of settled community life. Eastern families arrived, stable businesses opened, and law and order became the most compelling demand — all of which was incompatible with the old "roaring" lifestyle. As things calmed down, these new Western settlers started to drink much as did the Easterners whom they had left behind — which certainly did not mean that temperance was the order of the day.

The nineteenth-century farmer was the one who really tamed the developing frontier regions. The agricultural frontier had been pushing steadily west since the Revolution, usually following the fur trappers, miners, and cattlemen by a number of years. Farmers started to fill up Kentucky, Tennessee, and the Old Northwest well before 1820, and they moved across the Mississippi soon afterward; by mid-century, Americans were flocking to California (with its lure of gold), the Oregon Territory, Kansas, and Nebraska, leaving only the Great Plains region to be settled after the Civil War. But farming was not an easy way to make a living. It involved back-breaking work, with families dependent upon their own muscle power and the weather for success or failure. Life could be very lonely and, at least initially, spartan. The constant chores left little time for socializing, and the family's energies were bent toward the awesome problems of survival.

The farming frontier consequently saw relatively little of the riotous drinking behavior of the fur trappers and other rougher sorts. Yet, there was still plenty of drinking. One traveling evangelist noted in the 1850s that "a house could not be raised, a field of wheat cut down, nor could there be a log rolling, a husking, a quilting, a wedding, or a funeral without the aid of alcohol." But if alcohol formed an integral part of the farmer's daily life, disruptive drinking was a threat. Frequent intoxication diverted too much attention from maintaining a homestead. Thus, drunkenness was a luxury the average, struggling farmer could ill afford. For this reason, the drinking habits of most Western agriculturalists were more akin to the patterns familiar in the East than to the binge drinking of their ruder Western predecessors.

This is not to say that alcohol was not important on Western farms; on the contrary, frontier farmers first raised the issue of whiskey as a national question after the Revolution, albeit in a novel way. As part of their self-sufficient lifestyle, many of the trans-Appalachian farmers in the decade after independence continued the profitable colonial practice of turning much of their grain into whiskey. This was particularly true in the western counties of Virginia and Pennsylvania. These regions never lacked for passable whiskey, and they sold their product far and wide. Trouble started, however, when the new national government, in need of funds to carry out its programs, placed a tax on distilled spirits. Alexander Hamilton, the new nation's first secretary of the treasury, rightly foresaw a bonanza in revenues on distilled liquor, although there are also hints in the documents that temperance sympathies in men like Hamilton and James Madison of Virginia helped place whiskey on the taxable list.

At any rate, western Pennsylvania farmers protested the levy, which they saw as unfair (it may have been) and economically disastrous (it certainly was). Protest turned to open rebellion in western Pennsylvania after 1791, when some of the inhabitants and their supporters organized to resist the tax and drove federal collectors from the region. President Washington now faced a dilemma. He did not want to act the part of tyrant in the republic or move precipitately against the "whiskey rebels" for fear of giving his Jeffersonian political opponents — many of whom also criticized the tax — an issue. Yet he felt obligated to uphold the authority of the fledgling central government. Finally, after waiting until even a few Jeffersonians believed that things had gone too far in Pennsylvania, the president dispatched a strong militia force. Opposition melted in front of the invading army, and the federal tax measure was sustained, along with national government prestige. But from that date on, "moonshiners" began dodging revenue agents, placing America's beloved whiskey at the center of one of the nation's oldest illegal businesses.

But the Whiskey Rebellion did not deal with the question of temperance or, for that matter, with drinking habits. Rather, it was simply a further confirmation that hard liquor was available everywhere and that drinking had reached unusually high levels by the late eighteenth century.

Scattered evidence also indicates that drunkenness was far more prevalent after independence than it had been in the colonial era. If modern research that suggests a relationship among high average levels of consumption, availability of liquor, and rates of problem drinking is generally accurate, it can safely be assumed from literary records of the period that the young United States had more than its share of people in their cups. The Reverend Dorchester, one of the most diligent recorders of nineteenth-century drinking, certainly thought so, terming these years "the darkest period of all." He even compiled a sizable number of slang terms for getting drunk, including "half shaved," "cut in the craw," and "high up to picking cotton." Given these terms, everyday citizens were obviously aware that there was a lot of "high up to picking cotton" going around.

The same contemporary sources also indicate that early in the nineteenth century not very many persons saw disgrace in a binge; few, unlike Dr. Rush, considered such behavior a real threat to the moral fabric of the republic. Behavioral norms had in fact evolved to the point that imbibing citizens could take in stride quite a bit of what we would today consider problem drinking. This phenomenon was partly a reflection of the newer noncommunal, individualistic orientation that was emerging with the Revolutionary era—an outlook that put greater emphasis on personal liberty, self-reliance, and equality of opportunity among free citizens unfettered by unreasonable social and governmental restraints. This more latitudinarian world view stood in stark contrast to the community centered ethos of the colonial period and to the republicanism of Benjamin Rush, which emphasized a society of moral-political harmony and common purpose. Politically, this credo became more apparent with the election of Thomas Jefferson in 1800 and perhaps reached its zenith with the presence of Andrew Jackson in the presidency after 1828. The new mood exalted the rights of the common person, fostered a diversity of ideas, and preached the hatred of any form of privilege; it encouraged people to employ their wits and seek their fortunes individually, restrained only by their natural abilities. This emphasis upon the common person was also reflected in some aspects of American religious feeling. It was an era of revivalism, which stressed individual compacts with God as opposed to ritual or group covenants. The self-sufficient individual, not the community, thus became an integral part of the emerging Jeffersonian-Jacksonian value structure.

With this emphasis on more personal freedom in all areas of life, many Americans (although by no means all) sincerely felt that as long as their conduct hurt no one else, it was nobody's business what they did. Accordingly, as long as drinking harmed no one but the drinker, why worry or, more to the point, why make the behavior a national issue? In its day, this was a plausible position, despite the republicanism of the Founding Fathers. The fact is that many of the ill effects of drink so obvious in our postindustrial age were not as visible in the early nineteenth century. It was not necessarily a less complicated world; however, in a largely preindustrial milieu, drunken drivers in automobiles or alcoholic blackout by pilots at the controls of aircraft were not known. Thus, in the early 1800s, the idea that the problem drinker could cause serious social disruption had occurred to relatively few people; drinking behavior, even when disruptive, remained largely a matter of individual choice.

In this age of nascent democracy, drinking and beverage choice served to enrich the egalitarian ethos. For some citizens, downing American whiskey took on connotations of national feeling. "Good rye whiskey," one patriotic toper advised in 1814, "or high-proof apple-brandy," rather than wines or imported spirits, were the drinks for loyal men and women of the republic. Corn whiskey, particularly bourbon, earned yet more honors as a national drink. Harrison Hall, one of the most prominent distillers of the early 1800s, never tired of singing the praises of corn spirits. The French sipped their brandy, he noted, "the Hollanders swallowed gin; the Irish glory in their whiskey"; the English had their beloved porter. So, Hall reasoned, "why should not our countrymen have a national beverage?" Hard cider had its partisans for the honor, especially in New England. Whether enjoying cider or bourbon, however, many drinkers consciously identified their preferred beverage with a keen sense of nationhood, and they thus saw their imbibing as a patriotic act.

The social context of drinking, as historian W. J. Rorabaugh effectively argued, also captured the mood of the times. A personal binge, for example, was in a sense (albeit a perverse sense in some eyes) an assertion of individuality, of freedom from communal restraints. Even the drunkard, in essence, was a pluralist—free under the laws of the nation to pursue his or her own lifestyle no matter what others thought. After all, might the alcoholic not argue, was the nation not conceived in and dedicated to liberty? On the other hand, sharing drinks took on connotations of friendship and equality; refusing liquor could be a real insult. One minister who rode a circuit in the trans-Appalachian West remembered a parishioner saying that "if I did not drink with him, I was no friend of his, or his family, and he would never hear me preach again."

Captain Frederick Marryat, a British officer touring the United States in the 1830s, found that refusing a pull on the jug occasionally could be dangerous. "Stranger," went a local greeting (or so the captain reported), "will you drink or fight?" We can assume the captain either took the drink or won the fight, as he lived to write about the incident. But if he took the drink he was probably wise—for there is at least one grisly story of a group of Kentuckians who roasted one of their number to death when he refused to join them for a hospitable dram.

Perhaps no one saw the symbolic leveling role of drinking in the new democratic order better than did Jacksonian era politicians. The age took its politics seriously, and parties and candidates spared no pains to win the loyalties of the voter. They raised the old colonial practice of treating to an art form. A campaign of the 1830s, recalled by the governor of Illinois, was typical of the period. "Treating," he noted, was critical to electoral success:

In many counties the candidates would hire all the groceries in the county seats and other considerable villages, where the people could get liquor without cost for several weeks before election. The voters in all the neighboring country turned out every Saturday to visit the towns, see the candidates and hear the news. The candidates came also, and addressed the people from wagons, old logs, or stumps newly cut, from whence comes the phrase "stump speeches." The speeches being over, then commenced the drinking of liquor, and long before night a large portion of the voters would be drunk and staggering about town, cursing, swearing, halloing, yelling, huzza-ing for their favorite candidates.

But treating was more than a crowd pleaser; it was also a way for candidates to demonstrate their ties to the people—by drinking with them. Politicians in the Midwest, for example, knew the story of an old Baptist preacher, seeking a state governorship, who went "electioneer-

St. Louis Art Museum

The County Election, *by George Caleb Bingham (1851–1852). Bingham's classic rendition of the local political process offers one of the best views of drinking as a symbol of "democracy." Whiskey seems as much a part of the electoral procedure as voting itself: On the left, one well-heeled citizen enjoys a glass of the obviously bountiful liquor supply; left center, another voter is too inebriated to stand without assistance; on the right, yet another groggily hangs his bandaged head. The banner leaning against the column reads "The Will of the People the Supreme Law"—concern for what such a hard-drinking electorate might will in fact helped trigger the neorepublican temperance movement.*

ing with a Bible in one pocket and a bottle of whiskey in the other; and thus armed with 'the word of the Lord and the spirit' he could preach to one set of men and drink with another, and thus make himself agreeable to all."

In the presidential race of 1840, the Jacksonian opponents of William Henry Harrison printed an article alleging that the old man would be better off in a log cabin with a jug. The insult was a monumental blunder. In the "log cabin campaign" that followed, Harrison's managers played up the imagery—it had a certain common touch that voters liked. Harrison's supporters even passed out thousands of small bottles of hard cider just to make sure the voters remembered who their best friend really was. Harrison won handily.

Even earlier, at rough-hewn Andrew Jackson's inauguration gala in 1829, the imbibing crowds in the White House had become so rowdy that officials feared the revelers would tear the place apart. The solution was masterful: The staff carried the liquor out to the lawn; the gathering followed (naturally); and the mansion's doors swung shut. Few doubted, then, that America was in good hands as long as its leaders were willing to have drinks with the populace.

There is a final note on this point. It is worth speculating whether democratic ideology itself was not an important factor in America's drinking habits. The rise of this individualist ideology and the dramatic increase in drinking were parallel phenomena. "Rugged individualism," with its emphasis on self-reliance, while the staff of liberty for many, did not necessarily reflect an easy way of life. It threw families on their own initiative without the support of the old communal values and institutions in times of trouble.

Some social scientists have suggested, as well, that this lifestyle also helped shape perceptions of masculinity. The so-called rugged individualist won or lost the game of life on his own, and he did so by not complaining about trials or failures along the way. And certainly there were trials and failures enough in the early nineteenth century. New business ventures were risky; the acquisition of wealth was largely unregulated; and agriculture was subject to myriad hazards. The panics of 1819 and 1837, to cite only two examples, adversely affected thousands in all economic sectors, most especially the small-scale farmers and entrepreneurs who were so central to the individualist-egalitarian ethos of the age of Jackson.

There was, in sum, plenty to keep even self-reliant families anxious about in life. And it is well documented that anxious people drink. Al-

*The inauguration gala of Andrew Jackson, 1829. The original cap-
tion read: "President's Levée, or all Creation going to the White
House, Washington." By all accounts, the party was lively, with the
"treating" of the period thoroughly enjoyed by the guests.*

*The "log cabin campaign,"
1840. General William
Henry Harrison, who in reality was anything but from
a log cabin, was "just folks"
in this political cartoon. The
scene was complete with two
barrels of hard cider, a door
"always open to the travel-
ler," and a dog who recognized the general's former
comrades from the Battle of
Tippecanoe—fought back
in 1811!*

cohol, in turn, reduces anxiety; in fact, social drinking has always served as a means of reducing inner tensions and easing inhibitions. So it is just possible — although we will never be sure — that the pressures of life in the dawning era of individualism, coupled with the decline of traditional communal restraints against individual intemperance, explains at least in part the phenomenal drinking of the early nineteenth century.

Immigration and Antebellum Drinking

But even as Americans enjoyed their liquor in these turbulent years, events were in motion that would diversify their drinking habits and dramatically change the nation's views on the consumption of alcohol. In the first half of the nineteenth century, the United States witnessed a new start in the wave of mass migrations from Europe. As time went on, the impact on drinking patterns (and attitudes) of this floodtide of immigrants became increasingly pronounced.

The Irish were the largest single group of pre–Civil War immigrants. Fleeing poverty, political oppression, and, during the 1840s, the Great Famine, almost two million Irish landed in the United States between 1830 and 1860. Overwhelmingly, they were poor, and while some of them moved west or south, most remained in or near Eastern ports of entry. Cities such as Boston, New York, and Philadelphia contained major Irish populations by the 1850s. The immigrants lived virtually on the bottom of society's social scale. Crowded into squalid tenements, the Irish generally provided a cheap and plentiful labor supply for the industrializing Northern economy. Theirs was a hard life, made more difficult by massive social discrimination.

Native-born Americans had little love of the Irish. In addition to being poor, the newcomers were almost invariably Roman Catholic, and many of them clung to a personal value system rooted in deference to the church and to the Old World hierarchical social order that their church supported. For many Americans, this was enough to label the Irish as unacceptable aliens. The United States was largely a Protestant nation and had mistrusted anything connected with the Roman Catholic church ever since the beginning. This anti-Catholic bias exacerbated the already sharp cultural differences between natives and immigrants, particularly in areas with large Irish populations, and the natives often did their best to exclude Catholics from the American social, political, and economic mainstream. Indeed, cities like Charlestown, Massachusetts, and Philadelphia saw serious anti-Catholic rioting before the Civil War.

Some nativists went so far as to found an American Party, the Know-Nothings, dedicated to preserving the republic and its institutions from what they viewed as an onslaught of hostile immigrants with alien, antirepublican customs. From this narrow-minded perspective, anti-Catholicism was a social reform — and the nativist a reformer and a patriot looking backward toward a purer republic. The Know-Nothing party itself had considerable success in some regions before the Civil War. Thus, the "melting pot" phenomenon was not a major part of first-generation Irish experiences in the United States.

Responding to this hostility and to deeply held ethnic and religious preferences, many Irish resisted Americanization. In social and political activities, as well as in worship, they looked to themselves for support and protection. The Irish ultimately founded their own parochial schools, their own social organizations, and even their own militia regiments, and when they entered American politics, they did so in blocks under the tutelage of Irish ward politicians. In addition, many Old World customs and social relationships, such as obedience to church and local authority (a trait that greatly helped Irish political managers) not only remained alive but took on new vitality as signs of cultural strength and unity. Such, in particular, was the case with Irish drinking.

In Ireland, heavy drinking, which was often undistinguishable from problem drinking, had been an integral part of life. Much of this activity, as a number of sociologists have explained, was rooted in the "bachelor group." These groups provided a tight social network for men who, in land-hungry Ireland, had few opportunities to own enough land to make a living and, therefore, to raise families. The Great Famine exacerbated this pattern. Before the famine, the practice of subdividing land equally among sons had reached the point that parcels were too small to support families, except through intensive potato culture. With the famine, one solution was to delay marriage; another was to migrate across the Atlantic. For these men and there were many of them, young and old, who were driven to the brink of economic despair — drinking within the group turned into a communal ritual of belonging. The hours spent downing traditional Irish whiskey, gin, and malted beverages were vital to social stability for landless Irishmen. Drinking within the group was also a form of de facto social control. In a manner of speaking, it kept Irishmen "off the street and out of trouble" — or at least out of trouble unrelated to alcohol. In contrast, one could never be sure about what nondrinkers were doing. Out of sight of the bachelor group, they often were suspected of sexual promiscuity or other undesirable behavior. Thus, heavy drinking was as engrained in the Irish as it was among nineteenth-century native Americans, and it was a central element (as with the early colonists) in the cultural baggage of those emigrating to the United States.

In America, however, Irish drinking took on greater symbolic and emotional significance. Faced with an openly hostile environment, and both unable and unwilling to Americanize, the immigrants seized upon drinking as a major symbol of ethnic loyalty. That is, they drank hard to assert their Irishness; the harder they drank, the more Irish they supposedly became. Such drinking practices received the avid encouragement of many Irish-American leaders. For one thing, this pattern supported poverty-stricken widows, who could sell whiskey out of tenements without a license so long as ward politicians looked the other way. Local political bosses, who, to the dismay of native Americans soon dominated urban Irish politics, also frequently worked out of city saloons and saw to it that enough free drinks were passed around to keep the Irish vote loyal. (Treating was by no means a monopoly of native American politicians.) A large number of Irishmen went into the traffic as publicans, correctly perceiving a path to prosperity in the drinking habits of their brethren.

All of this made it relatively easy for anyone prone to alcoholism to get into real trouble. With heavy drinking openly accepted and drunkenness seldom classed a major vice, the Irish apparently did suffer from a much higher rate of inebriety than did other groups. Popular opinion held that the Irish and liquor were virtually synonymous, and the drunken Irishman became one of the major social stereotypes of the nineteenth century. To a degree, even the Irish-Americans accepted this image, although some ethnic spokesmen acknowledged that this did nothing to improve Irish status in the eyes of other Americans. "We are known," wrote one such person after the Civil War, "as a religion of saloonkeepers, of men who drink and men who provide the means of drinking." This view of the Irish eventually changed as social stigmas against them lessened and as second- and third-generation sons and daughters moved into the mainstream of American life; yet in the antebellum years, established neorepublicans viewed the drinking habits of the sons of Hibernia with alarm.

The Irish were not the only newcomers to arrive by the thousands before the Civil War. The antebellum flow of emigrants from Germany was second only to the tide from Ireland. Between 1830 and 1860, 893,000 Germans entered the United States. Over three million more arrived before the end of the century. Their initial assimilation experiences generally were happier than those of the Irish. German colonies dotted most major cities in the East and Midwest, and many German migrants either were skilled workers, who took the better industrial jobs denied the Irish, or had the financial means to open their own businesses. Thousands more were sufficiently well-to-do to acquire farms. There were some nativist grumblings about them, but the fact that fewer German settlers were Catholic and their relative success in adapting to American lifestyles spared them much of the prejudice directed at the Irish.

The Germans, like the Irish, also brought their traditional drinking habits with them. They preferred beer, but not the warm, heavy brew of the colonial period (which still had its partisans in the nineteenth century). The German drink was "lager beer," and the best was made from only water, hops, and malt. *Lager* means to ripen, and lager beer was allowed to age to a mellower flavor than that of previous American brews. German brewmasters began arriving during the 1840s and quickly reproduced some of their old country products.

As the beverage became popular with native-born Americans, lager beer quickly evolved to meet their preferences. Native Americans drank more and faster than did the Germans, habits that demanded a lighter and colder beverage than the original lager. Consequently, as one liquor dealer of the period noted, "a new American type of beer came into being"—the light-bodied, cold, golden brew popular today. Alcohol content in these beers ran roughly between 3.5 and 8.25 percent, and their flavor compared well with that of German products. Being plentiful wherever there were German-Americans, and fairly cheap to produce, beer became a favorite of wage earners of all national origins.

Distribution costs of lager, however, were high—barrels and kegs were bulky and heavy and hauling them any distance proved uneconomical. Local, family-oriented brewing therefore became the rule, and breweries were familiar parts of the urban landscape by mid-century. Cities with large German colonies, such as St. Louis and Milwaukee, experienced a boom in brewery construction, often under the eye of old country architects. Some owners, most of whom were German, eventually made fortunes as national distributors.

Anheuser-Busch, Pabst, Schmidts, Coors, Schlitz, and indeed most of modern America's popular beer labels are legacies from these early German-American brewers. The popularity of lager beer marked a resurgence in the use of nondistilled liquor. And although most of the nation still drank considerably more hard liquor than malted brews, the Reverend Dorchester was perceptive when he termed the years of German immigration the "beer invasion."

An antebellum brewery and beer garden in Fort Wayne, Indiana—evidence of the German influence in the Midwest.

The Germans were steady drinkers and downed their beer as eagerly as native Americans imbibed their whiskey. A German social gathering was scornfully described by a *New York Times* journalist:

> The object is to drink just as much beer as you can hold, smoke just as many cigars as you can bite the ends off of, and see who can sit in his chair the longest. It is an institution worthy [of] the gods. And, bless us, how the beer pours down! "It's up we all stand, and down she all goes"; and "Here, waiter, fill 'em up again." The man who can drink the most . . . is the best man. There is nothing to eat — and who would eat when he can blow off the foam and have her filled up again? . . . The bill of fare was varied and extensive. Following is a translation: Beer, Cigars, Beer, More Beer, Cigars, Beer, Beer, Beer, Beer, Beer, Beer, Beer, Beer, Beer, Beer, Beer, Beer, Beer, Beer, Beer.

But unlike the Irish, the Germans did not gain reputations as drunkards. Drinking to the point of frequent intoxication was not part of the German tradition, and as the German-Americans blended with native American society more easily, they had less reason to use facets of their Old World culture as defense mechanisms. Thus, there was no ethnic compulsion to drink to demonstrate one's Germanness. Indeed, except for their preference for lager beer rather than bourbon or rye whiskey, the Germans drank alcohol in much the same fashion (and at much the same rate) as did the native-born population.

Immigrant drinking in general, however, contributed significantly to a further diversification of American drinking patterns. Just as many native American communities did not assimilate the Irish and German newcomers, established ethnic patterns of alcohol use (with the exception of beer drinking) failed to enter the mainstream. Drinking habits took on a patchwork appearance in the United States, with different groups imbibing in different ways. By the 1840s and fifties, American tippling was more heterogeneous than it was in any of the more culturally homogeneous European nations.

Library of Congress

While the influx of immigrants diversified American drinking patterns, traditional beverages retained their popularity. For example, cider production was important in New England, the Middle Atlantic states, and some parts of the Midwest and South; innovations in cider mills (as this Pennsylvania advertisement indicates) commanded attention, and "apple bees," with plenty of cider on hand, were popular autumnal get-togethers in some regions.

The Antiliquor Response: The Origins of the Temperance Movement

As acceptable as drinking was to most Americans, it nevertheless had its critics. There was no temperance movement at the dawn of the nineteenth century, but animosity toward drinking excesses was clearly on the rise in certain quarters. Methodists, who along with the Quakers in the 1780s had denounced the use of distilled spirits for religious reasons, spread the tenet of abstinence from hard liquor as their sect experienced an explosive growth in numbers after the Revolution. Individual ministers of other religious groups also denounced strong drink on moral grounds, and Benjamin Rush himself remained the major public champion of temperance until his death in 1813. There were even a few organized efforts to deal with specific problems. In Litchfield County, Connecticut, for instance, some two hundred of the "most respectable farmers," challenging the wisdom of the day, concluded that drinking on the job did more harm than good and, in 1789, discontinued the customary liquor rations for farm labor. In 1808, a small group in Moreau, New York, founded the nation's first temperance society, also citing the deleterious impact of liquor on farm productivity.

Indeed, as these first temperance groups were being born, the United States was getting ready to enter an era of intense social reform activity — activity that merged temperance with goals as diverse as school reform, abolition, and women's rights. This ferment, growing out of the times, left the young republic in turmoil over a host of new social forces — forces that moved the nation steadily toward its modern character as a pluralist democracy. Thousands streamed toward the frontiers and beyond the influence of Eastern institutions; the increasingly powerful Jeffersonians (followed by the Jacksonians of the 1820s and thirties) offered citizens a democratic ideology stressing unfettered individualism as the basis of freedom, as opposed to the communal ideals of traditional republicanism; the arrival of major immigrant populations, unfamiliar with American values and having their own creeds and customs, also seemed likely to affect the character of the young nation; and around the corner loomed the industrialization process, with unknown consequences for the largely agrarian order of the postrevolutionary generation. While no one could predict where these trends would eventually lead, many Americans rejoiced at the apparent evolution of old social relationships and values and saw in the dawning age new and greater political and economic opportunities for all citizens. On the other hand, the specter of change also left a great many people, especially older native American families, perplexed and apprehensive.

Those who questioned the wisdom of these potentially radical changes were the nineteenth-century heirs of the old republicans—the neorepublicans of the stripe of Neal Dow. Like Benjamin Rush, former President John Adams, and others of the Revolutionary generation (many of whom were still alive in the early 1800s), they worshiped basic political liberty and the institutions of the republic, but only in the context of a stable social-moral order governed by men of sufficient character and virtue to appreciate what was needed for the welfare of all citizens. They were by no means against progress—many would play active roles in nineteenth-century commerce and industry—but they feared that, without proper social controls, the forces inherent in dawning American individualism and pluralism would sweep away the Revolutionary heritage. As reformers, they looked backward in seeking to provide for a stable, moral future.

For many neorepublicans, safeguarding society depended, as they frankly admitted, upon social and governmental leadership by men such as themselves—men of proven distinction, who would set high examples of personal conduct and had the courage to act vigorously in defense of accepted standards. Historians have termed this strain of thought the "stewardship tradition"; that is, a moral elite would act as stewards for the rest of the people, guiding and correcting their behavior. The elite would also lead a mass reformation in American values, thus assuring a citizenry of sufficient virtue to sustain the republic in the face of potentially disruptive pluralist influences. Such reform ultimately stressed the elimination of all social evils, at least those that bothered the neorepublicans.

These moral stewards honestly thought that they knew best how to order the affairs of other men and women. And they were equally convinced that reform would be a vital step in fulfilling the old republican dream of establishing the United States as a beacon of promise for the rest of humanity. If they could see to it that Americans acted in a manner worthy of their destiny, Providence itself—working largely through the major Protestant denominations—would guide the fortunes of the nation. Lyman Beecher of Connecticut, a staunch Calvinist minister and a prominent neorepublican reformer, revealed much of this faith in one of his calls for national reformation. "If it had been the design of Heaven to establish a powerful nation in the full enjoyment of civil and religious liberty," he wrote in the early 1800s, "where all the energies of man might find full scope and excitement," and "to show the world by one great successful experiment of what man is capable," where else would God do it "but in this country!" From this perspective, to labor for reform and for a perfected republic was to labor for the Lord, and hundreds set to the task with determination and confidence.

The reform impulse flowed into a number of channels and became a hallmark of the American experience before the Civil War. Any condition or situation labeled evil generated an effort — and frequently a formally organized national society — to set it right. Temperance was only one facet of this general phenomenon: Peace, abolition, the elimination of profanity and Sabbath-breaking, women's rights, mental health, the rekindling of orthodox Protestantism, concern over immigration (including, in its extreme forms, some of the anti-Catholicism noted earlier), education, and other causes all attracted champions. Temperance reform, however, as the period advanced, became one of the most popular causes. As drunkenness lay demonstrably at the root of other social ills, or at least symbolized such aspects of rampant pluralism as immigration and the roughhouse lifestyle of the American West, the attack on intemperance appeared particularly important. How, for example, could the nation logically promote better care for the mentally ill or the imprisoned if it allowed people to drink themselves to insanity or to a life of crime? Why reform public education when children returned each day from school to besotted parents, or end poverty when the poor squandered their pay on liquor? It seemed impossible to cure national ills without acknowledging the centrality of the liquor question, and legions of reformers quickly came to accept what Rush had pointed out long before: The elimination of drunkenness would prove crucial to avoiding internal civil disruption — thus literally preserving the republican experiment itself.

These neorepublican considerations were fully evident in the first major attempt to unite scattered temperance voices. That movement came into being in 1811, at the annual meeting of the general assembly of the Presbyterian church in Philadelphia. An aged Dr. Rush, then only two years from death but still a zealous guardian of the republic, sent the assembly one thousand copies of the *Inquiry* for distribution. He also urged the gathered clergymen to take a strong protemperance stance. In his appeal, the old physician was concerned less with theological matters than with the social-moral influence of organized religious groups. The churches in general, and the Presbyterian church in particular—one of America's oldest and most prestigious sects—carried immense weight with the public, and Rush knew that any cause espoused from the pulpit would become a cause to be reckoned with.

The Presbyterian clergy did not let him down. They, too, were concerned with the social forces being let loose upon the land. As members of a denomination long identified with the fortunes of the republic, they also feared the loss of national stability and of time-honored values and social relationships. Accordingly, the assembly issued a statement denouncing the drinking habits of the day, lamenting that "we are ashamed but constrained to say that we have heard of the sin of drunkenness prevailing—prevailing to a great degree—prevailing among even some of the visible members of the household of faith." The clergy then appointed a committee to report on how to best restrain "the excessive and intemperate use of spiritous liquors." Rush was delighted, especially because these actions attracted considerable public notice.

Presbyterian leaders next rallied their state congregations. Throughout 1811 and 1812, church groups in New England and the Middle Atlantic states offered prayers, resolutions, and sermons in the nascent battle against drink. In Connecticut, the state Presbyterian association struck directly at American drinking practices. The association called not only for preaching against intemperance but also for excluding spirits from the family diet and from church gatherings; parents were urged to warn their children against liquor and "farmers, mechanics and manufacturers" to end liquor rations for their workers. Men such as Lyman Beecher also wanted temperance literature distributed and societies formed to promote public morality. After some preliminary planning, the Society for the Promotion of Morals appeared in 1813 to combat the related vices of intemperance, Sabbath-breaking, and profanity. The same year and with similar goals in mind, some of the most prominent sons of Massachusetts founded the Massachusetts Society for the Suppression of Intemperance, the first statewide temperance organization.

Thus, the seed planted at the Presbyterian assembly of 1811 had taken root. Over the next decade, the temperance movement increased in strength and tempo. The Presbyterians, however, did not work alone. In 1816, the Methodists pledged to redouble their temperance efforts, and their ministers spread the gospel into the Midwest and South. Congregationalists, a number of Baptists, a few Anglicans, and many of the evangelical sects that flourished in the early 1800s took up the crusade as well. In fact, the chief credit for popularizing the temperance message before the mid-1820s must go to the Protestant churches, whose social influence and sheer numbers began to have a national impact.

A formal national temperance movement emerged in 1826: the American Society for the Promotion of Temperance (later known as the American Temperance Society). Leadership rested firmly in the hands of socially prominent clergy and laymen, whose proclaimed purpose was the reformation of the nation under the guidance of "holy men" who would "induce all temperate people to continue temperate" through abstinence from ardent spirits. The early temperance movement, then, was *not* a prohibitionist crusade; in adopting this moderate approach, the new society had taken a page right out of Benjamin Rush. Rush, whose memory the society revered and whose writings became movement gospel (he would eventually be known as the "Father of Temperance" and the "True Instaurator"), had counseled precisely such a course. Permitting the measured use of nondistilled beverages would prevent the drinking excesses associated with hard liquor.

Armed with this moderate doctrine, the Society for the Promotion of Temperance performed admirably. It virtually assumed the national leadership of temperance activities. The society helped organize local units, sent lecturers into the field, distributed literature (including the *Inquiry*), and served as a clearinghouse for movement information. Within three years, in large measure inspired by society proselytizing, 222 state and local antiliquor groups were at work across the land. The crusade was by no means at peak strength numerically, nor did it have any appreciable political influence at this stage; yet temperance reform now constituted a burgeoning national movement.

"Pure Water": Temperance Becomes Total Abstinence

As the temperance movement gathered momentum, additional reform motives—sometimes intertwined with neorepublican concerns for stability and national perfection—broadened the appeal. For example, the movement was a direct beneficiary of a series of religious revivals that swept the nation in the early nineteenth century. Many of the revivalists included the national perfectionist message in their calls for individual redemption and salvation, with temperance serving the cause of both. Some stressed temperance only as a means of avoiding sin and thus setting one's course toward salvation. Much to the delight of reform leaders, who saw benefits for the cause despite their elitist distaste for the revivalists, thousands of Americans swore off ardent spirits as an article of religious faith.

Fear of alcohol addiction, the enslavement to drink that Rush had described, was instrumental in bringing about a crucial change in the meaning of temperance—the shift from temperance as abstinence from distilled beverages to temperance as total abstinence. Even before the 1820s, some temperance advocates had insisted that prohibition was the only logical way to eliminate drunkenness: Alcohol was alcohol, they argued, whether in the form of beer, wine, cider, or distilled spirits; if alcohol was addictive in one beverage, why not in another? Beers and wines, from this more extreme perspective, were especially pernicious. They promised safety and health while they slowly brought about the drinker's doom. There was "no safe line of distinction between the *moderate* and the *immoderate*" use of alcohol, a Methodist report noted in 1832. That moderate use led to immoderate drinking "is almost as certain as it is insensible." The report ended by questioning "whether a man can indulge . . . at all and be considered temperate."

The most forceful statement of this position came in Lyman Beecher's *Six Sermons on Intemperance*. Beecher delivered them from the pulpit in Litchfield, Connecticut, in 1825. In 1826 he published them, and the *Six Sermons* took their place with Rush's *Inquiry* as temperance movement classics. Any drinking, he argued, was a step toward "irreclaimable" slavery to liquor; people simply could not tell when they crossed the line from moderate use to inebriety—could not tell, that is, until too late. Look out, he said, if you drank in secret, periodically felt compelled to drink, and found yourself with tremors, inflamed eyes, or a "disordered stomach." "You might as well cast loose in a frail boat before a hurricane, and expect safety," Beecher explained, and "you are gone, gone irretrievably, if you do not stop." But most could not stop; the power of alcohol was too strong. This fact, he noted, coupled with the abolition of the liquor traffic, would at least end the country's alcohol problem, as the "generation of drunkards" would "hasten out of time." Total abstinence, Beecher concluded, was the only sure means of personal salvation and societal stability.

The temperance movement controversy over total abstinence gave rise to one account of the origin of the term "teetotaler." In Hector, New York, the local temperance society debated the matter in 1826. To compromise, it allowed members a choice of pledges, one foreswearing all liquor, the other just distilled spirits. However, those going completely dry received a T—for total abstinence—next to their names on the society rolls, thus becoming known locally as "T-totalers." The term spread generally as other societies introduced total abstinence pledges.

Yet most leaders in the temperance movement were leery of total abstinence. From observation, if nothing else, reformers knew all too well that Americans loved to drink—and asking them to abandon whiskey seemed radical enough. Anything more, they believed, would offend the public and weaken the temperance cause, making the movement useless as a means of perfecting the republic. In fact, the founders of the American Temperance Society, while privately favoring total abstinence, dared not make it a tenet of the new organization for fear of outraging both the public and the mass of their colleagues in reform. There was, after all, the moderation legacy of Benjamin Rush, and even some old temperance leaders remained "ardent advocates for the culture of the grape . . . as a preventive of the ravages of intemperance." Accordingly, when a motion to espouse total abstinence came before the first national temperance convention in 1833, it went down to a quick defeat—although the gathering closed by heralding "pure water" as the only truly safe substitute for ardent spirits.

The proponents of total abstinence, however, steadily gained ground. Local societies increasingly fell into line. Seemingly convincing medical indictments against all beverage alcohol put holdouts on the defensive. In 1835, for example, reformer Edward C. Delevan of Albany, New York, published an expose of local brewers, claiming that they distributed unsanitary beer and ale. Hauled into court, as Dorchester explained, Delevan successfully proved that the brewers had used water from "a common receptacle for dead animals; that it received the drainage of slaughter houses and a glue factory." The publicity was terrific, and it did not enhance the reputation of beer. The same year, the national society released its own report on the nature of alcohol and concluded that, after all, there was no less danger in wine or beer than in whiskey or rum. Teetotalers hailed the report, and no one admitted that it contradicted Rush's moderationist dictum; they reasoned instead that they were simply advancing the ideas "so carefully nursed by our good Dr. Rush" to a higher plane.

On this basis, teetotalers carried their point. At a subsequent national temperance convention in Saratoga, New York, in 1836, the delegates formally endorsed total abstinence as the movement's interpretation of temperance. There was still some resistance among the rank and file, but by the end of the decade the issue was virtually closed. Temperance reform, for the first time, had gone fully "dry."

Rutgers Center of Alcohol Studies

The Drunkard's Progress from the First Glass to the Grave, by N. Currier. Currier's 1846 print is, in effect, a graphic version of Rush's earlier "Moral and Physical Thermometer." The artist depicted the same gradual addiction process, with similar social and health complications.

More remarkable, however, was the extent to which the rest of the nation followed suit. In 1835 the national temperance society estimated that two million people had renounced the use of distilled liquor (causing some four thousand distilleries to close), while nearly a quarter of a million persons had become total abstainers. Membership in temperance organizations had climbed to about 1.5 million. Thousands of others without any temperance affiliation or signing any pledge, also cut back on their drinking, even if they did not stop entirely. The cumulative effect sent national liquor consumption plummeting. From a high of just over seven gallons of absolute alcohol per capita annually in 1830, consumption estimates fell to slightly more than three gallons by 1840 — the largest ten-year drop in American history.

But abstinence pledges and depressed consumption rates only signaled a deeper shift in attitudes toward drinking. The traditional notion holding alcohol a positive good and drinking a normal and necessary part of life was coming apart under the relentless pressure of the temperance movement. The majority, to be sure, still drank, but the dry minority was larger than ever before by the end of the 1830s. Indications of strength were legion. Few employers, for instance, still provided their workers with eleveners or four o'clock drams, and many a harvest was coming in without benefit of liquor. Some employers, including a few of the new railroads, where a mistake on the job could be costly and deadly, had begun to fire anyone found drinking on duty. Increasingly, too, there were objections that drinking was something immigrants, as opposed to "true" Americans, did. Prominent citizens such as Senator Henry Clay of Kentucky gave well-publicized formal dinners without any of the customary libations, and these "cold water" parties created a popular stir. Drinking, in sum, no longer enjoyed its traditional high status.

Soon there were legal assaults on drinking. Since the colonial period, publicans had operated under licenses granted by county courts or municipal governments. The arrangement was essentially financial (it gave local authorities a steady source of income) rather than social (a control against drinking-related problems). However, the authorities could close a troublesome tavern by refusing to renew its license. Temperance advocates seized on this power and pushed for a wholesale rejection of new licenses and nonrenewal of expired ones. The local prestige of reformers brought some success but many tavern owners — often men of influence themselves — fought back with energy, frequently with the support of politicians who loathed the idea of losing license revenues. The legal result was generally a standoff. Wets prevailed in some areas and drys in others, with the status of some regions alternating with local changes in political leadership. Attacking licenses was a slow and frustrating way to stop drunkenness, but many reformers found pleasure in entering electoral struggles against the traffic, and they gained valuable experience in the techniques needed to transform temperance from a moral to a legislative movement.

Minimal political success emboldened some reformers to open a wider legal front. If the traffic was an evil, they reasoned, then society had every right to do more than revoke licenses—citizens should abolish drinking in defense of the common good. Prohibition thus seemed a logical step. In his *Six Sermons*, Lyman Beecher had argued that it was "vain to rely alone upon self-government and voluntary abstinence. Many may be saved by these means; but with nothing more, many will be lost and the evil will go down to other ages." Other temperance advocates explained that even reformed alcoholics still faced the enticements of the "rumsellers," to which the addictive nature of alcohol left them vulnerable. Under the circumstances, the Reverend Leonard Bacon argued that "you might almost as well persuade the chained maniac to leave off howling, as to persuade him to leave off drinking." There was only one remedy: "Remove the cause of it." The temperance movement thus translated abstinence from a voluntary, personal moral decision into a legislative mandate to save society as a whole. Stability, in this view, meant legal as opposed to moral suasion.

Yet support for prohibition in the 1830s was often haphazard. Most dry workers knew that coerced abstinence was many steps ahead of popular opinion, despite widespread sympathy for more moderate temperance ideas. To press the question too soon, they feared, could provoke an unfavorable reaction, particularly if an unwilling public saw prohibition as an invasion of civil rights. It was a dilemma for drys, but the stakes, a sober republic and all its consequent moral and civil blessings, seemed worth the gamble. They would risk offending the few to guarantee the safety of the many. Theodore Parker of New England, one of the greatest of the antebellum reformers, admitted that prohibition indeed seemed "an invasion of private rights." But he reasoned that it was "an invasion . . . for the sake of preserving the rights of all." While he believed that a drink was fine "when rightly used," Parker was convinced "that nine tenths" of the alcohol used was actually "abused." "The evil is monstrous," he concluded, "so patent, so universal, that it becomes the duty of the state to take care of its citizens; the whole of its parts."

Prohibition had minimal support outside the temperance movement itself before the 1840s, but the political potential of the idea was not lost on the more astute politicians of the day. Whether they were for or against temperance, few government officials were willing to offend dry leaders gratuitously. In fact, many highly placed national officials lent the movement a sympathetic ear. In 1832, for example, the Reverend Justin Edwards, the most active agent of the national society, prevailed upon Secretary of War Lewis Cass to end liquor rations for the army. That same year, the House of Representatives played host to a congressional temperance meeting, which solemnly denounced the manufacture of hard liquor as "incompatible with the obligations of social and moral duty, by every patriot and especially by every Christian in the country." While the legislators promised no legal action to enforce their resolutions, they did claim the right to make law on temperance issues should national well-being so require. Their statement on this count clearly revealed the continuing force of traditional republicanism: They affirmed both the right and the duty of a righteous citizenry to marshall public virtue—sacrificing personal interest for the good of the whole—in defense of communal safety. "The liberties and welfare of the nation," the assemblage recorded, "are . . . indissolubly connected with the morals and virtue of the people; and that, in the enactment of laws for the common benefit, it is" the duty of Congress to protect "the public morals from corruption." Benjamin Rush could not have stated the proposition any better.

How much of this proclamation was mere cant to satisfy dry constituents is hard to determine, although there is no reason to doubt the sincerity of many of the legislators. Some of them, such as Theodore Frelinghuysen of New Jersey and George Briggs of Massachusetts, were true believers, and in 1833 they helped organize the American Congressional Temperance Society. At the same time, politicians on all levels ended treating in their campaigns, which garnered plaudits from the dry leadership. The practice, an American Temperance Society report noted, had been unworthy of the leaders of a "great republic." And even if much of this early political support for temperance was mere expedience, it was powerful testimony to the rising influence of antiliquor forces.

Redeeming the Lost: Revivalists and Republicans

While the temperance movement mulled over the question of prohibition, events transpired that temporarily took the antiliquor initiative away from the established reform societies. A dry revival, led by men with no prior temperance connections, swept the nation in the 1840s, catching reformers almost completely by surprise. This remarkable dry explosion was the "Washingtonian movement," founded by six Baltimore topers in 1840. Sitting in Chase's Tavern one evening, or so tradition has it, these gentlemen turned to a discussion of their tippling ways, which they admitted were undermining their lives. As a consequence—and perhaps as a lark—one of the group, charged with reporting back to his companions, attended a nearby temperance lecture. The delegate emerged from the lecture a new man, not only taking the pledge himself but also persuading his friends to do the same. They decided to work for the reform of other drinkers, and calling themselves the Washington Temperance Society (in honor of the first president), they drew up a total abstinence pledge.

The group succeeded beyond its wildest expectations. Over a thousand men took the society's pledge by the end of the year, and "missionaries" then carried the Washingtonian theme to New York City, where they attracted thousands. After this, the Washingtonians came to represent a full-fledged revival. Societies patterned on the Washingtonian model sprang up everywhere; churches opened their sanctuaries for meetings; and Washingtonian lecturers, such as the spellbinding John B. Gough and John Hawkins, joined the ranks of the most sought-after speakers in the country.

Members worked fervently to hold one another to the pledge. They rushed to the aid of those who relapsed. If necessary, they helped fellow members find new jobs or temporary financial support. This work with the alcoholic was critical in the Washingtonian view; for beyond taking the pledge, the society stressed that the lifestyle of drunkards had to change. If they were to lose forever their passion for liquor, they had to avoid the social situations that had led them to drink in the first place. Under Washingtonian guidance, legions recovered—perhaps 600,000 by the late 1840s. Of these, about 150,000 ultimately remained abstinent. This meant, of course, that 450,000 relapsed at least to some degree; as one temperance historian put it, however, to save so many of a class generally thought hopeless was in any case "a glorious fact of moral triumph."

The Washingtonians were unlike other regiments in the antidrink army. Their emphasis was on saving individual alcoholics, not general social reform. To them, alcoholism was a problem of the isolated drinker, not part of a broader social malaise or a matter of ideological neorepublicanism. Helping the drunkard was the end in itself. At a time when the formal temperance movement was advocating prohibition, the Washingtonians remained cool toward legislatively oriented solutions to the problem. Indeed, to keep the focus on alcoholics and their problems, Washingtonians often closed their meetings to clergy and to members of other temperance organizations.

Its singular purpose probably accounts for much of the movement's stupendous growth. More than any other source, the Washingtonians offered hope to individuals too often dismissed as irredeemable. Whereas even the church "had passed them by as hopeless," wrote the Reverend Joel Parker in the 1840s, "God raised up reformers from among themselves, and now the multiplied and moving tales of woes and sins, and recoveries of poor, lost drunkards, are telling with amazing power upon hearts that were accounted to be beyond reach of the Gospel." Too many temperance advocates in other societies had little personal interest in the drunkard, Illinois legislator Abraham Lincoln observed in 1842. The Washingtonians were different. "Those whom they desire to convince and persuade are their old friends and companions. They know they are not demons," Lincoln said, "nor even the worst of men." In their charitable approach, Lincoln was sure, lay the Washingtonians' popularity.

Yet the meteoric rise of the Washingtonians held the seeds of their eventual decline. Like all other revival phenomena, the movement lost momentum, and by 1844 its activities were on the decline. By 1847 almost all the local societies had stopped meeting (although the Boston chapter continued to gather until 1860). More important than declining momentum was the loss of church and non-Washingtonian temperance support. The established churches, which had been allies, had come to resent Washingtonian opposition to their presumed leadership of the dry struggle, and they began to close their doors to movement activities. This prompted Washingtonian attacks on the church, which in turn exacerbated bad feelings. Some clergy envied the success of the lay movement, hurt that ex-alcoholics proved better reformers than learned ministers. "As [the clergy] were neither the originators nor the leaders in the movement," wrote one temperance man, "they felt themselves ignored, [and] therefore refused to have any affiliation for, or lend any assistance to it." At the same time, and for the same reasons, the older temperance societies also began to withdraw support. The societies worried further that the Washingtonians had drained off energies that might otherwise have flowed to them and that the revivalist oriented group lacked the institutional structure and the wider reform vision necessary to preserve the republic. The neglect of legal authority in the fight against liquor was a mistake, they insisted. Even a generally sympathetic temperance observer felt compelled to note that the "triumph of moral suasion was short and doubtful." In that the emotional appeal of the Washingtonians had diverted attention from the societies working toward legal suasion, their activities were actually an "evil." It was true that the Washingtonians had neither long-range programs nor a central organization to sustain what they had won. To save drunkards and then to see thousands of them relapse because liquor was still freely available made less and less sense to the stewardship oriented societies. In their eyes, the Washingtonian experience was proof that real progress could be attained only through legislation.

It is questionable, however, to what extent the Washingtonians actually disappeared. Some of the most influential lecturers, like John B. Gough, stayed in the field (although many eventually adopted a prohibitionist posture), and many old Washingtonians ultimately joined other temperance societies. But the most immediate Washingtonian legacy was a proliferation of fraternal temperance orders. Beginning

A Sons of Temperance membership certificate.

in the mid-1840s, as the Washingtonian tide ebbed, many of the revivalists and other temperance sympathizers swelled the ranks of such groups as the Sons of Temperance, the Good Templars, and the Temple of Honor and Temperance. Before the Civil War, hundreds of thousands of people had enrolled — for the purpose of safeguarding themselves against drink — in fraternities "more binding in . . . character and more perfect in . . . unity than the previous Washingtonian societies."

These fraternal orders were similar in structure. Most had elaborate oaths and abstinence pledges. Regalia and ceremonies were governed by "worthy patriarchs" and subofficials, who ruled with extensive by-laws and constitutions. Most of them initiated some kind of insurance benefits (in effect, they were analogous to dry Elks or Moose lodges). Sometimes, there was an organizational publication; some of these, like the *American Temperance Magazine*, published by the Sons of Temperance, were well edited and had major circulations. Local chapters owed allegiance to state or national organizations, and some lodges admitted women. Still others either enrolled blacks in integrated meetings or established them in separate lodges. Although many of these orders were short-lived, a few survived well into the twentieth century (the Good Templars society still exists).

Typical lodge constitutions stated that the members had come together "to protect [themselves] and others from the evils of intemperance, afford mutual assistance, and elevate [their] character." Brothers and sisters kept watch on one another to enforce the abstinence pledge, and some organizations had members seek out drunkards in order to aid in their rehabilitation. Breaking the pledge was grounds for expulsion, but in practice this measure was used only as a last resort. Most lodges punished lapses relatively mildly, enjoining their tippling members to sign a new pledge and to pay a small fine; moreover, expelled members could apply for readmission. The prospect of aid during a drinking-related crisis, after all, was one of the chief motives for joining. For brothers or sisters to turn their backs on another member — who might have been a friend or relative — would have made no sense.

A major effect of the Washingtonian revival was the stimulus it provided the prohibition drive. No single event did so much to focus public attention on the liquor question in so short a time. Despite their differences with the Washingtonians, dry reform leaders took full advantage of the situation. The traditional societies built up their memberships and influence as preceptors of public morality. They were further heartened as the new fraternal orders fell in under the prohibition banner. As it turned out, the Washingtonian rank and file—many of whom were former drunkards—moved into the new fraternities, but they did not usually lead them. The highest posts generally went to respected elite citizens of local communities, the bulk of whom were in full sympathy with the moral-social order envisioned in neorepublican ideology.

Thus, while the goal of personal deliverance from drinking problems remained central to the fraternal orders, they also stressed prohibition. The destruction of the traffic, they felt, would not only prevent drunkenness but also secure the stable moral society in which the sober mind could employ its talents. And with the strength of the fraternities added to that of the societies, not to mention those friendly to temperance ideals but lacking formal affiliations, the late 1840s saw a groundswell of prohibition activity.

In fact, prohibition sentiment had reached critical mass, the movement becoming, save only for abolition, the most powerful antebellum reform effort. Thousands of people, who before had merely dreamed of a dry republic, now saw this goal as within the realm of possibility. They began to bombard state legislatures with demands for the abolition of demon rum. Among some politicians, support for prohibition was already there. As early as 1846, temperance forces in Maine, under the leadership of Neal Dow, had persuaded the legislature to outlaw the manufacture and sale of distilled liquors. Although the law lacked penalties harsh enough to compel full compliance, the response of the legislators was enough to make temperance advocates in other states optimistic.

On the other hand, many political leaders—including some with temperance loyalties—were appalled at the prospect of thrashing out temperance questions in the political arena. In the 1840s, neither of the major political parties could boast any real unity on the great reform issues of the day. The Whigs, formed in the 1830s as an anti-Jackson coalition, had strong attachments to traditional republicanism, and significant elements of the Democratic party had also moved down the road of moral reform. But both parties were beginning to feel the strains of the growing antislavery crusade, making it increasingly hard to keep the party faithful in line—and the last thing party managers wanted was another divisive issue. Most political leaders, not to mention the masses of voters, recognized that there was no national consensus on prohibition. A great many people favored this goal, certainly vast majorities in some areas, but millions of Americans still prized their right to drink. Nationally, they probably still outnumbered their dry countrymen. The possibility existed that a drive for prohibition would evoke determined resistance, further fragmenting a republic already being torn asunder by the slavery question.

This fear proved well founded as opposition to prohibition appeared on a number of fronts. The liquor industry, wealthy and formerly respected, fought back in desperation. In particular, the brewers counterattacked with genuine hatred, feeling especially wronged. (Until the movement switched to total abstinence in the late 1830s, the brewers had seen themselves as temperance allies.) They held that beer, as Rush had suggested, was a wholesome substitute for ardent spirits. Teetotalism, however, drove them to common cause with the distillers, and together they financed proliquor candidates and, not infrequently, bribed politicians to support their interests. But such tactics often backfired. Brought to light in temperance exposes, they seemingly confirmed reform arguments that the traffic was a cancer on the republic.

Recent immigrants also formed a major opposition block. The reformers had found considerable early sympathy in some German communities. However, when presented with total abstinence, most Germans clung stubbornly to their lager. Nor would the Irish give up their drinking. In return, dry frustrations with the immigrants frequently took on an antiforeign cast, and temperance and nativist reformers often joined forces in political contests.

Nor did the South have much use for prohibition. The movement never fully died in the slave states, but it declined quickly as Southerners found that many firm abolitionists were also dry: William Lloyd Garrison, for example, one of the most strident of the antislavery voices, cried out as well for prohibition (his brother had died an alcoholic); Neal Dow, one of the most active prohibitionists, was almost as ardent in his abolitionism. Prohibition, in short, was a real political problem, destined to upset as many people as it pleased.

The experience of Father Theobald Mathew when he visited the United States illustrates how touchy a political issue prohibition had become. A gentle and pious Irish priest of the Capuchin order, Father Mathew led a series of spectacular temperance crusades in Ireland and Britain, emerging as one of the most beloved Irishmen of his time. So successful was he that the American Temperance Union (a coordinating body of state and national society officers formed in 1836) ignored his Catholicism and agreed to help support his stay in America. The hope was that he would build prohibition sympathy in general and get the temperance message through to Irish immigrants in particular. After initial hesitation, caused in part by anti-Catholic riots in Philadelphia, Father Mathew launched his American venture in 1849. Before leaving the United States in 1851, he had pledged thousands to total abstinence on a pilgrimage that took him through New England, the Middle Atlantic states, the South, and as far west as Arkansas. While he met many of the nation's leaders, his ministry was principally among the poor. Irish Catholics were especially drawn to him. His work gave new vigor to the struggling Catholic Total Abstinence Union, which was trying valiantly to promote temperance among Irish-Americans. From a strictly temperance perspective, almost everyone had reason to applaud Father Mathew.

But temperance was not the only perspective. Years before his tour, the Irish priest had denounced slavery, a position that endeared him to many American reformers. Upon coming to the United States, however, Father Mathew chose to address only the temperance issue; he was, therefore, soundly vilified by a number of Northern reformers. Nor, because of his antislavery sympathies, was he any more popular with many Southern leaders. This became evident when Congress chose to honor him by inviting him to sit at the bar of the Senate while in Washington, D.C. — the first foreigner since the Marquis de Lafayette to be accorded such a distinction. Father Mathew took his seat, but not until a number of Southern senators, led by Jefferson Davis of Mississippi, the future president of the Confederacy, scathingly attacked him as an agent of abolitionism. He certainly was not; but just as certainly his American experience was a sign of how seriously antebellum temperance battles could be affected by other issues.

Despite the controversies that swirled around their cause, the prohibitionists were tireless workers. Throughout the late 1840s, they incessantly lobbied their state legislatures and often allied themselves with other reform groups or political factions that sought dry votes for their own ends. In some states, prohibitionists leagued variously with antislavery Democrats, who were warring with the dominant pro-South wing of their party, and with elements of the Whigs, who were already beginning to lose their party cohesion under the stress of the sectional controversy. The societies and fraternal orders also supported these political efforts, lending votes, literature, organizational skills, and lecturers. Even commercial publishers gave a helping hand, albeit

A scene from an early edition of Timothy Shay Arthur's Ten Nights In A Bar-Room. *Mary Morgan—daughter of Joe Morgan, a drunkard who eventually emerges as the story's hero—is trying to lead her besotted father home. In the musical stage production of the novel, this is the point at which Mary sings, "Father, dear father, come home with me now." It also is the end of poor Mary: The enraged barkeep, Simon Slade, hurls a glass that mortally wounds the girl— the tragedy that prompts Joe finally to go on the wagon and to campaign for prohibition.*

The sixth in a series of eight prints, The Bottle, *by George Cruikshank (1847). Although Cruikshank was British, his work was highly regarded in the United States, and* The Bottle *series had several American printings in the nineteenth century. This reproduction, and the seven others, were used to illustrate a volume of Timothy Shay Arthur's* Temperance Tales *(1848). Arthur in fact wrote a short story around them ("The Bottle and The Pledge") in that book, in which he traced the progressive impact of alcohol addiction on the socioeconomic status, health, and moral values of a single family, the James Latimers. The original caption with this print read: "Quarrels Between Mr. And Mrs. Latimer, And Brutal Violence Between Them, Were The Natural Consequences Of The Too Frequent Use Of The Bottle."*

Rutgers Center of Alcohol Studies

for handsome profits. They brought out an entire genre of dry novels, short stories, plays, and illustrated materials (generally known as "Temperance Tales") that glorified prohibition and warned of the dire medical, social, and moral consequences of drink. Beginning in the 1840s, the tales were best-sellers, a fact further indicating the intense popular interest in prohibition.

Enthusiasm and political pressure finally came to a head in 1851. Neal Dow's Maine Law of that year gave prohibition advocates their first great legislative breakthrough, and they moved quickly to follow up on their victory. In August 1851, another temperance convention met in Saratoga Springs and issued a battle cry for the passage of Maine Laws throughout the nation. Lobbying at the state level redoubled, and prohibition became the goal of what was now clearly one of the most comprehensive political efforts the nation had ever seen. After an enthusiastic campaign directed in part by old stalwart Lyman Beecher, Massachusetts went dry less than a year later. Maine Laws next carried the day in Vermont, Minnesota Territory, and Rhode Island (1852); Michigan (1853); Connecticut (1854); and Indiana, New Hampshire, Delaware, Iowa, New York, and Nebraska Territory (1855). Similar measures almost won in Wisconsin (where prohibition twice cleared the legislature in 1855, only to meet a governor's veto), Pennsylvania, and New Jersey; across the border, the Canadian provinces of Nova Scotia and New Brunswick added their names to the dry column as well.

Politicized morality thus seemed well on its way to rolling back the tide of over two hundred years of American drinking habits. By the mid-1850s, many dry reformers were congratulating themselves on having destroyed the old consensus on drinking as a positive good, and they eagerly looked forward to national prohibition. Their confidence appeared fully justified. During the 1850s, enough Americans had stopped or moderated their drinking to drop national annual consumption levels well below three gallons of absolute alcohol per capita. These were the lowest rates in the nation's history, and temperance advocates everywhere nodded in agreement when the Reverend John Marsh, one of the more effective agents of the movement, proclaimed the days gone "when drinking was universal; when no table was thought . . . properly spread unless it contained a supply of intoxicating drink; when no person" was held respectable who failed to "furnish it to his guests," when no man thought of refusing liquor or of working without it, when "Ministers of the Gospel . . . were abundantly supplied by their people; when drinkers and rumsellers were unhesitatingly received as members of Christian churches." And they were equally sure that the day was almost at hand when the purified republic would no longer tolerate demon rum anywhere within its borders.

Dry Debacle

But those who prophesied a dry millennium were wrong. The Maine Laws in fact marked the high tide of temperance influence in the antebellum years—a tide that ebbed quickly with the approach of the Civil War. By the late 1850s, masses of people feared a violent confrontation over slavery and the preservation of the Union. Most Americans, including some important temperance leaders, increasingly gave the impending sectional struggle a higher priority than they did the battle against the traffic. Popular interest in the cause, so keen in the early fifties, was fading fast by the latter part of the decade as "Bleeding Kansas," the Dred Scott case, John Brown's Harper's Ferry raid, and Southern rumblings about secession began to dominate newspaper headlines. Also aiding the disenchantment with prohibition were a number of European medical reports that concluded that alcohol, while dangerous in excess, was not deleterious in moderation. All this caught the temperance movement off guard. Opponents of prohibition took heart.

Indeed, political prohibition fell apart at a speed that astonished even its enemies. The demise of the Whig party was a major blow. When the Whigs collapsed in the early 1850s under the strain of the slavery controversy, antiliquor leaders lost an important ally. The new Republican party, which rose to prominence after the death of the Whigs, offered little solace. There was some initial cooperation with the drys; however, Republican regulars soon chose to focus solely on the question of the spread of slavery. They did not want to defuse their efforts by linking the once mighty prohibition crusade with their stand against slavery. The political clout of temperance thus declined precipitately, and in state after state Maine Laws crumbled to dust. Legislatures either repealed them outright, or modified them to permit liquor sales with minimal interference, or allowed them to languish virtually unenforced.

Events in Maine were typical of those in other locales. The original Maine Law lasted only a few years. It was replaced in 1858 by a measure that kept prohibition on the books in name alone. There was neither popular nor political support for a stiffer law, and even Dow admitted that any effort to achieve real prohibition would have to wait until the nation had sorted out its sectional differences. Indeed, by the time Confederate guns opened on Fort Sumter in April 1861, prohibition had all but collapsed as a major public issue.

Yet the legacy of the prohibition struggle remained. The movement had indelibly etched total abstinence on much of the popular mind. It had convinced many that the dry doctrine held the key to the stability and prosperity of the republic. And if its political manifestation, prohibition, had fallen on hard times, thousands remained loyal to the idea nonetheless. In fact, the antebellum movement set an important precedent: Few temperance advocates in subsequent years would seriously advance any other method than legal prohibition as a solution to the liquor question. An equally important result of the antebellum crusade was an atmosphere of uncertainty over alcohol's future role in American society. Inasmuch as drinking had been an issue in the colonial period, it had been a matter of preventing abuses of a practice acclaimed as a social and medicinal necessity. In the antebellum decades, however, beverage alcohol became a national bone of contention. Yet no firm consensus against drinking emerged from the turmoil (the decline of prohibition demonstrated that), and the country found itself with divided attitudes toward alcohol use among its native-born citizens, its rapidly growing immigrant population, and those who disavowed all alcohol use. America, once content with its tippling (and deeming it not a social problem of great consequence), was now adrift on the issue. Thus, Americans entered the post–Civil War era confused, if not ambivalent, about what to think or do with respect to the onetime "Good Creature of God."

CHAPTER THREE

Search for Consensus: Drinking and the War Against Pluralism, 1860-1920

Mental suasion for the man who thinks,
Moral suasion for the man who drinks,
Legal suasion for the drunkard-maker,
Prison suasion for the statute-breaker.

—A. L. Benton
The Century of Temperance Reform (1885)

Hillsboro, Ohio, 1873

In 1873 Eliza Jane Thompson was the picture of domestic tranquility. A respected matriarch of fifty-seven, she had known little but happiness and security all her life. The daughter of former Ohio Governor Allen Trimble and the wife of James Thompson, one of Ohio's most successful attorneys, she had always enjoyed both wealth and social prominence. When she and her husband settled in Hillsboro, a prosperous and pleasant town in southern Ohio, they quickly became pillars of the community. Over their many years together, James Thompson poured his energy into his legal practice while his wife became a devoted homemaker, maintaining an attractive house, taking an active interest in church affairs, and rearing eight children. Eliza Thompson imparted to the children her own devout Christian faith and high moral tone and provided them with the same sense of stability and family loyalty that she had known as a child. As a mother and wife she had much to be proud of, having lovingly done all for her family that society expected from a woman of her social station. At any other time, Thompson could have expected to grow old in peace amid the respect of her neighbors and the love of her husband and children. But 1873 proved not to be any other time.

In that year Dr. Dioclesian Lewis came to Hillsboro. Lewis was a homeopathic physician, educator, and reform lecturer of some renown. His particular cause was physical education for women, but his oratorical repertoire included a range of other topics, including temperance. This, in fact, was the subject he chose for his December speaking engagement in Hillsboro. During his presentation (or in discussion afterward, we are not sure) he recalled that long ago his own dear mother, Dilecta Barbour Lewis, had met the liquor traffic head-on in a novel way: She pleaded with a hardened publican to stop selling to little Dio's drunken father; the saloonkeeper refused; and, in desperation, Dilecta Lewis led a band of women into the bar to pray—a tactic that melted the publican's heart and prompted him to take the pledge and forsake his evil ways. Lewis told his story with stirring emotion.

The impact on the women in the audience was electric. Like Dilecta Lewis, many of them feared the saloon. The cooling of temperance ardor during the Civil War had allowed the taverns to operate with few restraints, and many bars in Hillsboro, as in other Ohio communities, were unlicensed establishments of dubious reputation. What of the health and morality of their husbands and sons if, in the face of temptation, they should frequent such places? And what of their own social status and security, or that of their children, if their menfolk drank themselves to ruin? It was a fate too terrible to contemplate — but now, perhaps unwittingly, Dr. Lewis had suggested a means to deal with such fears.

In a meeting convened the following day, a body of Hillsboro women reached a momentous decision. They would do as the brave Dilecta Lewis had done in the face of a similar threat. Together they would march into the local dens of iniquity and there pray that the saloonkeepers would see the light and close their doors. They knew, moreover, that they would not be acting in total isolation. Women elsewhere had begun to take matters into their own hands. There had been a smattering of "pray-ins" at bars in Illinois, Michigan, Massachusetts, and Ohio between 1858 and 1871; while 1872 had seen a number of Ohio women filing suit against publicans under the state's Adair law, which allowed the wives of alcoholics to sue for damages against taverners selling to their besotted husbands. But the Hillsboro women also realized that what they planned for their town would take these protests yet another major step, as they intended not to quit until they had forced local officials to eliminate all illegal liquor sales. They were ready to act — all they needed was someone to lead them.

They chose Eliza Thompson. Thompson was known for her temperance sympathies. Her family had been dry, and in 1836 she had been the only female to attend the National Temperance Convention in Saratoga Springs (she had accompanied her father, who was a formal delegate). However, Thompson had no reputation as a social activist and had not even attended Dio Lewis's lecture. Thus, the call to leadership took her by surprise. Yet in their selection the women of Hillsboro had a point: Thompson's family background made her one of the most socially prominent women in the state, and her presence would lend the cause a prestige it otherwise would have lacked. With some trepidation, Thompson agreed to serve. On December 24, she led about seventy women into the streets.

They prayed that day in front of drug stores, major sources of so-called medicinal liquor, and day after day, until the middle of June, when they marched again, kneeling in front of hotels, taverns, and anywhere else liquor was sold. Bartenders, druggists, civil officials, and the citizenry in general were astonished. Many were sympathetic. All the druggists except one signed the women's pledge to end liquor sales, and the abstaining druggist, who sought a court injunction against Thompson's army, succeeded only in giving the women more publicity. The saloons themselves were almost defenseless. Illegal in the first place, they could hardly ask for the protection of the law—and who was going to arrest the likes of Eliza Thompson anyway? Hillsboro had never seen anything like it, and neither had the rest of the country, which gradually realized that something extraordinary was going on.

Indeed, as word of events in Hillsboro reached other regions, more women, often the wives or daughters of civic and social leaders, took their Bibles in hand and put hundreds of saloons under siege. Usually these demonstrations were peaceful, but irate publicans or saloon patrons occasionally hurled insults or even physically assaulted the "praying bands" (as the women called themselves). Yet the persistence of the

Library of Congress

The "Woman's Crusade," as dramatized by Currier and Ives in an 1874 engraving. Actually, very few of the crusaders resorted to violence; prayer and reproach were their standard techniques.

women was remarkable. They forced localities to close scores of illegal taverns, persuaded a few saloonkeepers to shut down and join their cause, conducted tearful conversions of drunkards, and induced thousands of topers to sign the pledge. The upheaval—which soon became known as the "Woman's Crusade" or the "Woman's War"—continued throughout 1874, gathering momentum as it spread across the land; by the end of the year many of the women had decided that it was to be war, whatever the sacrifice, to the end.

The fight would go on, they vowed, until the liquor traffic was destroyed once and for all. With this goal in view, many of the praying bands coalesced into formal "leagues," later called "unions," to consolidate the gains of the crusade and to carry on the good work on a more structured basis. In December 1874, a women's convention, including

Library of Congress

Another view of the Woman's War, from Harper's Weekly, *1874. Even when the crusaders failed to close a saloon, arrests and setbacks often built sympathy for the temperance women— a cause aided by illustrations such as this Thomas Nast sketch. Nast's swipe at the ethnic Germans of Cincinnati is rather obvious.*

Eliza Thompson (now honored as "Mother Thompson" for her stand in Hillsboro) met in Cleveland and founded the Woman's Christian Temperance Union (WCTU). As one participant recalled, they had "buckled on the armor for the long campaign" and served notice that the temperance movement was gathering steam once more.

For Thompson, however, the crusade was over. Cleveland was her last venture; she would pray in saloons no longer. She left the WCTU to younger women and returned to Hillsboro, where she died peacefully in 1905. Yet her brief reform career had helped fire a movement that, in her lifetime, came to dominate the nation's social and political concerns. To explain why, however, demands another look at the longstanding neorepublican dream of the good society; only this time we must trace its contours through an era of extremely complex social-industrial change.

With the Civil War, Americans faced the full onslaught of industrialization, and the process wrought monumental changes. Railroads were soon to span the continent; new technologies and financial structures brought vital new industries and such miracles as the incandescent light and the automobile; and vast new employment opportunities opened, all of which improved wages for some amid inhumane working conditions—and resultant labor strife. Urbanization soared as the native-born and the new waves of immigrants mingled in teeming industrial cities. In short, industrialization dramatically hastened the coming of the modern pluralist society.

The post–Civil War era was both an exciting and a frightening time. It was also an era of national adjustment, with people desperately trying to make sense of the new trends shaping their lives. Historian Robert Wiebe called their efforts a "search for order." His characterization provides a helpful perspective. Many contemporaries feared that the forces loosed in the urban-industrial revolution would plunge the nation into chaos unless vital economic, social, and governmental reforms quickly put society back on an orderly path. This reform impulse appeared in various guises, as different groups searched for order in diverse ways. Businessmen, for example, sought a rational and efficient economy through financial, technological, and management innovations; Progressive reformers worked for restraints on abuses in the marketplace; and professional groups of businessmen, lawyers, physicians, engineers, and academics, to cite only a few illustrations, pressed for recognition of their special skills and their unique contributions to the new industrial society. All these voices expressed a desire to impose a certain discipline on national character and life—to build an atmosphere of stability in which to enjoy the benefits of a new age rather than live in dread of potential disruptions.

Such was the social milieu of Eliza Thompson's crusade. The post-bellum temperance movement became part of the larger response to urban-industrial America, and it had some original ideas on the question of the moral-social order. The antiliquor reformers wanted nothing less than to remake the nation in their own image, purging the land of alien and hostile influences while incorporating into their fold all who accepted the time-honored message of the sober republic. It was the familiar neorepublican vision, and it retained its essential truths even in the post–Civil War world. If astonishing change and pluralism were seemingly ripping society apart, this view of reform — embodied in legal prohibition — would serve to pull the nation back together again. It would also rekindle the public virtue necessary to insure societal unity and stability. On this foundation, America's traditional values and institutions could rest more securely, safely guiding the nation as it adjusted to the industrial age.

Drinkers and Reformers: The Origins of Postbellum Temperance

While the Civil War had sidetracked the temperance movement, sparks of vitality lit even the crusade's darkest hours. Many local societies remained active—and so did the American Temperance Union. Union agents proselytized with surprising success in the Northern army, where some regiments actually founded their own temperance societies. (The army had never restored the liquor ration, but regulations permitted commanders to issue spirits almost at will and many of them did.) Colonel—later General—Neal Dow raised several Maine "temperance regiments." And only five months after Appomattox, dry leaders with an eye to the future replaced the old union with the National Temperance Society and Publication House. Thus, the crusade survived the Civil War years—and with considerable muscle still intact.

As if to demonstrate further the resilience of these reformers, political activities quickly resumed. Groups in Michigan, Ohio, and Illinois launched third-party prohibitionist efforts; and in 1869 a convention of temperance veterans, disappointed by the lack of Republican and Democratic interest in temperance, founded the National Prohibition

The Fruits of Temperance *and* The Fruits of Intemperance, *by Currier and Ives. "Temperance Tales" genre graphics, like these 1870 prints, remained popular as the dry crusade emerged from its Civil War period doldrums.*

Party. In 1872, James Black tallied 5,608 votes as the first Prohibitionist presidential candidate. His loss to General Ulysses S. Grant was not surprising, but the party message was clear: The lull in temperance activity was over. If any doubts lingered, they shortly disappeared with the explosion of the Woman's Crusade and the phenomenal rise of the WCTU.

From the beginning, the new movement was more forceful than its antebellum precursor had been. The call to action was loud and clear. Drys openly compared the importance of their crusade to that of the prewar antislavery movement. If abolitionism and the Civil War had freed the land from the curse of human slavery, they announced, they would liberate it from the curse of enslavement to drink. Our "next emancipation," the Reverend Dorchester promised, would be the freedom "from the bondage of alcohol."

And "the question" of such a noble cause was not going to be, as Edward B. Sutton assured the nation, just a matter of popular opinion: "The question is not," the Michigan clergyman and Prohibition Party member proclaimed, "is public sentiment ready for prohibition, but is prohibition right? Public sentiment was not ready for the Ten Commandments when they were first given." Echoing the words of New England Transcendentalist and reformer Theodore Parker, Sutton concluded that an individual's right to drink would have to give way to society's right to self-preservation. There was no liberty to drink when "it means the subjugation of a nation to the worst enemy man ever had." Temperance workers were now more willing than ever before to impose their views on society for its own good, regardless of the opposition.

In fact, the impulse to cleanse society as thoroughly as possible overshadowed the battle against drinking itself. This trend probably reflected the success of the antebellum crusade in reducing alcohol consumption, for the dizzying levels of prewar drinking were gone (the high was about seven gallons of absolute alcohol per capita in 1830). By the 1850s, the drinking-age population was consuming only some two gallons per person annually, a figure close to modern consumption estimates (the 1985 level was close to 2.6 gallons). So the national binge had ended before the Civil War, and postwar assaults on alcohol generally came not against drinking patterns or consumption rates per se but against drinking as a symbol of rampant pluralism, individualism, and potential social disorder.

A look at reactions to postbellum drinking confirms this view. Drinking patterns in the late nineteenth century retained the heterogeneous character they had exhibited in the antebellum years. If anything, the variations in drinking styles became even more pronounced as millions of new immigrants landed between the late 1860s and the early 1900s. The Irish and German waves continued, along with major contingents of other Northern Europeans. By the turn of the century, however, the greatest numbers were coming from Southern, Central, and Eastern Europe. This influx raised the number of foreign-born in the United States to 13,515,900 souls by 1910, up from 4,138,700 in 1860. A high proportion of these newcomers, such as the many Poles, Jews, and Italians, hailed from wet cultures; and like every immigrant group before them, they imported their drinking customs.

What is usually not known is that the new immigrants did not generally contribute to national alcohol problems. Indeed, some probably helped contain them. The Italians, for example, used wine extensively at mealtimes and in social contexts. But while drinking was an integral part of their tradition, they maintained strict customary sanctions against drunkenness. Jews also enjoyed alcohol as a normal part of their culture, incorporating ritual drinking into wedding ceremonies and other religious observances. Like the Italians, however, the Jews proscribed intemperance. Both these ethnic groups represented voices for drinking moderation; and while they probably had fewer total abstainers than did other communities, their rates of alcoholism were among the lowest (if not the lowest) in the country.

Library of Congress

Beer drinking spread rapidly from German communities to the rest of the population. Brewers tried to put the beverage in the most favorable light possible— whence this print's emphasis on family, health, friendship, and the nation.

At the same time, the continuing influx of Europeans helped to give drinking — and some of its ancillary pursuits — a highly ethnic cast. While the distilling of spirits remained largely in native hands (although there were important exceptions), the Irish and Germans made heavy inroads in other areas of the traffic. Saloonkeepers were prevalent among both groups and, for that matter, bars in many urban settings became differentiated in ownership and patronage by ethnicity. German breweries continued to boom, and sophisticated advertising efforts claimed ever more partisans of lager beer. Members of all social strata enjoyed the brew, but its low price made it especially popular as a working-class beverage. As such, the rise in the drinking of lager paralleled the rapid growth of the postbellum urban industrial work force. Consequently, by the late 1870s beer consumption was more than double the level of the 1860s; it had tripled by the 1880s; and by the 1890s beer was well on its way to challenging native American whiskey as the nation's most popular alcoholic beverage.

Wine also demonstrated a modest growth in popularity. Although viticulture lagged far behind distilling and brewing, wine had a traditional place in wealthier American homes. A number of immigrant groups, moreover, notably Italians, Jews, and some Germans, preferred wine to other drinks. The best wines were imported, but domestic products gradually began to improve in flavor.

Small vineyards were scattered throughout the states, but California became the largest wine producing region. Until about 1820, the "mission grape" — cultivated since its introduction by the Spanish in the mid-1700s — was the only California variety. But after the United States seized the area from Mexico as part of the Mexican War of the 1840s, within a generation immigrants from the wine producing regions of Europe had some fifty Old World varieties flourishing in the Western state's hospitable climate and soil. Frenchman Paul Masson, for example, had established a prospering vineyard by the second half of the century, and became noted for producing one of the best California champagnes. Secondo Guarti, from Italy, turned fifteen hundred acres of virtual dessert into lush vineyards (he ultimately received the title of *Grande Officiale*, one of the highest distinctions the Italian government could bestow). Guarti's efforts were typical of the energy and skills Italians brought to the California wine industry during the postbellum years. By the 1880s, America had over 130,000 acres of vines under cultivation — mostly in California, but New York vineyards were also growing — and a few wines had received favorable international attention. The future of viticulture looked very promising.

Yet it was precisely this foreign image associated with drinking that alarmed many temperance workers. Much of the antebellum temperance campaign had drawn life from native-born citizens, and a sentiment often expressed was that drinking was "unrepublican." With the prevalence of drinking in the postbellum immigrant population, such feelings intensified. Much of the nation's tippling, or so the Reverend Dorchester insisted in the 1880s, was rooted in "the reactionary tendencies" of "the free-and-easy drinking customs of Europe." While he acknowledged that America welcomed all immigrants who became "law-abiding citizens" and that "narrow prejudice" should not cloud the issue, he felt compelled to point out that much of the country's liquor trade was "in the hands of a low class of foreigners," whose names topped the doors of most saloons, beer gardens, and "low groggeries." Other temperance workers agreed that too many people in the new ethnic communities did not want to assimilate American values; drinking consequently threatened the republic's unity and stability from that direction.

But if ethnic drinking aroused concern, temperance advocates also denounced drinking on the part of middle- and upper-class native-born citizens. There were still those who shamelessly (in temperance eyes at least) cultivated an appreciation for fine drink. Social drinking, while much reduced from antebellum levels, nevertheless remained a fixed custom in many households, and plenty of businessmen still ordered a bourbon or a beer over lunch. Those who could afford them guaranteed a lucrative market for imported wines and spirits. The peculiarly American "cocktail"—a mixed drink, often including nonalcoholic ingredients—also gained in popularity.

Americans were mixing cocktails—the origin of the term is obscure—by the early 1800s, perhaps to improve the harsh taste of some crude whiskeys, and a great many recipes became standard during the last half of the century. "Professor" Jerry Thomas, for example, one of the most creative New York City bartenders of his day, invented (if that is the word) the "Tom and Jerry" and the "Blue Blazer" in those years. A turn-of-the-century edition of *The Women's Dictionary and Encyclopedia* (edited in part by the original Fannie Farmer and promising its readers "everything a woman wants to know") explained the mixing of no fewer than fifty-eight cocktails, including Sours, Martinis, and Manhattans.

The wealthier native-born American did a lot of drinking in opulent "saloons." The saloon—from the French *salon*—was deliberately christened to conjure up an image of elegance and taste, and many such urban establishments in the late nineteenth and early twentieth centuries more than filled the bill. Furniture, woodwork, and carpets created a luxurious ambience. Original artwork frequently adorned the walls, as did mirrors worth thousands of dollars in themselves. Some of the poshest watering spots were hotel bars, such as those in the Palace in San Francisco, the Palmer House in Chicago, and the old Fifth Avenue in New York. Others were part of restaurant operations. Luchow's and Delmonico's in New York, for instance, were noted as much for their luxurious bars and well-stocked wine cellars as for their savory cuisine.

Smaller saloons, catering to drinkers of more moderate means, but

Library of Congress

New Year's Eve, 1906. Temperance workers frowned on such celebrations. For solid citizens—especially women—to drink enthusiastically in public, drys felt, set a deplorable example for the rest of the nation.

This map appeared in Senator Henry Blair's Temperance Movement: or the Conflict between Man and Alcohol *(1888). Each small rectangle on Manhattan Island represents a licensed saloon, of which Blair located 9,168. He estimated a roughly equal number of unlicensed establishments, all of which the senator considered ample cause for alarm.*

The bar of the Hoffman House, New York City, late 1880s. The
Hoffman House, one of New York's most elegant saloons, was a favorite watering hole of the city's political and cultural elite. The man
sitting against the wall, beside the picture Nymphs and Satyr by
Bouguereau, is supposedly New York Governor David B. Hill.

boasting similar charms, were common outside the larger urban centers. Patrons often developed fond attachments for these places—there is a surprising number of sentimental histories of individual saloons. Looking back from the prohibition years, H. L. Mencken, a denizen of some of Baltimore's better establishments, once mused that in the building of these bars civilization had reached one of its highest art forms.

Drunken comportment, of course, was unacceptable in the middle and upper classes: One drank to be sociable, to relax, to enjoy oneself—but only in moderation (at least publicly). Nevertheless, drys maintained their healthy contempt for even moderate drinking. Given their belief in the inevitability of alcohol addiction, they considered moderate drinkers well on the way to doom. If anything, temperance leaders intensified their indictments, adding poor citizenship to their list of charges. The example of middle- and upper-class drinking was one the republic, threatened by hordes of undomesticated Europeans, could ill afford. Like Benjamin Rush, postbellum temperance advocates feared that liquor would corrupt the most responsible elements in society, set an anarchical example for the lower classes, and, finally, lead to a general collapse of civic virtue and to a new form of tyranny—that of the traffic. The so-called refined, well-to-do drinker therefore was as much a threat to the fabric of the republic as were whiskey guzzling Westerners, tippling immigrants, and poverty-stricken drunkards.

The New Society, Booze, and Social Disorder

Aside from these symbolic dangers, there were also immediate practical concerns. The dramatic social changes inherent in rapid industrialization and urbanization placed traditional dry worries over alcohol and such civil maladies as poverty, vice, crime, disease, and violence in a new and more visible context. Poverty, to cite only one illustration, was a major fact of urban life. Late nineteenth-century economic fluctuations, language barriers among immigrants, and limited work skills kept thousands periodically unemployed or locked into poorly paid jobs. Equally worrisome, many people spent too much of what little they earned on liquor, and through drinking they often lost their jobs, thus impoverishing not only themselves but also their families. Even dispassionate studies of the matter—by urban reformers, municipal officials, and newly professionalized social workers—put alcohol at the root of a minimum of 20 percent of urban poverty cases. Such personal tragedy, of course, was not confined to the industrial poor; yet the relative novelty of seeing so many instances of drinking-related poverty made a distinct impression on the middle-class public. Indeed, by the turn of century many students of urban affairs, such as social critics Amos Warner and Robert Hunter, and Progressive reformers like Jacob Riis and Evangeline Booth (of the Salvation Army)—who did not share temperance-related xenophobia—agreed that the liquor question must be tackled if the urban-industrial order were to be a fit, safe environment. These were not dispassionate observers, however, and some insisted upon serious reforms.

The rise of "skid rows" in many cities was yet another sign of the prevalence of alcohol problems. The term derived from Seattle's Skid Road (a name still used there) that track lumbermen had built to "skid" timber downhill. As Seattle grew, the section of town near Skid Road deteriorated, becoming a low-rent district of seedy bars frequented by derelicts and transients. Skid row soon became a popular term for similar areas in other cities, such as New York's Bowery.

Skid rows first appeared around the Civil War, in large part the product of high unemployment, which had resulted from unstable economic growth and labor surpluses caused by heavy European immigration. Forced by economic necessity, down-and-outers drifted into the poorest sections of town—to skid row. For the middle and upper classes, the skid row lifestyle was pluralism at its ugliest, and the so-called skid row bum quickly became the popular stereotype of the alcoholic. He was the diametric opposite of the steady, virtuous citizen who held the social and political fabric of the republic together. (Modern social research has demolished this stereotype: Most skid row inhabitants are not alcoholics, and as of the early 1980s probably no more than 3 or 4 percent of American alcoholics lived in skid row circumstances.)

Along with the skid row bum, the most ominous symbol of the dangers of drink became the urban saloon. Not that temperance workers liked rural or Western saloons any better, but the city version was more visibly associated with the ills of an industrializing society and thus seemed to be more immediately threatening. Most urban saloons were a far cry from Delmonico's, the Palmer House, or any of the elegant establishments that H. L. Mencken recalled so fondly. The majority were neighborhood bars, and too many were simply ginmills. The worst were dives serving as centers of drunkenness, crime, profanity, prostitution, gambling, and political corruption. Their patrons, frequently immigrants and unskilled industrial workers, held few values in common with those of the temperance movement.

In most major cities, political bosses used saloons as their headquarters and employed regular patrons to stuff ballot boxes (these same bars often served as polling places) or to terrorize opponents. Similarly, the rise of organized prostitution paralleled the growth of the urban ginmills. In Philadelphia, for instance, an 1876 canvass found 8,037 legal and illegal drinking establishments in the city: At least 3,782 of them had direct or indirect connections with "houses of ill fame." Some of the most notorious red light districts, such as Chicago's Gold Coast and the infamous Barbary Coast of San Francisco, had national reputations. The saloon, then, seemed to mock temperance conceptions of public virtue and stood starkly at odds with traditional American mores. It constituted, as one historian aptly noted, a veritable "counterculture," dangerous as well as inherently evil.

But the traffic did not worry very much about its image. In fact, it insolently faced down complaints. Large brewers owned most of the local saloons and used them as outlets for their beers. Breweries were highly competitive, and they openly encouraged heavy drinking. Notably, bartenders frequently took advantage of treating—not the political variant but the practice of buying rounds of drinks for the entire group of patrons, a chain often started by publicans themselves. In some respects, treating mirrored the old pretemperance notion of drinking as a source of camaraderie. Treating brought "a feeling," as one member of the traffic put it, "of independence and equality, in each individual." Buying a round of drinks demonstrated to friends that the purchaser could "keep his end up." It also brought the saloon a fortune, as the same source noted: "This habit of buying for the other fellow was always more in evidence among the wage-earners on their pay-days than it was among the people who could better afford to indulge in generosity."

Still other techniques kept liquor flowing. Many saloons lured customers with offers of a "free lunch"—usually well salted to inspire drinking (the saloon "bouncer" was generally on hand to discourage hearty appetites). New patrons also were given free drinks. As one Brewers' Association spokesman explained, this tactic extended even to children: A few cents spent on free drinks for boys was a good investment; the money would be amply recovered as these youths became habitual drinkers! At the time, many Americans, and by no means just

The Cosmopolitan saloon, unknown location in the West in the late nineteenth century. The Cosmopolitan was fairly elegant by Western standards, and it had all the elements—gambling and roulette tables, spittoons, and a portrait of a nude—that spurred antiliquor reformers to indignation and action.

The postbellum years saw the solidification of the stereotype of the "skid row" alcoholic. This print, probably from just after the Civil War, clearly captures the popular view of the destitute and dissipated drunkard.

temperance workers, regarded such practices much the same as our own generation would consider a modern drug-pusher giving children "free samples."

The saloons nevertheless scoffed at reform efforts. They had plenty of money for political wars and plenty of votes, which, as the *Liquor Man's Advocate* noted in 1874, they were ready to use. "Every saloon averages eighty regular customers," the paper observed, "and these eighty customers have eighty votes, and, if properly managed, every bartender might influence these eighty votes to a given point, decided by bartenders *en masse*." The saloon thus accorded temperance workers a perfect target. In the 1870s, these drinking establishments became the bête noire of the WCTU.

Members viewed the saloon as a danger to their families, to the republic's values, and to their status as women. In the social context of the day, these fears were not unreasonable. At the very time that the pre-Civil War temperance movement was taking shape, many Americans (with some notable exceptions) had already assigned fairly definite social roles to men and women. In the classic middle-class family—the accepted standard of the period—men went to work and provided for the family's financial support; women were expected to be homemakers and mothers. As such, women also became the chief preceptors of national virtue. That is, through the example of their own purity of behavior, they were to wed their families and communities to similar standards, thus guaranteeing the present and future welfare of the American family and of the republic itself. Ideally, their perfect piety and domesticity earned women the special affection of society (and had a great deal to do with forcing nineteenth-century women onto the proverbial pedestal).

Frances Willard (1839–1898). Once called the "Uncrowned Queen of American Womanhood," Willard was worshiped by many WCTU members and was able to marshall the organization behind a wide variety of other reforms. Shortly before her death in 1898, she may have formed doubts about the social usefulness of prohibition, and she clearly did become convinced that alcoholism was as much the result of poverty and other social and personal problems as it was a cause of those problems.

Rutgers Center of Alcohol Studies

Yet the security of a woman in this scheme was fragile. If a husband failed as a breadwinner or a child strayed from the fold — real possibilities amid the turmoil of the industrializing age — the entire household could be impoverished or disgraced. Family tranquility depended on financial prudence and loyalty to accepted behavioral standards, traits the saloons seemingly mocked. In fact, bars appeared to invite family catastrophe: They introduced children to drunkenness and vice and drove husbands to alcoholism; they also caused squandering of wages, wife beating, and child abuse; and, with the patron's inhibitions lowered through drink, the saloon led many men into the arms of prostitutes (and, not incidentally, contributed to the alarming spread of syphilis). If any of these disasters occurred, a displaced homemaker had no social welfare system to cushion the blow.

Thus, the women of the WCTU hated the saloon. Indeed, their dawning crusade adopted the motto "home protection." In his entertaining account of the temperance drive, John Kobler cynically referred to home protection as "organized mother love"; in a sense, he was correct. Yet as the WCTU waxed stronger, barkeepers would find little humor in attempted witticisms about their role in society. In attacking the saloon, WCTU members were dead serious about what their president, Frances Willard, referred to as the "politics of the mother heart."

The saloons also angered thousands of citizens outside the formal dry organizations. Parents routinely warned their children to steer clear of bars, and young women were known to cross streets or detour for blocks to avoid walking past tavern entrances. The middle class was sincerely alarmed. By the turn of the century, some of the more perceptive saloonkeepers realized that matters had probably gone too far. The saloon had drifted away from the traditional republican moral code. A few taverners urged their brethren to stop their excesses, and they tried to promote the saloons as "workingmen's clubs" where patrons could take a relaxing glass with their fellows before going home. A number of contemporary studies sympathized with this idea, and several historians have since reinforced the notion that the social functions of the saloon were of real importance in many parts of the nation. But mounting popular hostility made it impossible to redeem the image of the saloon; the public had found a new and dangerous enemy.

Concerns over social disorder, as exemplified by the saloon, also won the temperance cause some firm support among the nation's new industrial leaders. If drink posed a threat to the family unit, it could be equally dangerous in a modernizing technological society. For one thing, industrialists feared that an alcoholic employee could play havoc in a complex workplace. This had been a concern before the Civil War, but the subsequent rise of a mass industrial base, reflected in the production of assembly-line goods, gave the issue added importance. The increasing sophistication of manufactured goods made even drunken consumers dangerous: A medical journal noted in 1904 that "inebriate and moderate drinkers are the most incapable of all persons to drive motor wagons" and that society should restrict the operation of its new automobiles to "total abstainers." Hence, John D. Rockefeller, Henry Ford, and William Randolph Hearst, who knew quite a bit about the consequences of poor judgment and accidents in the rising technological age, became prohibitionists. Many other business leaders echoed their concerns. Charles Edison, for example, son of inventor Thomas Edison, became an advocate of more humane working conditions, in part on the theory that satisfied workers would not frequent the saloons that ringed the Edison factories.

To an extent, drinking also symbolized wastefulness, which people like Ford and Rockefeller found offensive in and of itself. As historian Richard D. Brown noted, such men believed that steadiness, thrift, and clear thinking were essential in an industrial world. They measured their own lives by the efficient use of time and resources: appointments kept, production schedules met, money properly invested, and personnel and materiel marshalled on time. The practice of whiling away hours in saloons, which had been harmless enough in the pre-industrial era, was to be avoided on principle. Besides, they claimed, booze clouded the businessman's mind. Thus, the first item in "Andrew Carnegie's Advice to Young Men"—even before "never speculate" and "save a little always"—was "never enter a bar-room, nor let the contents of a bar-room enter you." Money spent on drinking was money wasted, they insisted. According to the industrialists, wages should be put into savings, investments, and manufactured goods—which they produced! With this in mind, Henry Ford promised to fire any employee who drank, even at home, and declared that "booze had to go when modern industry and the motor car came in." Alcohol could come back, he said, only if America was "willing to abolish modern industry and the motor car." Ford was so adamant that after the enactment of National Prohibition in 1920, he threatened to halt automobile production should the nation ever think of repeal. Rather that, he warned, than pay wages that would end up in saloon coffers. Kindred sentiments characterized the thinking of many temperance workers and seemingly gave the entire crusade added relevance as citizens searched for order in the early twentieth century.

The Dry Offensive: The 1870s and 1880s

As dry leaders surveyed what they considered the rampant social and political disorder of postbellum America, they came to a rough consensus on how to attack the problem. They refurbished the holistic antebellum view of social evils as interrelated — with intemperance at the center of most of them. Thus, these new temperance workers were convinced that their neorepublican vision of the good society could become reality only through a broad-based reform effort. They would deal with all problems simultaneously. As such, Senator Henry Blair of New Hampshire, who in 1876 offered Congress the first National Prohibition amendment to the Constitution, also championed women's rights and education. Neal Dow, who renounced the Republicans when they equivocated on temperance and ran for president himself as a Prohibitionist in 1880, campaigned as well for education, suffrage, the income tax, and the direct election of senators. The temperance movement thus saw itself as part of the war against all evil and social chaos.

Among the most insistent of these neorepublican reformers were the women of the WCTU. Under their first president, Annie Wittenmeyer, they concentrated mostly on temperance work, but the union turned to other activities when Frances Willard took charge in 1879. Willard was an extraordinary leader. A devout Methodist, she had pursued a distinguished career in education (she was the first dean of women at Northwestern University) before turning full-time to temperance. Passionately committed to women's rights, she was also convinced that liquor was an especial threat to the status and morality of women. "When a man would rob a woman of her virtue," Willard asked at one point, "or a woman is about to sell herself in the most degraded bargain that the mind can contemplate, what does he give her, and what does she take? STRONG DRINK!" Willard presided over the union until her death in 1898, by which time its members numbered in the hundreds of thousands. The WCTU represented the first mass entry of women into American reform work and politics.

Willard ran the WCTU as a well-oiled reform machine. In doing so, she not only reflected similar moves toward systemized operations in business but also structured the union in the orderly image she envisioned for the rest of the country. Willard recognized that more women could be mobilized if the WCTU espoused concerns besides drinking. The women's organization ultimately established forty separate departments, with their own superintendents and reform activities. Mary Hunt, for example, supervised a national effort to introduce "Scientific Temperance Instruction" into public school curricula, thereby spreading the WCTU message on the health and social impacts of drinking to millions of children. By 1884, a department was disseminating information on narcotics; another was pursuing world peace; while yet another was cultivating "good citizenship" among immigrants, blacks, and Indians (the union spoke of this last work as "Americanization," in which members tried to pattern the views of others after their own middle-class values). Willard herself directed the Social Purity Department, which sought laws against seduction, rape, prostitution, and sexual intercourse with women younger than eighteen. Many WCTU members were also suffragists and social workers, all of which made Willard's call for a union "do everything" policy a dynamic reality.

Rutgers Center of Alcohol Studies

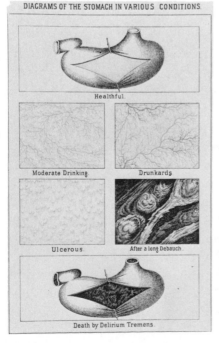

DIAGRAMS OF THE STOMACH IN VARIOUS CONDITIONS.

Healthful.

Moderate Drinking.

Drunkards.

Ulcerous.

After a long Debauch.

Death by Delirium Tremens.

"Scientific temperance instruction" relied heavily on visual representations of the physical damage allegedly caused by alcohol. Among the most popular graphic materials were Dr. Thomas Sewall's illustrations, which the doctor supposedly drew from dissections in 1842. Sewall's pictures purported to show the progressive deterioration of the stomach lining under the influence of alcohol, and they were standard aids in teaching school children about alcohol during the last half of the nineteenth century.

The union also lent a hand in hard-nosed politics. The first major battleground was Kansas, where in the 1870s and 1880s members had become incensed at official refusals to close illegal saloons. They supported the efforts of Republican Governor John St. John, a fiery postbellum reformer, to dry up the state and helped him win two tumultuous campaigns. But the Republicans feared a split between the GOP's wet and dry adherents, and the division helped deny him the election in 1882 — after which the governor became a Prohibition party stalwart. But before his Kansas fortunes declined, St. John, with WCTU and other dry support, had forced the passage of the first postbellum prohibition law.

Similar campaigns soon got under way in other states. Middle-class women, often with children in tow to illustrate the cause of home protection, descended on legislators and demanded dry laws. And they

Library of Congress

The war against the saloon had much of its basis in the WCTU's concept of "home protection," and temperance mothers frequently brought their children to antiliquor demonstrations to stress the point. Who with any compassion, they reasoned — and with great effect on public opinion — could support the saloon against the ranks of the young?

Rutgers Center of Alcohol Studies

had plenty of help: National WCTU headquarters in Evanston, Illinois, and the National Temperance Society and Publication House in New York barraged the nation with prohibitionist literature. The Prohibition party and the fraternal temperance lodges (which claimed more than 400,000 members) also actively lobbied state officials. Dry sentiment took new root under this pressure. By the late 1880s, the Dakotas, Rhode Island, Iowa, and Maine had joined Kansas in prohibition; the wets fought in desperation to turn back the antiliquor tide in many other states.

Although temperance waxed strong in the 1880s and regard for even moderate drinking reached new lows, the political fortunes of prohibition ultimately fell far short of total victory. Worse yet, some of the prohibition forays started to fizzle. Willard's Home Protection party of 1881, and its fusion with the Prohibitionists as the Prohibition Home Protection party in 1882, went nowhere. Nor, aside from some local victories, did the Prohibition party itself. The hostility of the major political parties was a formidable problem. Party managers, some of whom recalled the antebellum chaos arising from prohibition, wanted to avoid the liquor issue. Party loyalties were strong after the Civil War, and few Republicans or Democrats, many of whom were otherwise loyal to temperance, were willing to break ranks over any single issue, no matter how important. Not even the Populists, in their spectacular third-party bid of the early 1890s, were interested in a joint campaign with the WCTU when Willard approached them.

The Republicans, however, finally decided they had to offer the drys at least a token of sympathy, for in 1884 they learned through bitter experience not to offend temperance workers without cause. The GOP presidential candidate of that year was James G. Blaine, a man allegedly corrupt and avowedly wet. He lost the election in part because he failed to carry New York, where Prohibitionist candidate St. John drained off twenty-four thousand votes that otherwise probably would have gone to Blaine. This came on top of the so-called Burchard Alliteration fiasco, in which the Reverend Burchard, campaigning for Blaine, had denounced the Democrats as the party of "Rum, Romanism, and Rebellion" — in front of an audience partly of Irish Catholics! It was not one of the more intelligently run Republican campaigns, and in order to mend fences with drys, party leaders began inserting noncommittal references to temperance and local home protection laws into GOP platforms (best described as adjusting to political reality). For the time being, these gestures were satisfactory to all but the most ardent reformers and mild enough neither to offend most wets nor to bind the party to the antiliquor cause.

The resultant cooling of third-party political prohibition activity was deceptive in that it hid a real turn in popular opinion against the demon. School children throughout the land were learning the lessons of scientific temperance instruction—and would, or so dry leaders hoped, grow up to vote as they had been taught. With increasing frequency, physicians and scientists also were lending their support to the temperance cause, warning the public that alcohol was indeed a hazard to health.

The liquor industry tried to respond. As early as the late 1870s, the American Brewers' Association sponsored a number of studies purporting to show that beer was not a major cause of intemperance—the real culprit was whiskey. This effort did the brewers' image little good, however, merely demonstrating that they were feeling temperance pressure. Americans, in sum, were hearing the antiliquor message one way or another, and many of them were becoming believers.

An even more telling sign came from the ethnic populations, often heavily urban and Roman Catholic. Despite the undeniable hostility toward the Roman church on the part of many native-born drys, Catholic participation in the temperance movement, given impetus by Father Mathew's antebellum ministry, had become a larger phenomenon than most historians have realized. Throughout the latter part of the century, a number of priests engaged in social work campaigned vigorously for prohibition, citing liquor as a prime source of urban poverty. Indeed, many Catholic clergy were no happier than their Protestant counterparts about parishioners in the traffic. In 1884, for instance, a council of Catholic leaders issued a series of resolutions, later approved by Pope Leo XIII, urging all Catholic publicans to abandon saloonkeeping. They should find, the statement declared, "some other more decent method of making a livelihood." Some prelates also pointed out that because so many recent immigrants were Catholic, the church was one of America's best means of introducing the new arrivals to the dry values of their adopted country. Archbishop John Ireland of St. Paul, Minnesota, for example, noted that while many Irish and Central and Southern European immigrants had indeed brought their old drinking ways to the United States, American Catholic leaders were changing things fast. In "The Catholic Church and the Saloon" (1894), he stridently denounced the traffic and explained that over the years the Catholic Total Abstinence Union had built a membership in the tens of thousands and that some dioceses had excluded all liquor dealers "from office, or even membership, in Catholic associations." Old charges that Catholics were "lenient toward intemperance and . . . the saloon" lacked substance, Ireland stated flatly, and he insisted that the church shared the nation's desire to control the liquor menace. "The American saloon," the archbishop wrote, was "a personification of the vilest elements in our modern civilization." It was a mortal danger to "virtue, to piety of soul, to peace of family, to the material, moral, and intellectual welfare of the people, to the free institutions of the republic." No native Protestant could have summarized the temperance position better. Dry leaders rejoiced. Americanization, it seemed, was having an impact.

The mood of many temperance workers was decidedly positive. Frances Willard averaged over a speech a day in these years, usually in front of enthusiastic audiences. Daniel Dorchester failed to see any real setbacks in the slowed pace of legislative progress, and he predicted an inexorable march to a dry millennium. And Senator Henry Blair, the old stalwart of constitutional prohibition, argued in his *History of the Temperance Movement* (1888) that the course of history would henceforth be decided on the basis of the struggle between the two types of people in the world: those who drank and those who did not. A great reckoning was coming, he claimed, just as one had come earlier between slave and free states in the Civil War. The utter rout of liquor and its partisans, Blair proclaimed, would usher in a new era of stability and harmony. Thus, the deflation of temperance spirits that followed the dry failures of the 1850s and sixties was replaced with a new vigor.

Helping the Fallen

While temperance reformers pursued their myriad activities, a considerable number of Americans turned their attention to the individual alcoholic, the individual whose drinking problems had prompted some of the antiliquor response in the first place. If the alcoholic — or just the heavy drinker — had been something of a socially accepted individualist in the Jacksonian years, the early temperance movement undercut such popular tolerance during the 1850s. Instead, many Americans

As the temperance movement gathered steam, "taking the pledge" came to represent not only a personal promise to abstain from drink but also an act of affiliation with the crusade. This elaborate postbellum pledge form is replete with cameos of movement heroes and heroines—reminders of those whose ranks the signer would join.

adopted a view of the drunkard as a physically and economically broken derelict, a socially disruptive person whose lifestyle was at variance with accepted mores, whose very existence was an impediment to the coming of the sober republic. After the Civil War, this image crystallized in the skid row stereotype. And given the fears for the sanctity of the middle-class home, the demands of industrial efficiency, and the premium on good citizenship in a rapidly changing society, the individual drunkard's aberrant behavior and apparent lack of regard for neorepublican values was intolerable, at least in temperance eyes.

As long as the traffic was there to entice drinkers to alcoholism, and as long as moderate drinkers were on hand to set a bad example for others, temperance workers knew there would be drunkards. Aware of both the temptations drinkers faced and the addictive nature of alcohol, many drys conceded that society simply could not hold alcoholics individually responsible for their sad condition. The blame lay with a society that permitted liquor sales and sanctioned drinking. They also held that rescuing alcoholics — because they were less sinners or criminals than victims of society and the traffic — should be a vital part of the temperance movement's activities. After prohibition was the law of the land, such a rehabilitation effort would be unnecessary; in the meantime, however, concerned citizens had to help drunkards — for their own good and for the good of the nation.

As in so many other fields of reform work, the WCTU took the lead in championing this cause. The same concerns for the family that prompted hatred for the saloon also generated genuine sympathy for the drunkard. Indeed, within the context of home protection, no other stance on alcoholism made much sense. Condemning the drunkard was in some ways unthinkable: If the saloon did tempt a father or son, was a WCTU mother to give up her loved one without a fight? For too long, remembered one veteran of the Woman's Crusade, wives and mothers "had seen the brightest and the best of their sons go down." Their purpose now was not only to keep drink from their families in the first place but also to fight the evil if it already afflicted a family member.

The WCTU remedy was "gospel temperance" — a moral suasionist attempt to spark a spiritual rebirth in alcoholics and to get them to keep a pledge of total abstinence. The task, as the *Union Signal* put it, was analogous to "Peter preaching to the gentiles." The women of the WCTU took their preaching seriously. Beginning in 1875, they sought out drunkards in private homes, hospitals, jails, saloons, and even workplaces. Gospel temperance became a national phenomenon, and claims that it had saved thousands for sobriety and for God by the late 1870s are entirely believable.

The WCTU also labored, in conjunction with leading gospel temperance drives, to establish "Reform Clubs." These groups, like the Washingtonians before them (and Alcoholics Anonymous today), were self-governing organizations of alcoholics (or any drinkers worried about becoming alcoholics) who had banded together to help one another stay sober. The clubs were thus a means of institutionalizing the gains made by gospel temperance and of preventing the backsliding that had followed the ebb of the Washingtonian enthusiasm.

Although the union established a number of these clubs, it preferred working with three other movements active in the latter part of the century. Beginning in the early 1870s, J. D. Osgood, a besotted Maine businessman who had reformed himself, founded a chain of clubs throughout New England and the West in alliance with local WCTU chapters. Osgood's following became known as the "Blue Ribbon movement," after the blue cloth badges members wore (the WCTU effort was already known as the "White Ribbon movement"). In similar fashion, Henry Reynolds, an ex-alcoholic Maine doctor, launched the "Red Ribbon movement." At the same time, another reformed drunkard, Francis Murphy, led a major temperance revival in the Middle Atlantic states and the Midwest, and he too left a trail of Reform Clubs. By the 1880s, probably several hundred thousand men and women had joined one of these clubs (we have no precise numbers), and while not all members finally triumphed over the bottle, most contemporary observers agreed that legions "of victims of strong drink . . . reformed, and thousands of desolated and wretched homes [were] made happy."

The majority of drinkers involved with gospel temperance and the Reform Clubs were men. Women also constituted a significant part of the national alcoholism problem, although the relative proportion of male and female alcoholics during this period remains unknown. Nineteenth- and early twentieth century estimates suggest that between one out of ten to one out of three problem drinkers were women. Historians are aware, however, that being labeled an alcoholic was a social catastrophe for women in Victorian America. Indeed, many Americans were unprepared to see women with drinking problems as "real women": The ideal woman was virtuous and pure; alcoholics were degraded. Women defended the home; alcoholics imperiled it. While mothers strove to raise their children in a morally upright environment, drunkards were constant impediments to this task. Alcoholism was considered to be so far from an acceptable standard of behavior for Victorian women that society could explain such conduct only in terms of extreme deviance. They had transgressed not only the norms of hearth and home but also the standards of what was supposed to be feminine and, therefore, as the Reverend Madison C. Peters put it in 1906, they presented "a deplorable outlook for the future of the Republic." This was something the nation would not forgive, noted Dr. Albert Day (an early specialist in alcoholism treatment). The public, he observed, invariably saw inebriated women as worse than drunken men. "A debauched woman is always, everywhere, a more terrible object to behold than a brutish man. We look to see women," Day said, "a little nearer to the angels" than men, "so their fall seems greater."

The stigma imposed by this double standard led to the now familiar "hidden alcoholism" among women. Alcoholic women kept their condition to themselves for fear of social disgrace, only to deteriorate physically as a result. In 1876, for instance, the president of the New York WCTU claimed that many women, including "half the ladies of wealth and fashion," routinely "disguised" their drinking out of the social fear of being identified as alcoholics. It was, as one doctor put it, "regarded as a great disgrace for a woman to be intemperate." Delay in seeking help, he added, accounted for the relative severity of alcoholism in women when the problem finally came to light.

Medical comment went further during the closing years of the nineteenth century. Some doctors claimed that women alcoholics were "more or less chronic," or less capable of rehabilitation than men. The results of inebriety, these physicians concluded, were "more far-reaching and more dreadful" in women. In the early 1900s, one detailed study of hospitalized alcoholics reported that only 29 percent of the women recovered fully, as opposed to 44 percent of the men. The medical complications in the women were more severe (35 percent of the women displayed the brain disorders of Korsakoff's syndrome, for example, compared to only 14 percent of the men), and over twice as many women as men died from alcoholism (15 versus 7 percent).

The special plight of women alcoholics did not escape the attention of the reformers. As early as the 1860s, some temperance and medical authorities argued that the prevalence of alcoholic women justified the construction of sanitariums especially for them. In 1874, the first national convention of the WCTU called for local, state, and federal funding of "Homes for Inebriate Women" throughout the country. And although major public support was not forthcoming, the union maintained its interest in the idea well into the twentieth century. A privately funded asylum for women, Temple Home, did open in 1876 in Binghamton, New York, where it apparently prospered for a number of years. In 1874, Connecticut chartered the Women's National Hospital in order to provide for women alcoholics and "opium eaters"; while the effort collapsed in 1885 because of conflict between hospital promoters and the state legislature, all concerned recognized that society was not facing up to a major untreated female population. In fact, the female alcoholic of industrializing America remained one of the saddest examples of the society's Victorian attitudes and, for many reformers, represented a constant reminder of the necessity of abolishing the liquor trade.

Antiliquor reformers, however, were not alone in their concern about alcoholism treatment. While the WCTU and other dry groups dealt with problem drinkers in their orderly fashion, a segment of the medical community was urging a remarkably different approach to alcoholism. Often faced with the health complications of drinking, physicians had long been interested in alcohol-related issues. There was, for example, an extensive debate over the medical efficacy of alcohol, with some doctors taking the position that alcohol was pure poison and others holding that drink was not as hazardous as temperance workers alleged—and even useful in treating some conditions. This controversy raged until the early 1900s, when, under severe pressure from the temperance movement, the medical profession (or at least that part of it represented by the American Medical Association) finally adopted a dry posture.

Still other physicians were concerned less with the debate over prohibition—and medicinal liquor per se—than with the proper medical treatment of the alcoholic and the scientific investigation of alcoholism. Ever since the work of Benjamin Rush and the English doctor Thomas Trotter in the late eighteenth and early nineteenth centuries, a steadily growing number of physicians and laymen had viewed chronic drunkenness as a disease—an idea that became rather generally diffused in the medical community in the decades before the Civil War. By the 1840s, many temperance workers (as has been seen) had also accepted the disease concept, which further popularized the belief that intemperance was a medical, as well as a moral and social problem. By this time, the progressively debilitating nature of the malady was also familiar: The symptomatic course from moderate drinking to addiction and craving had gained wide recognition, although these ideas lacked any empirical foundation.

These early notions came into sharper focus shortly after the Civil War. Over the ensuing years they evolved into concepts roughly comparable to those that have become widely accepted in the last half of the twentieth century. The impetus for much of this new interest in the concept of alcoholism as a disease grew from the labors of Dr. Joseph E. Turner, originally of Bath, Maine. He accepted the disease concept as holy writ, and his theoretical contributions to the understanding of alcoholism were therefore minimal. On the other hand, Turner launched a crusade calling for the medical treatment of alcoholics and urged the construction of "inebriate asylums" for that purpose. Only in these institutions, he claimed, could alcoholics get the professional care that would enable them to break the chain of addiction. And with genuine foresight, he stressed an equally important justification for the asylums: Turner believed that studies of patient populations would lead to breakthroughs in the medical battle against alcoholism.

In 1864, after a twenty-year campaign, Turner opened the New York State Inebriate Asylum in Binghamton, New York. Turner himself was superintendent, but his tenure became an exercise in frustration. He proved unable to cope with management, personnel, and financial problems, and the institution's board ousted him in 1867. But Turner never stopped being a missionary for medical treatment, and before he died in 1889 his gospel had inspired many. Support for special asylums gradually spread, and by 1900 over fifty public or private facilities had opened for the purpose of treating alcoholics—many of them operated by individuals who considered Turner the "discoverer of a new realm of scientific medicine."

While Turner pursued his crusade, other physicians—most of whom knew or had worked with Turner—took some equally important steps on behalf of the disease concept. In 1870, a group led by Drs. Joseph W. Parrish and Willard Parker founded the American Association for the Cure of Inebriates (soon renamed the Association for the Study of Inebriety). Rather than espouse the neorepublicanism of the temperance movement, the new association embodied the professionalizing spirit of the age—members sought to establish addiction treatment and research (both for alcohol and for narcotics) as a medical specialty, just as groups like the American Bar Association or the American Historical Association would be staking out their special claims to expertise in their respective fields. Most association members were asylum doctors or administrators who sought not only professional recognition for themselves, but also public support for asylum construction and the removal of inebriates from the penal system in favor of compulsory treatment programs. Thus, inasmuch as it led to the founding of the association, the impulse toward order that had prompted heightened fears of the drunkard also operated to marshall the nation's first medical effort to treat male and female alcoholics.

The association grew fairly rapidly in the last half of the century and finally acquired considerable lay and professional recognition, developing close ties with the temperance movement along the way. Originally, some religiously oriented reformers feared that emphasizing medical approaches to alcoholism might divert attention from the moral and social crusade, but these feelings vanished when the association willingly acknowledged the importance of spiritual elements in alcoholism treatment and endorsed prohibition as a means of preventing inebriety in the first place. Many of the member doctors were strong temperance advocates. Thomas D. Crothers, for instance, a longtime association officer, became deeply involved with WCTU alcohol education activities and wrote for many dry publications. Willard Parker, an association founder and one of the nation's foremost surgeons after

Dr. T. D. Crothers, an officer in the American Association for the Study of Inebriety, also directed his own asylum. Walnut Grove, in offering elegant surroundings to patients, was similar to many other private asylums of the day—and to most such facilities today.

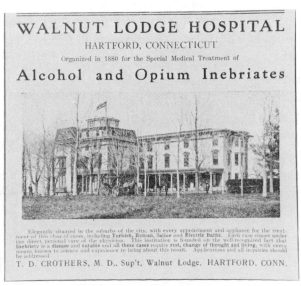

WALNUT LODGE HOSPITAL
HARTFORD, CONNECTICUT
Organized in 1880 for the Special Medical Treatment of
Alcohol and Opium Inebriates

Elegantly situated in the suburbs of the city, with every appointment and appliance for the treatment of this class of cases, including Turkish, Roman, Saline and Electric Baths. Each case comes under the direct personal care of the physician. This institution is founded on the well-recognized fact that inebriety is a disease and curable and all these cases require rest, change of thought and living, with every means known to science and experience to bring about this result. Applications and all inquiries should be addressed

T. D. CROTHERS, M. D., Sup't, Walnut Lodge, HARTFORD, CONN.

the Civil War, also contributed to temperance publications. In turn, Frances Willard publicly supported asylum treatment activities, and Timothy Shay Arthur, perhaps the most famous temperance author of the age, ranked the work of the association with that of the WCTU in the fight against drunkenness.

The Keeley Cure

The most dramatic promise of relief for the drunkard, however, came from neither the association, nor the Reform Clubs, nor any other temperance source. Rather, the final decades of the nineteenth century saw thousands of alcoholics proclaim the miracles wrought by Dr. Leslie Keeley and his "Keeley Cure" (sometimes called the "Gold Cure"). Keeley, born in Ireland in 1834, grew up in New York and served in the Union army's medical corps during the Civil War; then he settled in Illinois. In 1880, he announced (based upon what research, if any, is unknown) that he had discovered a specific remedy for alcoholism and drug addictions. Soon he opened the Keeley Institute at Dwight, Illinois, and began treating patients. His activities received no particular recognition until 1891, when the *Chicago Tribune* published a series of laudatory articles on the doctor and his cure. This sparked a wave of popularity for Keeley, and drunkards flocked to Dwight—and then to branch institutes, which proliferated during the 1890s. By the turn of the century, every state had a Keeley Institute (and some had as many as three).

Keeley's secret was "Bichloride" or "Double Chloride of Gold" (whence the term "Gold Cure"). Pharmacology recognized no such substance, and Keeley never revealed his formula, but bichloride of gold was evidently a gold salt mixed with various vegetable compounds. Nor was Keeley's gold cure unique. Dr. J. L. Gray of Chicago,

An advertisement for "Dr. Haines' Golden Specific"—another so-called cure for alcoholism of the 1890s.

Rutgers Center of Alcohol Studies

for example, was one of several other practitioners to offer a similar cure for alcoholism during the 1880s, although he freely publicized his formula: Twelve grains "chloride of gold and sodium," six grains "muriate of ammonia," one grain "nitrate of strychnia," one-quarter grain atrophine, three ounces "compound fluid extract of cinchona," and one ounce each of glycerine, "fluid extract of coca," and distilled water—a teaspoonful to be taken "every two hours when awake." "Dr. Haines' Golden Specific" was another such cure. Distributed through the mails by the Golden Specific Company, this concoction sold well at the turn of the century. The directions for use of this vegetable compound urged wives to put it secretly into their husbands' food; presumably, miraculous results would follow.

Keeley's gigantic success stemmed from his business acumen in promoting the institutes. He argued that inebriety was the result of alcoholic or narcotic poisoning of the nerve cells, which, in turn, became addicted and required repeated doses of alcohol or drugs to continue to function. This idea was not really dissimilar from some of the theories advanced by association members who openly branded Keeley a

The Women's Auxiliary of the Keeley League of Illinois, 1893.
Keeley's cure involved the organization of former patients to spread
the "Bichloride of Gold" gospel. The leagues also may have served to
keep Keeley Institute "graduates" away from liquor, in much the
same way that the Reform Clubs did, and in that respect they helped
make the cure work.

quack. In retort, Keeley insisted that precisely scheduled doses of his secret compound could break addiction and that the most effective means of administering the cure was intravenous injection at one of his institutes (mail-order oral doses were clearly a second-best method). To keep a lucrative stream of addicts flowing into his establishments, Keeley and his branch managers became adept at organizing former patients (dignified with the title of "graduates") as missionaries on behalf of the cure. In the early 1890s, Keeley marshalled thousands of his patients into a "Keeley League," which held annual conventions and hired lecturers to spread the Gold Cure gospel. The league also staged a "Keeley Day" at the Columbian Exposition in Chicago in 1893; hundreds of graduates paraded in honor of their savior and his cure. There was even a league auxiliary of graduates' wives—the "Ladies' Bichloride of Gold Clubs." It was all good for business, a fact Keeley's sternest critics acknowledged. By 1918, one inquiry estimated that some 400,000 people had taken the cure.

Enthusiasm for the Keeley Cure, however, did not long survive Keeley's death in 1900. The last league convention was held in 1897, even before he passed away; as time went on, the relapses of graduates became all too apparent (thus damaging the credibility of institute promises to prospective patients). Medical charges that Keeley's methods were ridiculous also began to tell, and by the 1920s there were only eleven institutes left (although the original facility at Dwight continued to produce a profit). Eventually the remaining branch institutes either closed or ended their affiliation with the cure, and even Dwight (which is still operating today) dropped all pretensions of offering any specific remedy for inebriety. The Gold Cure, then, remains only as a curiosity of its period. In an age when relatively little was known about alcoholism treatment, thousands had turned to Keeley because he promised a miracle that few others dared offer.

Consensus: The Anti-Saloon League and the End of Pluralism

Despite the efforts of the association and the enormous popularity of Keeley, early medical attempts to help the alcoholic were rather limited. That left only the temperance movement, which was doing its best to put boundaries around potential social disruption as part of a larger American search for order. Reforming the drunkard was just one more way to curb the personal and family tragedies associated with alcoholism and to purify the alien lifestyles surrounding the traffic. Directly or indirectly, alcoholism rehabilitation contributed to the temperance movement's efforts to realize the neorepublican social model. At this time, it was part of a broader vision that led directly toward National Prohibition.

By the 1890s this vision was gaining momentum. Its promise had captivated millions of Americans. While there would never be full national consensus, a majority ultimately agreed that the temperance ideal was desirable as a national policy goal. Precisely when that majority coalesced is difficult to say. Several familiar strands, however, indicate that some sort of reckoning had become probable by the early 1900s.

The tide of popular opinion had been running against drinking for some time. By the turn of the century this feeling, particularly in its prohibitionist form, had become thoroughly intertwined with contemporary Progressive reform thought. Urban Progressives viewed temperance as a means to alleviate poverty and to clean up the political corruption spread through insidious saloons. Dry inroads among Catholics and immigrants, the impact of temperance education in the schools, the heightened outpouring of medical warnings against liquor, and the stress that leading industrialists placed on the need for prohibition all had started to converge.

The same years witnessed much commentary from the reform press, including such journals as the *Nation* and the Hearst newspapers, which came out firmly for prohibition, citing it as an indispensable link in the execution of other reforms. Even unreconstructed drinkers like novelist Jack London urged the abolition of the traffic for the benefit of future generations. The success of temperance advocates in bringing together so many diverse peoples in a common cause dramatically illustrated the movement's developing power and its potential role as a vehicle of national unity and order.

There were occasionally more spectacular signs of the evolving consensus against drink. In 1899, for example, Kansas saw Carry Nation launch her "hatchetation" (her word) campaign; in some of her sorties against saloons she rallied hundreds of supporters. Before her death in 1911, she had struck terror into the hearts of saloonkeepers from coast to coast and demonstrated something of the popular hatred of the traffic. In the end, however, Nation may have done little more than prove that every movement has its lunatic fringe. The formal temperance or-

While many temperance workers may have sympathized with Carry Nation's saloon-busting raids, temperance movement leadership generally looked askance at her techniques. They did not want the dry crusade either to lose prestige through bad publicity or to acquire a reputation for lawlessness. Nation's newspaper coverage, as this New York cartoon demonstrates, did nothing to assuage their fears in this regard.

ganizations (including the WCTU to which Nation belonged) looked askance at her theatrics, preferring less violent methods of influencing public opinion. By the turn of the century, the temperance movement did not need a Carry Nation.

The movement now had enough popular support to begin translating its ideals into the political arena, and it had finally found a technique that allowed that translation without running afoul of Republican and Democratic sensibilities. The solution was the Anti-Saloon League, which effectively organized a nonpartisan political base for temperance, swinging dry votes to anyone—Republican or Democrat—who promised to support prohibition. Instead of backing splinter groups like Willard's Home Protection effort or even the Prohibition party itself, the league convinced most antiliquor sympathizers that working at odds with the major parties was futile. Victory, league members argued, lay within the traditional two-party system.

The Anti-Saloon League was the child of the Reverend Dr. Howard Hyde Russell, who saw both the popular appeal of temperance and the past political mistakes of the crusade. He advocated not only a nonpartisan approach to prohibition politics but also the direct involvement of the pulpit on behalf of electoral contests against the traffic. Starting in Ohio, where Russell had sought help from the traditionally reform-minded students and faculty of Oberlin College, the league began to perfect its methods during the early 1890s. Working first through Methodist pulpits (and thereafter through other denominations as well), the league spread the dry message from the congregations to the ballot boxes.

Part of the message was "local option," which began to dry up Ohio on a county-by-county (or town-by-town) basis. The second tenet was nonpartisanship: The league proved that it could marshall votes for anyone — Republican or Democrat — who was willing to vote dry. Both the major parties rapidly awoke to the electoral power of the league, and it soon became apparent that the political fortunes of the antiliquor crusade would not have to depend on any single party — and certainly not on the small and ineffectual Prohibition party. In fact, Republican and Democratic managers learned that cooperation with the league could guarantee their candidates not only a large block of votes but also campaign workers and financial contributions. Throughout the 1890s, then, the Anti-Saloon League gathered momentum as it duplicated its Ohio successes in other regions, forming state chapters and a national organization (1895) along the way.

The growth of the league, of course, would have been impossible without the public groundswell of temperance support. But league activities both rode and cultivated this popular trend, which carried the organization to the heights of national political power. By the early 1900s, the league had become a skilled and well-financed lobby for state and federal prohibition, and it boasted a massive grass-roots following. Its annual budget, for instance, was well over $2 million, with 90 percent of the total coming in donations of $100 or less. And not all this backing was Protestant. A surprising number of Catholics — some of them priests imbued with the Progressive "social gospel" and active in urban social work — openly supported the league. Several priests, in fact, held state or national league offices. Other Catholics who did not favor the league often failed to oppose it for fear of reviving nativist rumblings against their church. The league's own American Issue Press churned out millions of publications, keeping members well informed and well armed with moral and political arguments. This association was so effective in rallying the public that by the turn of the century most other temperance groups, including the WCTU and the

Prohibition party (which had originally, and at times bitterly, resented the league's nonpartisan approach), had acknowledged the league's dominant role in the antiliquor struggle.

The man in charge of the national legislative effort was an Ohio prodigy, Wayne B. Wheeler, whom Russell had discovered at Oberlin. Wheeler, an utterly dedicated reformer, yearned for the sober, unified republic of temperance dreams. He was, as historian Norman Clark stressed, firmly grounded in the stewardship tradition; Wheeler believed implicitly that the dry crusade had the responsibility to lead the nation to ever greater heights of morality, patriotism, and citizenship. Wheeler also knew how to get what he wanted. He had, for example, orchestrated the successful local option campaign in Ohio, the league's first major victory.

Wheeler exemplified the league's nonpartisan political effectiveness. A Republican himself, he swung league votes to the Democrats in 1905 to defeat Ohio's wet Republican Governor Myron Herrick. In Washington, as the league's general counsel, he illustrated dry strength to wavering legislators by showering them with prohibitionist telegrams. "Wheelerism" became the byword for high-powered lobbying. Indeed, as one of his former aides, Peter Odegard, explained in *Pressure Politics* (1928), Wheeler pioneered many of the strong-arm lobbying techniques now so common in national politics. Under Wheeler's leadership, the league thus was both respected and feared on Capitol Hill. It became the most influential pressure group of its day.

All this meant that National Prohibition was looming ever closer. By the early 1900s, even the most skilled and dedicated proliquor forces found themselves unable to stem the popular tide. George Coes Howell, a reasoned and eloquent spokesman for the traffic, deplored what he labeled "ignorant emotionalism . . . directed by brilliant fanatics." Yet he knew what liquor supporters were up against: Prohibitionists had "promised a Utopia, wherein drunkenness was to be unknown" and other social evils would consequently be eliminated. Politicians who tried to stand up to the league risked defeat; wet voters, even in some large cities such as Los Angeles and Seattle, which had sizable working-class or ethnic populations, found themselves outnumbered in local political contests. Most Americans, as a number of recent and detailed state-level histories have shown, genuinely considered prohibition the issue of the day; if they were not thoroughly committed temperance workers themselves, they were at least willing to give the sober republic a fair try.

Matters had already begun to fall into place for the crusaders. By 1903, over a third of the nation lived under some type of prohibitory law — that is, thirty-five million people — a figure rising to forty-six million by 1913, or about half the populace. In Washington, dry congressional strength reflected these numbers, and 1913 saw passage of the Webb-Kenyon Act, banning the shipment of liquor from wet to dry states. The law was a real blow to the liquor industry, and the traffic correctly surmised that tougher measures were coming.

In 1916, after a tremendous push from all dry organizations, the general elections sent so many league endorsed candidates to the House and Senate that action on a prohibitory amendment to the Constitution was virtually assured. The Eighteenth Amendment easily received congressional approval in December 1917 and promptly went to the states for ratification. The amendment itself was a simple document. The first section prohibited the manufacture, sale, transportation, and importing or exporting of "intoxicating liquors" from or to anywhere within the United States or territories under its jurisdiction. The provisions would take effect one year after ratification, thus providing a grace period for the traffic to liquidate its holdings and wrap up its affairs. The second section provided for "concurrent" enforcement of the amendment; that is, both the federal and the state governments would have the power to police violations. Third, the article would be "inoperative" unless it was ratified within seven years.

No one seriously thought that the ratification process would take seven years to complete, and events transpired that gave the amendment an unanticipated boost. In April 1917, the United States declared war on the Central Powers; by December, when Congress acted on the Eighteenth Amendment, Americans were consumed by a patriotic frenzy that, among other things, vilified anything German. German-Americans were harassed, sauerkraut renamed "liberty cabbage," and the music of Beethoven and Wagner frowned upon. The government of Woodrow Wilson urged Americans to hate the enemy and to sacrifice for the cause of victory. Temperance workers, it should be noted, did not start this patriotic binge, but they were quick to take advantage of it.

World War I gave the prohibition crusade yet another chance to demonstrate its dedication to national unity and discipline. The reformers led and applauded efforts to dry up the armed forces. The temperance movement provided speakers to lecture the troops on good citizenship and patriotism. Dry advocates successfully fought the brewing and distilling of grains into beverage alcohol as an emergency food conservation measure (the Lever Food and Fuel Control Act). And antiliquor forces happily watched the public turn even more strongly against the brewers—most of whom had German names—in the new wave of war-inspired emotionalism. Indeed, the temperance movement fanned the fires of hatred directed at the brewers in a smear campaign that reflected little credit on the drys. On a more practical level, President Wilson, in December 1917, forbade the brewing of any beer stronger than 2.75 percent. While these war related measures (termed "war prohibition") delighted antiliquor forces, state ratifications of the prohibition amendment pressed forward. The thirty-sixth state ratified in January 1919, making prohibition part of the Constitution in record time; no previous amendment had ever passed so quickly and with so clear a mandate from the states. Ultimately, only Connecticut and Rhode Island refused to ratify. The nation was thus scheduled to go constitutionally dry in January 1920.

In reality, however, prohibition did not take that long to implement. In September 1919, Congress extended the wartime limitations on the use of foodstuffs in distilling and brewing, which severely limited the amount of legal alcohol in the marketplace. This action probably reflected a congressional desire to insure order and tranquility during military demobilization, especially during a period of intense fear of postwar social unrest and radicalism (it was the time of the "red scare"). But the measure was also part of a wider dry plan to see that National Prohibition got off to a good start. Under the aegis of the Anti-Saloon League, Congress added some real teeth to existing restrictions on liquor production. Specifically, the legislature defined "intoxicating liquor"—the wording of the Eighteenth Amendment—as any beverage of more than .5 percent alcohol. Wilson vetoed the bill, but Congress easily overrode him in October and scheduled the law to take effect three months later.

The enabling legislation in question was the National Prohibition Act, which quickly became known as the Volstead Act, named after Representative Andrew Volstead of Minnesota. Actually, Wayne Wheeler had drafted the legislation. Volstead, a stalwart neorepublican believer in virtue and sobriety, firmly held that law could indeed control national morality. He was as firmly committed to the stewardship ideal as was Wheeler, and had served only as a willing and convenient congressional sponsor. The act killed whatever wet hopes remained that light wines or beers might survive under National Prohibition (a number of moderate drys were also disappointed in this regard).

The Volstead Act even regulated the use of sacramental wines and medicinal liquor. Beverages kept in private homes, however—such as a farmer's naturally fermented hard cider—remained legal for personal use, provided none was offered for sale. With the passage of the Volstead Act, America's dry legal framework was largely in place and temperance workers looked forward to the burial of their insidious enemy, beverage alcohol, in January 1920.

Americans seemed to take all this in stride. The antiliquor victory had been building for years, and most citizens apparently accepted it. The talk of drying out the nation was nothing new, and the advent of constitutional prohibition seemed almost an anticlimax after so many decades of heated debate and hard work. The demon, in fact, died a largely quiet death on January 16, 1920. As notable a newspaper as the *New York Times* saw no reason to give its demise more than a single column.

"To the Heights of Mount Sinai"

Yet even in dying (for that is how matters looked in 1920), drink served a vital national purpose. Liquor—collectively drinking, the traffic, and all that alcohol stood for in the temperance mind—had been the enemy to generations of Americans wedded to the ideal of neorepublican virtue and stewardship. In the years following the Revolution, excessive drinking had threatened to undermine the glorious promise of independence and the young republic; after the Civil War, alcohol had stood in the way of the reform and perfection that the results of the sectional conflict had suggested were possible for a moral and liberty-loving citizenry. Indeed, postbellum antiliquor rhetoric of a "new abolitionism" was sincere. Temperance workers took their cause as seriously as the Revolutionary generation had taken the issue of republicanism or the men and women of the 1860s the Southern secessionist rebellion. Indeed, the antiliquor reformers saw themselves fulfilling the dreams of their forebears; the old dream of a unified republic sustained by public virtue, which had driven forward the Washingtons and Lincolns of earlier eras, would prove impossible without a latter-day victory over drink. The temperance wars were, therefore, every bit as crucial as the conflicts that had previously shaped the United States, or so claimed the dry reformers of the late nineteenth and early twentieth centuries. They saw themselves as every bit as heroic as the veterans of these earlier struggles. This belief helped sustain the movement through the Progressive years and toward final victory in the Eighteenth Amendment. The death of liquor, therefore, symbolized the fruition of reformist dreams unfolding since the late 1780s, the passing of the last hurdle on the path to the virtuous republic.

Thus, drinking in America now seemed only a part of an imperfect past, to be replaced by a new order that would justify all the arduous labor that had called it into being. The fact that National Prohibition did not enjoy unanimous support as it became part of the Constitution did not matter. Few people believed that Americans would violate the Constitution on a mass basis. And besides, as sociologist Joseph Gusfield argued, drys, and those who shared their ideals, could now claim that their standards were law, that their norms were the measuring rod against which all conduct would be judged in the future. Hence, anyone who did break the law would be labeling himself or herself a deviant, beyond the pale of acceptable behavior for "true" Americans.

Legal prohibition ended debate on that long contested point. In 1920, the neorepublican moral triumph seemed complete. Hard drinkers, immigrants, the traffic, the evils of industrialization, and all the other manifestations of rampant pluralism and individualism had not ruined the nation. Neorepublican ideals had not only proved durable, but in important respects they determined the very nature of social change. In a retrospective look at the temperance crusade, dry journalist W. R. Scott summed up the pattern this way: The old ideals had at last carried "the American people . . . up to the final heights of Mount Sinai." It remained to be seen what they would do at that elevation.

CHAPTER FOUR

Drier and Drier, and Wetter and Wetter: Drinking and the Pluralist Renaissance

---

Our country has deliberately undertaken a great social and economic experiment, noble in motive and far-reaching in purpose. It must be worked out constructively.

President-elect Herbert Hoover (1928)

The Eighteenth Article of Amendment to the Constitution . . . is hereby repealed.

Twenty-first Amendment to the Constitution of the United States of America (1933)

The White House, 1933

December 5, 1933, was a day of waiting. The Twenty-first Amendment, which would repeal the Eighteenth Amendment and end National Prohibition, was on the verge of ratification. Congress had sent the new amendment to the states in March, and thirty-three state conventions had quickly and overwhelmingly voted for repeal. So the pro-liquor movement needed only three more states—for a constitutional minimum of thirty-six—to assure victory. Ohio and Pennsylvania fell into line early on the fifth, and late in the afternoon the Utah convention neared a final vote. The nation watched carefully. In cities like Boston, Chicago, and San Francisco, speakeasy patrons waited with illegal drinks in hand. New York City's entire police force was on duty to control expected repeal celebrations in Times Square and in the thousands of drinking establishments ready to dispense legal booze for the first time in nearly fourteen years. In Maryland, the state legislature fired its "State House bootlegger," anticipating the enjoyment of "patriotically . . . legal liquor." Perhaps no one waited more hopefully than President Franklin Delano Roosevelt. The Columbia Broadcasting System had put the White House in direct contact with Salt Lake City, and the president was eager to announce at the earliest possible moment that the book had been closed on the sober republic.

There was some irony in the fact that FDR would be the one to announce the end of prohibition. Until he ran for president, he had not seriously championed the wet cause. Indeed, his wife, Eleanor, had once been a firm dry, disapproving even of her husband's occasional highball. And Roosevelt had seen the political grief that an openly wet position had brought his fellow Democrat Al Smith in 1928. So, initially the new president was in no rush to embrace legal liquor. But his party had forced his hand. Roosevelt's opponent for the nomination of 1932 had been none other than Smith, who called openly for repeal, as did most of the delegates to the Democratic convention. Encouraged by the Association against the Prohibition Amendment, they clamored for repeal, and the future president was forced to lead the cause lest he find himself a mere follower. But Roosevelt warmed to his wet role during the campaign, and he approved as the new Congress, while awaiting state ratification of the Twenty-first Amendment, amended the Volstead Act in April 1933 to permit the sale of light wines and beers of no more than 3.2 percent alcohol. Now all he needed was word from Utah, and he could finish the job.

Finally the waiting was over. At 3:32½ P.M. Mountain Time—
5:32½ P.M. Eastern Standard Time—S. R. Thurman of Salt Lake City
cast the deciding vote for repeal. National Prohibition was dead. FDR
probably got the word less than three minutes later. At 6:55 P.M., the
president signed an official proclamation of repeal. Yet after lauding
"this return of individual freedom," he went on to sound a note of cau-
tion. The demise of prohibition and the Volstead Act, he told the nation, were not signals for a new national binge. "I ask especially," he
added, "that no state shall, by law or otherwise, authorize the return of
the saloon, either in its old form or in some modern guise." Rather,
Roosevelt wanted an end to the illegal liquor traffic and "the education
of every citizen toward a greater temperance throughout the nation."
Any return to the "repugnant conditions that [had] obtained prior to
the adoption of the Eighteenth Amendment," Roosevelt warned, and
any social chaos that followed in prohibition's path would be "a living
reproach to us all."

Popular reaction to repeal and the president's message varied. The
more moderate temperance workers accepted the White House statement with resignation; some were philosophical. "Political Prohibition
cannot sustain itself," one of them concluded; in the future "only a
spiritual attainment by a vast majority of citizens . . . would make total abstinence a fact." If the temperance movement were to continue,
he observed, it would have to be on a nonpolitical basis. Predictably,
however, diehard drys thundered defiance. The Anti-Saloon League
screamed that repeal meant "War . . . NO PEACE PACT—NO AR-
MISTICE" and that temperance forces would soon be ready to resume
the "offensive against the liquor traffic." The proliquor roar was just as
loud in the bars of Chicago and New York. But, on the whole, Americans took the news calmly, seemingly more relieved than angry or ex-
ultant. Even in New York's Times Square the police reported no more
than the usual number of arrests for an average evening. The mood,
the *New York Times* reported, was that of "quiet restraint." Pauline
Sabin, the astute leader of the Women's Organization for National
Prohibition Reform, which had worked as hard as any other group to
make the events of December 5 possible, seemed best to capture popular sentiment on the occasion. Sabin expressed her hope that celebrations would "be short-lived, and that once the custom of drinking" was
again open and accepted "we shall settle down to temperance and
moderation."

Yet no matter how people initially reacted to the repeal proclamation, for those who stopped to reflect, the event was in many respects extraordinary. Since the days of Benjamin Rush, some five generations of temperance reformers had labored to build a dry America. However, their final victory had endured for less than fourteen years. While the Eighteenth Amendment had had undeniable popular approval behind it, once enacted, no other amendment ever had proved so controversial. Nor has any other amendment been repealed. And when repeal happened, few could doubt that the Twenty-first Amendment had ridden to success on an even larger wave of public support than had carried National Prohibition to ratification. The event was extraordinary and certainly ironic. How could such a turnabout have happened?

Wets and drys offered conflicting explanations of repeal. These versions, in which they frequently managed to vilify each other thoroughly, added more heat than light to the search for answers. Yet some observers recognized that fundamental changes had occurred in the moral-social perceptions that had given rise to the sober republic. Such changes not only concerned attitudes toward drinking and alcohol but in great measure reflected the national mood and circumstances that ultimately sent Franklin Roosevelt to the White House. To understand these developments, however, takes us back to America's initial experiences with its "noble experiment" and to the chain of events and feelings set in motion by the Eighteenth Amendment.

Drinking in the Sober Republic: Did Prohibition Prohibit?

Enforcement of the Volstead Act is one of the most misunderstood chapters in American history. Both professional historians and lay writers, looking back from the wet perspective of the post-repeal years, have pronounced the dry movement a failure. Indeed, they often have assumed that the prohibition years saw an upsurge in drinking, although admittedly illegal. In *Prohibition Mania* (1927), a book whose title betrayed its authors' feelings on the subject, Clarence Darrow and Victor Yarros "dismissed with unmitigated contempt" dry claims that American liquor consumption had declined. They insisted heatedly that guzzling was worse than ever. And the judgment of Robert Lewis Taylor, in his delightful biography of Carry Nation, is fairly typical of the modern public view: "On the night of January 16, 1920, the coun-

The early 1920s were happy days for the WCTU. The battle for repeal had not begun in earnest, and the future of National Prohibition looked bright. The decorated car, dating from 1922, was an entry in a local temperance celebration and reflected the dry crusade's upbeat mood.

try had gone to bed fairly sober; next morning it awoke, grabbed a red tin New Year's Eve horn and blew it without interruption for the next fourteen years, or until President Roosevelt picked up a pen and revoked the holy crusade."

More recently, however, a number of historians have effectively challenged this "soaking wet" image of prohibition, citing a variety of impressive statistical evidence to the contrary. In a penetrating 1968 article, historian John C. Burnham surveyed contemporary reports bearing on liquor consumption during the Volstead years. Some of his most significant findings came from data gathered in studies of the medical complications of problem drinkers, which showed sharp declines from preprohibition levels in hospital admissions for alcoholism, in the prevalence of alcohol-related psychoses, and in other drinking-related disease conditions. In addition, Burnham tallied the number of arrests for drunkenness, as well as the national cost of incarcerating public inebriates, and he found the figures to be considerably lower than comparative totals in the pre-Volstead era.

Nor was Burnham the first to reach such conclusions. As early as 1930, Yale economist Irving Fisher, a convinced dry, argued a similar case in The "Noble Experiment." Fisher claimed that prohibition saw a dramatic decline in the national death rate from alcoholism. Despite its admitted temperance bias, his work still stands up well. Fisher conceded that in wet states where Volstead Act enforcement was minimal, such as New York and Maryland, alcoholism mortality rates may have reached preprohibition levels by the late 1920s (but not earlier). He based these observations on Census Bureau, insurance industry, and public health sources, all of which he had studied carefully; his conclusions appear to be generally sound.

There are additional data: In 1943, Forrest Linder and Robert Grove compiled mortality figures for the Census Bureau in *Vital Statistics Rates in the United States, 1900–1940*. They found that from a high of 7.3 deaths from chronic or acute alcoholism per 100,000 population in 1907, the rate fell gradually (possibly as a result of the advent of state prohibitory laws and war prohibition) to 1.6 per 100,000 in 1919 and then to 1.0 in 1920, the first year of National Prohibition. The rates then climbed slowly again, probably reflecting the gradual increase in illegal (and often poisonous) liquor supplies (a point discussed later), peaking at 4.0 per 100,000 in 1927 — although in 1932, the last full year of prohibition, the figure was down once again to 2.5.

While it is difficult to link conclusively these alcoholism death rates with data on other diseases, Linder and Grove did chart a parallel trend in the death rate from cirrhosis of the liver. A number of researchers — albeit with debatable accuracy — have cited cirrhosis as an important element in the estimation of alcoholism rates (notably E. M. Jellinek in 1942, with many subsequent revisions of his technique over the years), so the Linder and Grove figures may be fairly accurate. They found that from a high of 14.8 deaths per 100,000 in 1907 (also the high point in deaths from alcoholism), death from cirrhosis roughly kept pace with the declining number of deaths from alcoholism, falling to 7.9 per 100,000 in 1919 and 7.1 in 1920. Thereafter, the rate never rose above 7.5 during the dry decade. Despite the problems inherent in reporting alcoholism statistics — there is no way to tell how uniform data collection may have been in compiling the *Vital Statistics* volume — the weight of the medical evidence strongly suggests that prohibition may have worked directly to reduce mortality from alcoholism and cirrhosis of the liver.

The social work community added its testimony as well. After surveying the field operations of the Salvation Army, Commander Evangeline Booth — perhaps one of America's most beloved practitioners of the social gospel — insisted that prohibition was doing the job among great numbers of urban poor. She argued in *Some Have*

Stopped Drinking (1928) that, although intemperance was still a problem in some quarters, drinking had fallen off drastically since the advent of prohibition. Poorer people were drinking less, Booth claimed,
and consequently the army found less urban poverty and fewer broken
homes resulting from wages sqandered on booze and from drinking-related violence. Martha Bruere reported similar findings in an even
more comprehensive survey of social workers, *Does Prohibition Work?*
(1927). Not only was liquor consumption down, but more wages—
which previously had gone for drink—seemed to be flowing into savings accounts or family necessities. Irving Fisher's inquiry also recorded
equally plausible evidence from still other urban social workers on this
matter.

In an important contemporary study, economist Clark Warburton—a convinced wet whose research for *The Economic Results of
Prohibition* (1932) had been supported by the Association Against the
Prohibition Amendment—also studied the urban poor. From findings
compatible with Fisher's and Bruere's, Warburton concluded that in
the early dry years, urban wage earners spent some $2 billion less on al-
cohol than they had before ratification of the Eighteenth Amendment.
This amount had roughly halved by 1929, but even that reduced figure
represented a substantial savings.

Perhaps the most impressive figures in support of reduced drinking
under the Volstead Act are the consumption estimates supplied by
both historians and contemporary authorities. In 1976, historian Norman Clark reviewed the literature and concluded that estimates that
placed annual absolute alcohol consumption rates at between 50 and
33 percent less than those of the preprohibition years were essentially
correct. Citing statistics published by the National Institute of Alcohol
Abuse and Alcoholism, he noted that immediately after repeal, in
1934, annual pcr capita consumption of absolute alcohol (among persons aged fifteen or older) stood at slightly less than a gallon, down
from 2.6 gallons in the 1906–1910 period. These data buttress the conclusion that Americans must have been drinking less than ever before
during prohibition, probably just under a gallon of absolute alcohol
per capita annually, a judgment sustained by historical consumption
estimates published in 1980 by the Rutgers University Center of Alcohol Studies (see the Appendix).

On the other hand, National Prohibition did not put an end to
drinking. Plenty of people knew very well where to look for a glass of

something stronger than water. It would be misleading to claim that the United States ever effectively "dried out." Many citizens (we will never know how many) had to go no further for liquor than their own cellars. They had either laid in an ample supply of alcohol over the years before 1920 or made huge purchases on the eve of prohibition; in any event, they faced the onset of America's "long thirst" well prepared. And as long as they did not sell their booze, they were free under the Volstead Act to keep it and drink it privately. H. L. Mencken, the caustic "Sage of Baltimore," who pledged his *American Mercury* magazine to "the return of the American saloon," was a prime example in this regard. Described as "ombibulous" (that is, he drank everything) by one admirer, Mencken supposedly had a splendid variety of beverages stashed away—enough, as it turned out, to keep him going until repeal in 1933. In New York City, the Yale Club was similarly forearmed by 1920; its members had the pleasure of popping corks and enjoying quality whiskey and wine throughout the prohibition years. But such preparations could backfire: In *The Cup of Fury* (1956), novelist-reformer Upton Sinclair recalled that his uncle, John Randolph Bland, was "a practical man." He "recognized the oncoming of Prohibition before the legislation actually became part of our Constitution," Sinclair wrote, and he cached $6,000 worth of "wines, whiskeys, brandies and liquors" against the coming thirsty years. Unfortunately or fortunately, when Uncle Bland moved to other quarters for the winter, thieves invaded his summer home "and carried off every case of his treasures."

There was also country liquor. Rural stills remained a traditional part of the American landscape. Operating illegally even before prohibition, their proprietors had notoriously little respect for the Volstead Act, and moonshiners continued to ply their trade with relative impunity. One West Virginia grandmother operated a still for thirty years (right through the Volstead era) and usually welcomed the arrival of law officers. They were, she recalled much later, some of her best customers. (Her son remembered that one of the worst hidings he got as a youth came after he and some playmates decided to play "revenooers" and smashed up one of his mother's stills.) In regions where relations with enforcement authorities were less cordial, backwoods distillers resorted to elaborate schemes to camouflage their operations. Revenue officials once padlocked a hollow California redwood that housed a still. But for every moonshiner caught, thousands got away and local recipes and skills survived the era almost as though prohibition had never existed.

Generally, the really wet areas were the major cities. Not only did metropolitan centers have large ethnic enclaves, some of which tried to keep traditional drinking patterns alive despite prohibition, but also cities offered the mass concentration of customers, transportation and storage facilities, distribution networks, and sales outlets necessary to make illegal booze operations highly profitable. The career of George Remus illustrates how such businesses worked.

Before prohibition, Remus had been a noted Chicago attorney (he was an early activist against the death penalty). No friend of steward-ship and moral neorepublicanism, Remus abhorred the notion of legis-lated morality embodied in the Eighteenth Amendment. With the ad-vent of the sober republic, however, he decided (for reasons not fully understood—but probably having something to do with easy money) to take advantage of what he saw as national folly. Moving to Cincinnati, and marshalling his considerable legal and administrative talents, he used bribery and fraud to procure enough licenses to distribute "me-dicinal liquor" (legal under the Volstead Act) on a scale that required him to purchase and operate a number of distilleries to meet customer demand. Then, to increase his sales, he "stole" liquor from his own dis-tilling operations and sold it for higher prices on the illegal market. Until the government put Remus out of business in 1922, Cincinnati and other Midwestern towns found him a reliable supplier.

Liquor flowed abundantly in Chicago. The city had always been tolerant of illegal saloons and bordellos, and prohibition had a mini-mal impact on these operations. As legal sources of beverage alcohol dried up, however, some of the more successful owners of illicit estab-lishments discovered the financial possibilities in liquor distribution. Johnny Torrio, for instance, relative of and advisor to "Big Jim" Col-osimo, one of Chicago's largest brothel owners, once sought to pur-chase an old brewery for use as a house of ill fame but decided that there would be more money in brewing beer. That decision helped make a lot of people connected with Torrio incredibly rich. And per-haps richest of all was Al Capone, a Brooklyn thug whom Torrio brought to prominence in Chicago. When Capone was at the height of his power, his illegal liquor, prostitution, and racketeering operations brought in hundreds of millions of dollars a year. To protect his em-pire, Capone had perhaps a thousand men working directly for him (some of whom he kept busy fighting off or eliminating rival gangs), as well as numerous city police and other officials on his unofficial payroll. The price was high, but wet Chicagoans had enough to drink.

There were plenty of other leaky seams in prohibition. Urban centers with large ethnic communities, such as Boston, New York, and Philadelphia, seldom went thirsty, and the entire state of Rhode Island, with a huge ethnic population, was notoriously lax in Volstead Act enforcement. Detroit was a major terminus and distribution network for illegal Canadian liquor, and it also supported a thriving urban moonshine operation. Detroit's reputation as a wet town was such that Larry Engelmann, historian of the Motor City under prohibition, termed it the "City upon a Still."

Nor were Detroit's urban stills unique. Most large cities had them, and some communities boasted hundreds of such small-scale operations. Owners called their stills "alky-cookers." Families could buy the equipment and get a still going for about $10, easily turning out several gallons of neutral spirits a day (children learned to supervise production when mom and dad were busy). Local gangsters, who frequently sold the cookers to the home distillers in the first place, picked up the booze on a scheduled basis, paying an average of $2 a gallon for the home brewed spirits. In Chicago, the Genna family, one of the most brutal of that city's mobs, originally ran the alky business; they organized Italian neighborhoods and turned their operation into a gold mine. The Gennas (and gangs like them) either sold the alcohol to a distributor, who would make gin from it, or made the gin themselves for resale. The most common recipe was simple: Mix the alcohol with 30 to 50 percent water, then add a few drops of glycerine and juniper juice to simulate the flavor of gin. The concoction went into bottles or jugs too tall to fill with water from a sink tap, but they fit under bathtub taps, whence the term "bathtub gin." The gin maker got about $6 a gallon from speakeasy owners or other retailers, who in turn sold the liquor by the glass for a whopping total of $40. It was good business for all but the consumer. (Prohibition probably made distilling more prevalent on a small-scale, family basis than at any other time since the frontier days of the late eighteenth and early nineteenth centuries.)

Other distilled spirits also found their way into the illicit market. Industrial alcohol, vital to the nation's economy, remained in production subject to federal regulation. The regulations, however, were less than airtight: Bootleggers stole considerable quantities of industrial alcohol, which was mixed with water and flavorings and sold at handsome profits as scotch, bourbon, and so on. Falsified production and storage records also enabled criminals to divert some of this legal alcohol to beverage use. Much of the industrial spirits supply was denatured—methyl alcohol, benzine, or other chemicals were added to make it impotable—but this precaution did not pose an insurmountable problem. Bootlegger financed chemists could remove the denaturant through redistillation ("washing"). Properly "washed" alcohol was drinkable but a carelessly prepared potion could blind or kill. Unfortunately, there were a lot of sloppy jobs.

Smuggling was another source of booze. "Rum Row" was active off the coasts of the larger metropolitan areas. Ships lined up, usually just outside the three-mile territorial limit, to discharge cargoes of British,

The crash of "aerial rum runner," New York State, 1922. The biplane was flying liquor in from Canada when it went down—without breaking any of the 150 bottles "of choice Scotch and Irish whiskey." The pilot, who escaped in a waiting car, may have been a woman: The police announced that their "latest clew [sic] is a powder puff" found aboard the aircraft.

Caribbean, and other imported liquor via smaller, faster vessels. At different times, the most profitable rows operated off the New England, Florida, Northwest, and New Jersey coasts—close, that is, to the most compact urban markets. It could be a tough and expensive business: The government could confiscate captured rum runners, and competitors were known to hijack rival ships on the high seas. But the rewards of success were huge, and the row attracted some colorful characters. Bill McCoy was perhaps the best known. He had a reputation for bringing in quality merchandise—the original "Real McCoy."

Glaring as these violations of the Volstead Act were, they did not support preprohibition levels of drinking, and they are certainly not cause to alter the conclusion that the Eighteenth Amendment radically cut American liquor consumption. There is no sign that drinking spread into areas in which it had not flourished before, particularly among the millions of citizens who had welcomed prohibition in the first place.

In fact, prohibition always retained considerable grass-roots support, even among some groups later depicted as soaking wet in ill-informed accounts of the Volstead years. College students, for example, apparently remained fairly temperate, at least through the mid-1920s—the wild sprees depicted in the novels of F. Scott Fitzgerald notwithstanding. While there were egregious exceptions, most colleges and universities were not scenes of riotous drinking. Indeed, the majority of reliable reports, including a careful survey in 1926 conducted by the Intercollegiate Prohibition Association, revealed considerable student support for the Noble Experiment. If anything, some of the worst drinking excesses on campus were the achievement of visiting alumni, whose actions the undergraduates often subsequently deplored. And there is good reason to believe these conclusions, as a *Literary Digest* poll (which was by no means biased toward drys) taken in 1926 produced virtually identical findings to those of the Intercollegiate Prohibition Association. Drinking in college during the prohibition years, then, apparently was not much different from drinking in the rest of the country—that is, it was confined to and condoned by a minority.

Contrary to the assertions of some social historians, there is little evidence to support the claim that women vastly increased their consumption of alcohol during the Volstead years. Middle- and upper-class "flappers" did, indeed, frequent the fancier speakeasies, where they received considerable publicity and created the illusion of a surge in female drinking. No doubt the lower-class speakeasies ("blind pigs") also attracted women, although they garnered less newspaper attention. But women had regularly accompanied men to many of the plusher liquor establishments in the days before prohibition, and women from wet families had also imbibed regularly. In working-class and poorer rural saloons, prostitutes had routinely hustled drinks to pick up customers in return for the use of rooms on the premises. So to claim that prohibition first brought women into drinking establishments in large numbers—or radically increased the population of female drinkers—is absurd. Moreover, there are no data in any of the survey sources assessing consumption rates—hospital and police records and social work case studies—that indicate increased drinking among women. On the contrary, there is every reason to assume that, like most other Americans, women as a group drank less during prohibition.

Besides, illegal booze was expensive and most drinkers—female or male—could not afford to consume alcohol at preprohibition rates. The Torrios, Capones, Remuses, and McCoys of the era were not philanthropists. Their work was risky, and their overhead expenses were immense: The costs associated with intercepted shipments (lost either to rivals or to enforcement agents), hired thugs, police payoffs, chemists, distillery workers, ships, trucks, and production equipment all mounted up—so those in the traffic charged plenty. In Northern cities, cocktails that sold for 15¢ in 1918 were 75¢ by the early 1920s. Domestic lager beer, which sold for about $10.50 a barrel in 1918, cost anywhere from 15¢ to $1 or more a *quart* by 1930 (that is, $160 or more a barrel, depending upon the quality of the beer). Domestic spirits, which averaged $1.39 a quart in 1918, soared to an average of $4.01 a quart by 1930. Prices on imported foreign beverages also rose significantly, and, as Clark Warburton pointed out, no doubt a large quantity of American made liquor was passed off as imported to fetch higher prices. In short, bootlegging activity was less a sign that drinking was rife than an explanation of why it was so hard to drink cheaply. And expensive booze alone, as a number of modern studies of liquor sales have shown convincingly, may limit alcohol consumption.

The high cost of illicit drink also had an impact on consumption patterns by type of product. By the 1880s, annual per capita absolute alcohol consumption was fairly evenly balanced between beer (45 percent) and spirits (47 percent), with wine in a distant third place (7 percent). By 1919, the figures read 55 percent for beer and only 37 percent for spirits—the beer invasion obviously had succeeded. But prohibition altered the situation, raising the relative proportion of distilled beverage consumption. Estimates derived from Warburton's calculations indicate that of all absolute alcohol consumed in the Volstead years, roughly 75 percent came in the form of whiskey, gin, scotch, or other spirits, with only some 15 percent in beer.

The change was probably a simple matter of consumer economics. The middle classes and wealthier drinkers, who could best afford to imbibe at high prohibition prices, shifted their habits relatively little— they had always been the greater spirits drinkers. On the other hand, blue-collar workers and poorer groups, who usually preferred beer, generally could not afford the higher prices; consequently, they apparently drank less. So the higher proportion of spirits consumed did not necessarily mean that vast new legions of people were now drinking distilled beverages—only that fewer Americans, particularly former beer drinkers, could afford to buy preprohibition amounts of liquor and that among those who continued to drink *proportionately* more preferred spirits. Actually, genuine lager was sometimes hard to obtain, and beer lovers had to settle for "needle beer." This was legal near-beer, brewed in the normal way but with the alcohol drawn off. Ethyl alcohol was then sprayed back into the beverage—"needling"—sometimes at the bar in front of the customer. This product was just not as good as real beer. Nor was most home brew, all of which no doubt contributed to the decline in beer consumption.

Prohibition also served to stimulate interest in nonalcoholic beverages. Temperance workers had long urged Americans to drink water, fruit juices, and soft drinks in lieu of alcohol. In fact, temperance tracts often provided recipes for "wholesome" concoctions. In *Give Prohibition Its Chance* (1929), a stridently political work, WCTU President Ella Boole included a lengthy appendix on the subject. No doubt many people responded to such advice, both during and after the anti-liquor wars, which, along with the high cost and illegality of booze, accounted at least partly for a surge in the popularity of "safe" beverages during the 1920s.

Coffee, orange and grape juice, and carbonated soft drinks all experienced consumption increases over preprohibition levels. The Welch Grape Juice Company, for example, sold a million more gallons of juice annually during the 1920s than it had in 1914. Orange production also rose dramatically, some 25 percent over prior levels, reflecting the heightened juice demand. Carbonated beverages, which had enjoyed a growing popularity even before the Eighteenth Amendment, also did very well, with bottling companies reaping handsome profits. People drank almost three times as much Coca-Cola in 1930, for instance, than they had in 1919. (There is a strong likelihood that at least some of these carbonated products—particularly the suspiciously popular ginger ale—ended up as mixers for illegal liquor.) Overall, milk experienced the largest growth in popularity. An average American living in an urban area typically drank around thirty-four gallons of milk in 1917, a figure that rose to over forty-nine gallons by 1930.

There were also a number of attempts to duplicate the taste of beer in nonalcoholic beverages. The most ambitious was "Bevo"—from the Bohemian *pivo*, or beer—by Anheuser-Busch. Bevo was made from water, yeast, hops, barley, salt, and rice; the drink had an alcohol content well below the .5 percent allowed by the Volstead Act. Anheuser-Busch ultimately sank some $15 million into the project, and for a while it looked as though Bevo would pay off. It sold well just before National Prohibition (1916–1918). Then, disaster struck. Bevo required large amounts of brewer's yeast, a by-product of normal brewing operations. When the yeast supply declined precipitately with the Volstead Act—causing a drastic change in the taste of the beverage—Bevo's popularity quickly dwindled.

Near-beer, marketed by a number of companies, was no more successful. The esters that gave this drink its flavor were drawn off with the alcohol in the final processing. Near-beer hence never won any real public affection. Perhaps its biggest partisans were those who bought it for needling, but even then near-beer was not nearly as flavorful as traditional lager.

The answer to the original question, then—did prohibition prohibit?—is in many respects yes. The Volstead Act did reduce the incidence of drinking and many of its associated health and social problems. The ironic twist, however, is that this result ultimately did not decide the overall public evaluation of the sober republic.

Not Quite Dry: Neorepublicans in a Changing America

Temperance leaders were generally satisfied with the initial implementation of National Prohibition. The visible decline in drinking and

Demolition of a New York City speakeasy, February 1933. Carry Nation had no monopoly on the destruction of "joints." These federal agents were equally skilled, although by 1933 the public tide had turned against such activities.

many of its related problems, which they had long promised the citizenry, appeared to be happening just as predicted. Just as important, the advent of the Volstead Act found that old temperance ogre, the saloon, only a shadow of its former self. Not that the saloon was gone — some of the illegal bars and speakeasies were every bit as pernicious as their preprohibition counterparts had been — but state and local regulations had cleaned up (or put out of business) many saloons in the years before the Eighteenth Amendment. The Volstead Act obviously enabled authorities to do even more. There was little denying a dry victory in this regard, as most of the public conceded. Thus, as prohibition began its tenure, partisans had every expectation of success.

At the same time, many drys were realists. They had no illusions about the unpopularity of the Eighteenth Amendment in some quarters, and few of them expected full compliance. Consequently, they accepted early violations of the Volstead Act — even some of the more glaring ones, like George Remus's operations — as opportunities to test public virtue. They looked hopefully to long-run effects, convinced that full public acceptance of prohibition and total abstinence would ultimately lead to a truly sober republic. It would all take a while. Old topers would either die off or go on the water wagon; Volstead enforcement, however, would gradually tighten, and American children — primed by Scientific Temperance Instruction — would grow up dry. Even ethnic urban centers, temporary wet islands in a dry country, would eventually come around as "Americanization" took firm grip.

As long as progress was steady, most drys were willing to wait for the millennium. Senator William E. Borah of Idaho, one of the most articulate antiliquor champions, predicted that prohibition would need at least a generation for a fair test of its effectiveness. Ella Boole, president of the national WCTU, also noted that true abstinence would take time; she added forcefully that the cause deserved patience. The drinking habits of three centuries could not die quickly, and sensible drys accepted that fact as they looked forward to their neorepublican nirvana.

Besides, temperance sympathizers reasoned that, with prohibition actually a part of the Constitution, Americans would ultimately fall into line on that score alone. Given their own reverence for the institutions of the republic, drys could not imagine their fellow citizens flouting the provisions of the nation's basic legal charter. Consequently, few drys at the outset of prohibition saw the need to coerce their countrymen. They believed that a relatively modest enforcement campaign would carry the day.

This optimistic line of thought emerged clearly in the government's first attempts to enforce the Volstead Act. The assignment became the responsibility of the Prohibition Unit (later Bureau), a division of the Treasury Department. The first prohibition commissioner (the head of the unit) was Ohio lawyer John Kramer, handpicked for the job by Anti-Saloon Leaguer Wayne Wheeler. Alcohol, Kramer promised, would soon neither be "manufactured , sold, nor given away, nor hauled in anything on the surface of the earth, or in the air." To make good this pledge, the commissioner deployed 1,526 agents — roughly one for every seventy-one thousand Americans or every twelve miles of the nation's approximately nineteen thousand miles of land or ocean borders. Moreover, the unit would police prohibition at a bargain price: Wheeler thought $5 million a year would suffice. Although Congress allowed $6,350,000 for the first unit budget, Wheeler noted that the enforcement tab would decline as the need for policing disappeared over time. Besides, drys were counting on state antiliquor enforcement to complement the federal effort. In short, the initial enforcement foray was predicated on abundant optimism. The assumption was that there would only be a small number of violators. No dry would have counted on an ever-expanding war with ever-increasing resistance.

Initial temperance optimism, however, was misplaced. With benefit of hindsight one can see that the persistent drinking in the early Volstead years—no matter how temporary dry leaders considered this phenomenon—represented not a dying custom but one of the first of a series of important social changes. Even as Commissioner Kramer and his colleagues in the Prohibition Unit prepared to enforce the Volstead Act, these new trends (however imperceptibly at first) began to undermine the Noble Experiment.

Perhaps the most telling sign was a cooling of public enthusiasm for reform in general. World War I had diverted some of the nation's attention from domestic crusades; equally important, the evident success of Progressive period reformers in ameliorating some of the more threatening problems of America's new urban-industrial culture had helped soften public cries for yet more controls. While few claimed social perfection had been reached in the United States, many basic reform measures were in place. American political institutions seemed to be flourishing, and big business, once so feared in many quarters, emerged from Progressivism as less a social evil than a source of national economic strength and prosperity for millions of citizens. Gradually, then, as old anxieties generated by industrialization subsided, the public came to better terms with their new society—and the old reform impulse lost much of its zealous quality.

The trend away from reform was evident in many areas of national life. The relative economic security of the age (the economy boomed during the 1920s) eased some long-standing fears about the integrity of the middle-class family—financial ruin seemed less likely. This development, coupled with the passage of women's suffrage in the Nineteenth Amendment (1920), tended to make home protection a less pressing concern. Old nativist anxieties over the massive waves of immigrants also declined. New quotas had reduced the immigrant stream to a trickle by the mid-1920s, and fears on this count were allayed to such an extent that by 1928 the Democrats could actually nominate an urban, wet Catholic for president. Thus, as the nation adjusted to profound changes, the social anxieties necessary to fuel massive reform crusades were no longer of sufficient force.

The impact of these changes on the temperance movement was staggering, although dry leaders were among the last to see either the pattern or its implications. They were proud of their movement's victories—the passing of the old-time saloon, the greatly reduced alcohol consumption rates—and at first could not perceive the paradox of the situation. Their very success in reducing the most visible dangers of drink allowed public attention to drift from the liquor question. With the drink problem evidently "solved" with prohibition—or at least greatly reduced in dimensions—popular interest waned. And for the same reasons, the drinking that went on no longer seemed especially dangerous or socially disruptive, hardly an attitude conducive to maintaining the antiliquor crusade at fever pitch.

From the very start of the Noble Experiment, some drys were afraid of the growth of just such an attitude. They warned their fellow neorepublican stewards against complacence. The Eighteenth Amendment, they cautioned, was not the end of the struggle but only a landmark along the road to final national abstinence. In the meantime, the struggle had to continue. They also knew full well that temperance had drawn support and allies from other reform camps. And now, for the first time, the temperance movement found itself largely alone in the field. More astute leaders began stressing the need to revive the old general reform atmosphere. Dr. Ira Landrith, president of the Intercollegiate Prohibition Association, voiced the typical call to arms, proclaiming continuous reform efforts a necessity if America were "to fulfill her mission as God's new Holy Land, and if Americans" were "to live up to their divinely appointed privilege as his Chosen People." Indeed, efforts to rally the antiliquor faithful included a series of reminders about the "bad old days"—evident in works like *When the Brewer Had the Stranglehold* (1930).

Yet efforts to rally flagging temperance zeal faced still other obstacles. As fears of social disorder receded, people began to shed their suspicions of that old nemesis of all good neorepublicans—a pluralist social order that would undermine national ideals. And there can be no doubt that pluralism was on the rise. The trend was visible in any number of America's social and political processes. For example, ethnic groups, particularly in the city machines, began wielding more influence in national politics. The role of women was also changing. Some studies have suggested that attachment to the home remained strong among most women during the twenties, but some women moved their horizons beyond the hearth, becoming active socially and politically. Certainly the Victorian image of woman's proper place had begun to lose some of its force.

Economic changes stimulated pluralism in the 1920s. Significantly, industrial growth was no longer dependent on the traditional values of thrift and sacrifice—the very traits that had enabled the early industrialists to ally with the temperance movement and to embrace its vision of a virtuous society. By the twenties, industry had its physical plant largely in place, ending the phase in its development most tied to the accumulation and savings of wealth by the public. Now business prosperity hinged not so much on funds for investment as on mass purchase of consumer durable goods. Hence, business leaders began speaking less about savings and sacrifice and more about spending—to indulge individual tastes on the enormous range of new products, from automobiles to refrigerators, that industry had made available. Advertising catered blatantly to individualism and enjoyment. Such appeals utterly neglected traditional notions of family or community centered duty and loyalty.

The products themselves abetted the same end. Home appliances, for instance, generally worked to give family members previously unheard of amounts of free time. Most notably, they reduced the need for centering individual energies mainly on home life. Indeed, the automobile, the telephone, the radio, and the movies clearly drew attention away from the family toward new experiences, acquaintances, and lifestyles—that is, toward the individualistic pluralism that the sober republic had resisted for so long. And as Americans became accustomed to the new social scenario, with its emphasis on diversity and individuality, the tenets of neorepublicanism, with its fears of disunity and social chaos, seemed less and less germane to the dawning age of consumerism.

Even with prohibition, drinking patterns fit naturally into this emergent pluralism. Tippling in defiance of the law became something of a symbol of individualism. As such, neorepublican social norms appeared increasingly outdated, unnecessary, and even repressive (an echo here of Jacksonian days). Reformer-educator Harry

Warner, for example, staunch dry though he was, explained at least some of the drinking he found on college campuses in just such terms: Students were incorporating alcohol into a newer, freer lifestyle. In a 1968 study, historian Paul A. Carter took this view one step farther. In a society beginning to emphasize consumption, Carter postulated, people also began to judge success and status—in themselves and in others—by the products they bought and used. Encouraged by sophisticated advertising, "the linkage between the little man and the great" existed "essentially in the goods they consume[d] in common." Consumption, Carter wrote, became "a surrogate for concrete accomplishment"—a state of affairs, it may be added, at striking variance with the work and thrift morality of the sober republic. In Carter's view, this new rage for status gradually applied even to drinking; for drinking, thanks in great measure to the Volstead Act, had indeed become an activity most visibly associated with the affluent (who could afford liquor), thus meriting emulation in a consumer-oriented society.

Hence, after decades of declining status at the hands of the temperance movement, beverage alcohol began to capture popular acceptance. Booze was by no means rehabilitated, but despite all the efforts directed against it, liquor would not die. This changing social milieu, with at least a latently more tolerant attitude toward drinking, provides a necessary background against which to view prohibition enforcement.

"Their Best Endeavors": Enforcing the Volstead Act

If, in retrospect, enforcement of the Volstead Act seems a fool's errand, it must be borne in mind that the trends running against prohibition became evident only gradually and, as will be seen, did not spark significant or organized resistance until the end of the dry decade. Yet it is equally true that Volstead enforcement quickly developed as something considerably different from the theoretically easy task that dry leaders had predicted. For instance, there was real trouble in the Prohibition Unit. By 1923, if not sooner, Kramer's early promises to rid the land of booze looked hopelessly naive. His undermanned force simply could not cope with sophisticated bootlegging operations. Worse, too many of the federal agents, who were not paid well and had been hired without civil service tests, proved incompetent or corrupt—or both. A few were themselves bootleggers. The costs associated with enforcement were also a disappointment: The inability to stamp out illegal American drinking served to drive up government costs, Wheeler's initial optimism notwithstanding. In 1923, the treasury secretary told Congress that his department needed a staggering $28 million to fund the Prohibition Unit adequately (so much for Wheeler's $5 million or less estimate), while a few years later one enforcement official suggested an annual figure of $300 million! This was not how the pattern was supposed to work.

Equally disturbing from the federal viewpoint was the general failure of concurrent legislation by the states. The 1920s was an age of financial austerity in government at all levels. While most states seemed eager to pass strict enforcement laws supporting the Volstead Act, they were not overly generous in funding implementation. Instead of paying the bill themselves, the states were inclined to surrender their enforcement responsibilities to the federal Prohibition Unit. There was an unexpressed but very real sentiment in the states, as historian Donald Chidsey put it, to "let Sam do it."

Some states showed outright unwillingness to cooperate with federal efforts. New York, for example, repealed its enforcement act in 1923, claiming it was ineffective, which was true enough—juries in wet areas often flatly refused to convict even the most blatant violators. Of some seven thousand New York arrests between 1921 and 1923, only twenty-seven resulted in convictions. Maryland never bothered to pass an enforcement act, while Nevada, Utah, and Missouri each allotted only $1,000 a year to support their laws. Rhode Island, which had refused to ratify the Eighteenth Amendment in the first place, did pass an act; however, the state enforced prohibition casually at best. And while authorities in some states did their best to police liquor violations, there was no denying temperance frustrations over concurrent legislation—or the fact that state and local intransigence reflected a growing popular resistance to the dry laws.

To give the drys their due, however, and without for a moment overlooking the shortcomings of Volstead regulations, there were some honest efforts to improve enforcement. Commissioner Kramer soon gave way to Roy Asa Haynes, who promised a more efficient administration. Officials also tried to weed out corrupt or incompetent agents (scores of men were fired); periodically, they brought in new regional administrators with reputations for honesty. Even while deficiences were there, the Unit's record was not one of total failure. Absolute alcohol consumption did remain at its lowest levels during the Volstead era. Warburton's consumption estimates reveal a gradual increase in drinking by 1923, as bootleggers extended their distribution networks; but the rise was not dramatic. Wine and spirits consumption actually declined on occasion in the later 1920s, as enforcement authorities kept the pressure on illegal suppliers. Even such wet strongholds as Chicago and Detroit continually felt the heat. In 1923, reform Mayor William E. Dever—to the surprise of the nation—cracked down on corruption in general and illegal booze in particular, substantially (albeit temporarily) drying out the city of Chicago. In 1929, Detroit's reputation as a wet metropolis and the premier port of entry for smuggled Canadian liquor finally prompted a massive enforcement campaign. A coordinated federal and local operation from 1929 to 1931 vastly reduced the amount of beverage alcohol available in the city, demonstrating that the prohibition agents could be an effective force.

But the battle against liquor would not be won or lost in the trenches, and the most telling exchanges of the period did not necessarily involve agents, bootleggers, or drinkers. The war for the hearts and minds of popular opinion—the war that really counted—was fought on other fronts. One of the most hotly contested issues was "personal liberty," a controversy that continued to gall the prohibitionists. The remarks of attorney Clarence Darrow were typical of wet sentiments in this regard: "Prohibition is an outrageous and senseless invasion of the personal liberty of millions of intelligent and temperate persons who see nothing dangerous or immoral in the moderate consumption of alcoholic beverages." It was useless, he asserted, to force abstinence on an entire nation in order to stop the excesses of a handful of problem drinkers. Drys bristled at Darrow's remarks, maintaining the neorepublican stewardship position that the rights of society come first and that dutiful citizens should obey the law for the benefit of the whole community. "Personal liberty," Irving Fisher insisted, "is . . . limited to boundaries set by the welfare of the social group"; a host of other temperance advocates took similar stands. Indeed, they thought that dry champions, even as early as the antebellum years, had satisfactorily demolished the wet "liberty" argument. Yet the debate persisted—and like drinking itself would not go away.

Perhaps the most vocal advocate of the personal liberty position was the Association against the Prohibition Amendment, founded by retired naval officer William H. Strayton in 1918. Although vociferous for liberty where the Eighteenth Amendment was concerned, the AAPA was not, however, a particularly liberal group. A thorough conservative, Strayton had been unhappy with most legislation of the Progressive period, which he declared had threatened such fundamental American tenets as states' rights, unfettered private enterprise, and minimal federal interference with the lives of local citizens. But he denounced prohibition as the most offensive reform of all. It was, he insisted, "a symptom of a disease" in the land, "the desire of fanatics to meddle in the other man's affairs and to regulate the details of your lives and mine." Those who joined Strayton's group—few in the beginning, but many more as hostility to the Volstead Act gathered momentum in the late 1920s—concurred. A federal government that could abolish drinking, they feared, could certainly launch other broad and sweeping efforts to regulate American life. Repeal of the Eighteenth Amendment, therefore, became the AAPA's goal.

In the early 1920s, however, few people outside the then small AAPA believed that repeal was even remotely possible. As confirmed a wet as Darrow—he once described himself as a "100 percent opponent" of prohibition—considered such a remedy out of the question. Dry strength in Congress and in the state legislatures, he readily conceded, was too great to sustain a repeal drive—which would have entailed yet another amendment to the Constitution. Although the flamboyant lawyer did not much like his bed fellow, Darrow was in accord with ultra-dry Senator Morris Sheppard of Texas on this point. As late as 1930, Sheppard was still insisting that because of the difficulties inherent in amending the Constitution, there was "as much chance of repealing the Eighteenth Amendment as there is for a humming bird to fly to the planet Mars with the Washington Monument tied to its tail."

The best that Darrow hoped for under the circumstances was some modification of the Volstead definition of intoxicating beverages, especially with respect to light wines and beer. In New York, Governor Alfred Smith took a similar stance. He urged the legislature in 1923 to pass a series of resolutions asking Congress to take a more flexible course. But even Smith, who was willing to make the strictures of prohibition a political issue, harbored no real illusions. For in Washington, D.C., Wayne Wheeler—that paragon of temperance dedication and pragmatism—was still calling the tune in Congress. Patiently and skillfully, he spearheaded successful drives against all wet initiatives, easily overcoming efforts to make wine and beer legal again. His opponents' fumbling, Wheeler once observed in a rare lapse of seriousness, was "asinine." So while the winds of change were starting to blow, they were not yet at gale force.

At the same time, the delay in making prohibition a practical reality and the persistence of wet opposition—particularly when it clearly represented a hefty minority—did become distinctly annoying to drys. As early as 1924, the Anti-Saloon League's *American Issue* felt compelled to remind the faithful that it was going to take "twenty years to make the United States actually dry." People were losing patience simply "because in a little more than four years the country is not bone dry."

Many temperance sympathizers were not reassured. They perceived only the worst motives at work in critics and violators of the Volstead Act. Temperance organizer Ira Landrith, for example, spoke for many partisans of the sober republic when he labeled bootleggers, their customers, and lax enforcement officers absolutely treasonous. No doubt they seemed to be in the eyes of the man who had earlier coined the national slogan, "A Saloonless Nation by 1920." Landrith did not bother to hide his anger or his conviction that the continuing persistence of illegal booze imperiled the republic: "Society," he announced, "ought to get the habit of classing" bootleggers and drinkers "all together" with the "Bolshevists" as threats to "the health of society and the perpetuity of popular government." Clearly, this was not the voice of a man confident that prohibition had secured the moral stability and good order in society for which the temperance movement had fought.

Other temperance advocates revealed similar doubts. The *Union Signal*, for instance, constantly monitored the activities of groups like the AAPA. It lost no opportunity throughout the 1920s to cast such organizations in a disruptive and unpatriotic light. The AAPA in particular, the WCTU journal charged, was intent on subverting the Constitution, bringing back the old evils of liquor-dominated politics, and setting intolerable examples of poor citizenship for both native-born citizens and immigrants trying to learn American ways. "The situation," one *Signal* writer declared in 1923, represented an unhealthy attitude in "a certain portion" of the public. The article concluded by calling "on those who recognize the benefits of prohibition to use their best endeavors to bring about a universal recognition of its value." The same year, Dr. Clarence True Wilson, a spokesman for the Board of

Temperance of the Methodist church, reached the identical conclusion. He stressed that making "the country distinctly dry would require a new educational campaign for law enforcement and for law respect that shall be as thorough as that by which we won prohibition." The optimistic projections of antiliquor advocates were giving way.

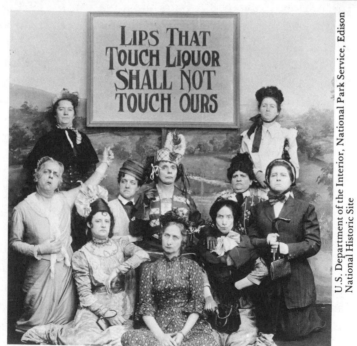

The struggle over Prohibition was not without its lighter side. The tub full of beer no doubt struck a fond chord in many hearts, although the WCTU probably saw little humor in the satire on temperance women.

From Reform to Reaction: The Sober Republic at Bay

Historian Jack S. Blocker noted that the rise of the Anti-Saloon League to temperance leadership after the turn of the century signaled a gradual, but significant, shift away from the crusade's broad base of reform activities. Instead, the league emphasized prohibition above all other goals, arguing that once the nation dried out, other issues — urban poverty, broken families, industrial accidents, alcoholism, the rehabilitation of problem drinkers — would naturally resolve themselves. Thus, while temperance groups like the WCTU did not abruptly abandon other interests, they no longer pursued them with their old vigor. This change in emphasis may have hastened the advent of the Eighteenth Amendment; in the long run, however, it was probably one of the neorepublicans' most costly blunders.

The broad reform base of the past had allowed temperance workers a sweeping overview of the ills of American life. Varied interests meant a wider perspective and a sense of balance in dealing with social and political issues. Yet, as the reformers narrowed their field of vision, they consequently also tended to put on blinders. And somewhere along the way, when antiliquor reform most needed the ability to stay in touch with and to influence popular opinion — that is, precisely when the stresses and frustrations of the Volstead wars began to take their toll on dry nerves — the crusaders gradually lost touch with the national pulse. Increasing rigidity, rather than flexibility, was their response. Temperance advocates had been used to leading the public, and the new and growing threat of failure served to exacerbate dry anxieties. It was the kind of situation that makes hard-pressed people lose their equilibrium — and even makes them small-minded if not petty and mean.

A variety of trends marked the movement's growing hostility toward anyone not firmly in the dry camp. Temperance attitudes in dealing with the drunkard represent a prominent case in point. As the final struggle for prohibition loomed on the horizon, for example, attention to such basic work as rehabilitation of alcoholics withered. Many crusaders began labeling rehabilitation as nothing more than a waste of time and energy; prohibition, they promised, would make such work unnecessary. It was better policy "to turn off the spiggot," one temperance worker suggested, than "to mop up the slop" afterward.

Whatever sense such thinking made, it had the effect of aborting many promising efforts in alcoholism treatment. Without adequate support, the Murphy Clubs and the Red and Blue Ribbon movements slowly declined. Gospel Temperance took a lesser priority with the WCTU and the "Lincoln-Lee Legion"—the moral suasionist arm of the Anti-Saloon League—turned into nothing more than a shadow. Neglect of alcoholics and their plight also proved a final blow to the Association for the Study of Inebriety. With public support for its special interest on the wane, this group was unable to maintain its professional standards and prestige and dissolved in the mid-1920s. Treatment, it seemed, was an idea whose time had passed.

The very real plight of the alcoholic now made little difference to zealous Volstead partisans. Indeed, as criticism of prohibition mounted, drys became increasingly hostile toward the alcoholic. They had always used drunkards, even when sympathetic toward them, as the epitome of human degradation. As the antiliquor consensus faltered, however, alcoholics (and drinkers in general) became convenient scapegoats for temperance frustrations.

Humane concern for the problem drinker's spiritual and physical health thus quickly gave way to bitter recriminations. The traditional neorepublican impulse to compel individual behavior in defense of public good asserted itself with a vengeance. Drys continually called for stiffer jail terms for incorrigible topers, and by the late 1920s there was considerable talk of amending the Volstead Act to make drinking itself a felony. One essayist, writing in a competition on *Law Observance* (1929) sponsored by automobile industrialist W. C. Durant, suggested that drinkers be exiled to concentration camps in the Aleutian Islands. Against the old reform goals of the temperance movement, such fulminating did not make for pleasant reading. These arguments reflected the crusade's increasing pessimism and vindictiveness.

This unfortunate trend was evident in other areas as well. Crusade leaders for example, Wayne Wheeler among them, continued to insist that the government maintain the practice of adding denaturants to industrial alcohol, despite protests that poorly washed moonshine was killing or blinding scores of Americans. This same emphasis on enforcing the law, whatever the human toll, led to a number of nasty incidents. In 1929, the WCTU's president, Ella Boole, learned of a raid in which prohibition agents had clubbed a suspected bootlegger unconscious and then gunned down his unarmed wife when she ran to his aid. "Well," Boole coolly observed, "she was evading the law, wasn't she?" No doubt she was—but that was not the point by 1929. Nor was the fact that, before Prohibition, legal liquor or the saloon probably had killed more Americans annually than all the nation's dry agents and poisoned moonshine put together did in the 1920s. The real issue was that, given evanescent public values, fewer and fewer Americans saw drinking as something that warranted either the needless poisoning of people or the shooting of dealers (much less their wives). The public simply became less tolerant of any movement, however high its ideals, that condoned such actions.

In the fluctuating social milieu of the 1920s, dry zealousness carried temperance workers ever further from the mainstream of public opinion. Some elements in the crusade became almost phobic in attempts to reassert neorepublican control. More and more temperance voices lashed out at all signs of national disunity and railed at the rising tide of what they perceived as social chaos in the form of rampant pluralism. Occasionally, they became truly vicious.

In the South, for instance, a number of temperance leaders raised the banner of racism in efforts to maintain white support for the cause. As historian Andrew Sinclair emphasized, some drys had long played on white fears of drunken blacks "getting out of control" as a recruiting ploy, but the later Volstead years saw this theme become especially pronounced. To cite one prominent example, Georgia Congressman William ("Earnest Willie") Upshaw—a man with impeccable antipluralist credentials and a long association with the Anti-Saloon League—routinely conjured up horrific scenes of besotted blacks rising in violence against whites should legal liquor ever return. Upshaw, known in Congress as "the dryest of the drys," combined his temperance views with overt support for the Ku Klux Klan and later with a virulent anticommunism. His fanaticism eventually alienated most white Southerners, but the fact that he and his allies commanded serious attention throughout the middle and late 1920s was yet another sign of how troubled the ideal of the sober republic had become.

On the national level, harried antipluralism carried bigotry into presidential politics. By 1928, national disenchantment with the Volstead Act was such that Democrats were willing to challenge prohibition openly in nominating Governor Al Smith of New York. Smith was not only a wet but also a Catholic and a product of the urban, ethnic politics of Tammany Hall—a blend, in short, of almost everything the sober republic had fought against at one time or another. The Republicans ran popular and capable Secretary of Commerce Herbert Hoover. Hoover considered liquor a genuine curse, but he also thought the Eighteenth Amendment unnecessarily rigid. Hoover felt obligated, however, to enforce the law of the land. Thus, many wets and drys perceived in the election a classic test of their respective strength.

The Anti-Saloon League mobilized on behalf of Hoover, hoping a GOP victory would at last pave the way to effective Volstead enforcement. The league went into battle, however, under a new general. Wayne Wheeler had died in 1927, and organizational leadership had passed to James Cannon, a Methodist bishop from Virginia and a lifelong Democrat. Cannon, a capable man, was ruthlessly dedicated to National Prohibition and for all it stood, but he had grave flaws. Whereas even Wheeler's ardent enemies generally had conceded that he was a gentleman, Cannon was arrogant and vindictive, as well as blatantly anti-Catholic (despite the work of so many Catholics associated with the league). Unfortunately the bishop gave full rein to his prejudices during the campaign, and in an effort to rally Democrats—particularly Southern Democrats—for Hoover, he openly played to native Protestant biases against Smith's religion.

It was not a pleasant campaign. Smith fought back, gamely denouncing such scurrilous bigotry. He attracted enthusiastic crowds in wet ethnic centers like Milwaukee and New York. Cannon, on his side, went as far as to spread rumors that Smith would invite the pope to take up residence in the White House. For sensitive drys who had worked closely with Catholics and immigrants on many temperance projects, the bishop was an embarrassment. For the public, Cannon's smear tactics cast a largely undeserved—but understandable—pall of bigotry and intolerance over the entire crusade. Cannon's tactics represented just one more sign that the temperance movement was losing touch with rising American pluralism.

Although Cannon and the Anti-Saloon League were quick to take credit when Hoover swamped Smith at the polls, few historians believe their impact was crucial. Students of the 1928 election have argued that Hoover probably was unbeatable, given several years of economic prosperity under the GOP. At any rate, as part of the popular mandate, it fell to Hoover to do what he could with prohibition, which he had once called an "experiment noble in motive and far-reaching in purpose" (a phrase the Democrats shortened to the "noble experiment"). Of all his responsibilities as chief executive, enforcement of the Volstead Act probably appealed least to the new president.

Nothing Hoover did as president helped. Soon after taking office, he appointed a National Commission on Law Observance and Enforcement (better known as the Wickersham Commission, after chairman and former Attorney General George Wickersham) to suggest remedies to Volstead enforcement problems. The commission went to work with good intentions, but its final report, issued after nineteen months of investigation, suggested that there would be as many problems as solutions in full-scale enforcement efforts. Because the report did not call for repeal of the Eighteenth Amendment, drys claimed a victory. Nevertheless, the report disclosed numerous examples of gross incompetence and corruption in the ranks of the Prohibition Unit, and the commissioners refused to issue a blanket endorsement of the Volstead Act. On the other hand, wets raged because the commission failed to call for significant liberalization of the Volstead laws. One proliquor congressman called it the "Wicked-Sham Report." So Wickersham's efforts (the only major federal policy review of prohibition enforcement) came to naught. In the meantime, the situation got worse.

The persistence of enforcement difficulties reflected a rapid collapse of the moral authority of the sober republic. The changing social context of the decade, which boded ill for sustained public support of the Eighteenth Amendment, was now clearly accelerating the decline of the Noble Experiment. And, at least symbolically, it is possible to date the temperance movement's final break with the majority of Americans with the passage of the Jones Act in March 1929. Named for its chief legislative sponsor, Senator Wesley L. Jones of Washington, the act was primarily the work of Bishop Cannon and the league; in it the nation saw the dry leaders reaching their wits' end. With Hoover's victory behind them, and with the Wickersham Commission still gathering evidence, Cannon and his allies — in violation of their own warnings of a few years earlier that drying out the country would take time — decided to plug all the leaks in the Volstead laws in one legislative coup. The new law amended Volstead penalties, which had consisted of six months' imprisonment or a $1,000 fine, to provide for first-offense jailings of five years *and* a fine of $10,000. Thus, the act popularly became known as the "Jones 5 & 10 law."

The Jones law represented a last desperate attempt by crusaders exasperated at continued opposition to using prohibition as the key to a stable national order. Even so, the Hoover administration, moved by a sense of political obligation to the league, did attempt to implement these new and needlessly harsh penalties. A wave of convictions resulted, directed mostly at small-scale bootleggers and drinkers who refused to disclose their sources of supply (a felony under the Jones Act). Courts and jails across the land quickly became clogged. The entire judicial system seemed to teeter on the brink of collapse. And while extreme drys applauded so much tough action, the public, including many moderate temperance workers, was dismayed. The jailings and the stiff Jones penalties made prohibition seem an instrument of oppression — a curse rather than a blessing to the good society that most crusaders had originally projected. It also appeared that the Jones Act would actually make prohibition a source of the very social turmoil and divisiveness that the old reformers had tried so hard to eliminate.

Significantly, drinking itself virtually disappeared as an important issue in popular perceptions of the Jones Act controversy. Rather, the question now was whether the nation would tolerate a gigantic police operation to support dry policies that growing numbers of Americans saw as out of step with the times. The answer, which came through loud and clear by 1930, was a resounding no; the sober republic was suffering a wave of major defections.

Industrial and business leaders, for instance, many of whom had been champions of the antiliquor crusade, began to abandon ship and even openly to denounce prohibition. Prohibition had appealed to them as a factor in bringing order to the nation when business and industry dreamed about a stable America. But now the disputes over the Volstead Act — and especially the anger following the Jones Act — made the movement seem a source of disorder itself. Furthermore, temperance values were now more clearly at variance with the consumption oriented lifestyle that business leaders considered essential to industrial prosperity. Eventually, such illustrious citizens as William Randolph Hearst and John D. Rockefeller, Jr., came out for repeal. Rockefeller defected only in 1932, but his statement on the matter revealed much of how business thinking on the sober republic had changed and how far the new pluralism had undermined the old longings for unity and moral orthodoxy. The nation had changed to the point that it was "unlikely," Rockefeller declared, "that any one [prohibitory] method will fit the entire nation"; to insist on holistic solutions, he concluded, would only undermine public respect for law. Citing similar fears, the

The Pabst brewery in Milwaukee, 1930. Repeal was by no means a sure thing in 1930, but Prohibition had become so unpopular that the Pabst Company, anticipating the national turnabout, invested almost $1 million to modernize this plant (which had been closed for ten years). Each vat could hold four hundred barrels of beer.

powerful Du Pont family of Delaware, also formerly dry, threw its support to the Association against the Prohibition Amendment. With such prestigious backing, the AAPA had gained much stature and power by the close of the 1920s.

Changing attitudes of women toward liquor, moreover, were a great disappointment to temperance workers. The dry crusade had played a major part in bringing women into the American political mainstream. Indeed, antiliquor reformers had generally (with some notable exceptions) been staunch defenders of women's suffrage, in the belief that the new voters would drive yet another nail into the coffin of the traffic. For this reason, they applauded the Nineteenth Amendment (1920), while many wets bewailed what they saw as another disaster. Neither wets nor drys had reckoned with other social changes then sweeping the nation. The vote — coupled with new mobility outside the home, increased free time, and diversification of lifestyles — was chipping away at the cult of domesticity. Some women were loosening their ties to Victorian roles as guardians of the home; others, even if they remained at home, were developing broader interests and pursuing outside activities. Perhaps with lowered national drinking rates, relatively fewer women were being brutalized or neglected by drunken husbands. The result was that the mores of the sober republic seemed increasingly dated in the eyes of many women, even if they did not drink. Like men, they were attracted to and felt generally secure in the new pluralist, consumer oriented America. The debate over drinking looked ever more irrelevant, and the Jones "5 & 10" penalties seemed ridiculous if not outrageous.

New attitudes among women soon took concrete form. The WCTU, for example, could no longer count on overwhelming female support. In fact, drys became enraged when an articulate proliquor women's group joined forces with the AAPA to urge repeal of the Eighteenth Amendment.

Pauline Sabin, a wealthy New York socialite with excellent political connections and formerly a prohibitionist and member of the Women's National Republican Club, launched the Women's Organization for National Prohibition Reform in May 1929. Sabin, who personified the emerging modern woman — worldly, sophisticated, smartly dressed, at ease with a career and pursuits outside the home — announced her intention to lead as many women as she could away from the WCTU fold. Sabin even turned dry rhetoric to her advantage. "The women of the country," she told a press conference, were starting to see "the deplorable effects of the operation of the law [the Volstead and Jones Acts] upon their country and their children." The "corruption and hypocrisy" stemming from prohibition, she insisted, were worse than legal liquor. Of all ironies, repeal was necessary "for the protection of the American home" and the return of "sobriety and honesty."

This was too much for the WCTU. "As to Mrs. Sabin and her cocktail-drinking women," responded Dr. Mary Armor, president of the Georgia chapter, "we will outlive them, out-fight them, out-love them, out-pray them, and out-vote them." It was brave talk, but Armor could not hide the real issue: The national mood was slipping away from the dry crusade.

Return of "the Demon"

After 1930, repeal was no more inevitable than National Prohibition had been in 1916 or 1917, but it was just as likely. Repeal was clearly an idea whose time had come, and any number of signs pointed in this direction. Popular disgust with the rigidity of temperance advocates continued to mount, encouraged now by a highly sophisticated public relations campaign directed by the AAPA. In fact, wet propaganda became more effective than its dry counterpart had ever been, and the image of temperance partisans as either rubes (an inaccurate characterization) or fanatics started to take root in much of the public mind. Nor did the movement do much to help itself. Temperance leaders continued to cling blindly to their all-or-nothing posture. Under these circumstances, even the most influential drys lost their effectiveness. Ella Boole actually suffered the indignity of being heckled at a national women's Republican conference. Worse yet for the dry image, Bishop Cannon was censured by his own church for involvement in an extramarital affair and in shady stock investments. Prohibition was thus ripe for the fall.

The final blow came with the Great Depression. The crash of the stock market in October 1929 and the subsequent economic malaise that saw almost a third of the country unemployed by 1932 plunged Americans into the gravest economic crisis in national history. The battle over liquor paled before the monumental social problems resulting from the depression. Just as an earlier generation of Americans had set aside the dry crusade with the coming of the Civil War, so their twentieth-century counterparts turned away from antiliquor agitation to tackle the awesome task of national economic recovery. The AAPA was quick to take advantage of the moment (just as the temperance movement had seized the initiative during World War I). The association pointed out that repeal would mean both the employment of thousands in a rejuvenated liquor industry and a bonanza in liquor taxes for fiscally starved governments. In effect, the depression crisis suddenly endowed repeal with as much popularity as the war crisis previously had given prohibition.

The drys never regained their balance. They no longer had effective leaders, their national constituency had shrunk to a shadow of its former strength, and even long-standing allies now insisted that solving depression problems was more important than continuing prohibition. Antiliquor influence in the government plummeted. Even President Hoover, who had promised a fair trial for the Volstead Act, now tried to put as much distance as possible between himself and the temperance movement. He had problems enough and did not need the albatross of the Eighteenth Amendment around his neck as the 1932 election approached. Thus, the dry reformers, so recently among the most powerful policymakers in the land, were now caught up, virtually hopeless, in events that they could not control.

Franklin Roosevelt's smashing victory over Hoover brought matters to a head. The campaign in 1932 was, more than anything else, a referendum on Hoover's handling of the depression, and the public rejected him. But in the campaign, the AAPA saw to it that prohibition faced popular censure as well. The wet organization enthusiastically backed the Democratic candidate, encouraging Roosevelt to build on the legacy of Al Smith and to call openly for repeal. The AAPA not only succeeded in its immediate efforts but also, as a result, paved the way for an initially cautious FDR to campaign as a wet champion. The election, therefore, realized all that wets had hoped it would. Repeal itself (1933) was almost an anticlimax.

CHAPTER FIVE

The Age of Ambivalence: Drinking in Modern America

———————◆———————

A Congressman was once asked by a constituent to explain his attitude toward whiskey. "If you mean the demon drink that poisons the mind, pollutes the body, desecrates family life, and inflames sinners, then I'm against it," the Congressman said. "But if you mean the elixir of Christmas cheer, the shield against winter chill, the taxable potion that puts needed funds into public coffers to comfort little crippled children, then I'm for it. This is my position, and I will not compromise."

—Popular anecdote

The collapse of the sober republic left Americans with no dominant attitudes toward beverage alcohol. Certainly there was no longer any governmental consensus on the liquor question. In the aftermath of repeal, national authorities seemed relieved to be rid of the burden of prohibition, and they sincerely hoped that the return of legal liquor would not create problems that might prompt another reform drive. The mandate of the Federal Alcohol Control Administration—created by President Roosevelt to oversee federal liquor regulations—was to do as little as possible and to hope for the best. Joseph Choate, Jr., director of the agency, promised in 1934 to let the states manage their own affairs in relation to liquor. He also offered the wishful hypothesis that drinking would no longer be a national issue once alcohol was legal again. The "illicit quality" of drinking under the Volstead Act, he speculated, had made it appealing to many people, but "with the legitimate opportunity to drink I believe the desire to drink—and to treat— will be less in many cases."

While Choate's suggestion rested on a questionable foundation in fact, the approach was novel: Where the old temperance movement had sought to eliminate drunkenness and social disorder through the concerted governmental suppression of liquor, Choate would proceed by keeping federal authorities out of the business of determining what people should drink. And at the time, with the shadow of prohibition still strong, the policy seemed to make sense. In fact, *anything* that allowed the government to steer clear of alcohol-related disputes appeared to make sense to the Roosevelt administration. Yet decisions that seem logical in one era (as the drys had learned through bitter experience) can look hopelessly inadequate in the next—and it was not long before many Americans once more found themselves wondering whether the nation could afford a strictly hands-off approach to beverage alcohol.

The Decline of Temperance

At first, Choate and others in the Roosevelt coalition were not certain that their liquor control policies would prove popular over time. They set to work amid a burst of public acclaim for repeal—but what would happen if this enthusiasm cooled? The magnitude of the proliquor triumph was not fully apparent even by the late 1930s, and many wets frankly predicted a continuing struggle with the prohibitionists. Yet

National Archives

Repeal found the brewers grateful to wet political champions. Here a wagon of Budweiser arrives as a gift for—and a tribute to—Al Smith at his Empire State Building office in New York City, 1933.

their fears were groundless. Although it took years of reckoning before what had happened began to sink in with finality, Americans gradually recognized that the death of the sober republic reflected changes in national values as profound as those that had made prohibition possible in the first place. It should not be surprising, then, that despite some brave temperance vows of counterattack, attempts to rekindle the dry flame went nowhere. Historian Jay Rubin showed, for example, that efforts to revitalize temperance as a patriotic measure during World War II—a method that had served prohibitionists well during World War I—fell on deaf ears. A call for a new constitutional prohibition drive by the Anti-Saloon League in the 1940s also never got off the ground. In fact, antiliquor groups found it hard even to get a hearing from most of the public.

This popular disenchantment with the dry movement hit the major temperance organizations hard. The Anti-Saloon League and the WCTU, once counting their memberships in the millions, dwindled precipitately. Some state organizations, particularly in the South and certain parts of the Midwest, remained influential on the local level, but there was no significant national offensive. By the mid-1960s, the WCTU was down to about 250,000 members, while the Anti-Saloon League had all but ceased to exist. Renamed the National Council on Alcohol Problems, League remnants now struggle on, but with few members. Thus, the national crusade, and all that it implied about the neorepublican mentality, truly came to an end with repeal.

This rapid demise flowed from the same evolution of social values that had finally brought repeal. If increasing tolerance for individual freedom during the 1920s was a measure of broadened acceptance of a dawning pluralist culture in the United States, the election of 1932 (and with it repeal) was emblematic of a dramatic shift away from neo-republican reform goals. The voters who elected Franklin Roosevelt were more than just middle-class citizens stung by the Depression; the alliance also represented a variety of ethnic, urban, and labor groups that, after years on the periphery of the American political arena, had finally emerged as a dominant force in national electoral affairs. From the New Deal on, those seeking political power would applaud (and play to) the pluralism denoting national life. Not surprisingly, organizations in ideological conflict with the new reality, a position the dying temperance movement epitomized, were doomed to minority and splinter group status.

The Return of "the Traffic"

While repeal spelled the end of the temperance movement as a decisive force on the American scene, it also marked the resurgence of the liquor industry. For the Roosevelt administration, it was a welcome revival. The predicted beverage alcohol tax revenues—a major wet promise in the struggle for repeal—poured into federal, state, and local coffers. The national government estimated that its $2.60 per gallon tax on distilled liquor would bring in close to $500 million a year. The windfall went largely to fund depression relief projects under the National Industrial Recovery Act. Ironically, demon rum, reviled by neorepublicans for over a century as the prime source of social disruption and havoc, was now cast in the role of social savior.

The passage of time has blurred the memory of how welcome these liquor revenues were during the Depression, as well as the creation of new jobs either directly or indirectly linked to the beverage alcohol industry. Since the 1930s, government has relied heavily on alcohol-generated monies. By the late 1960s, federal taxes on distilled spirits alone had topped $5.2 billion per year, a figure that rose to $6.5 billion per year in the 1970s. In fact, after personal and corporate income taxes, the levies on alcohol constituted the largest single source of federal revenue. In addition, hundreds of thousands of jobs and billions of dollars in business flowed each year from the production, distribution, and

The liquor industry was careful to point out the benefits of repeal as an antidepression measure. In this 1934 photograph, an employee of the Continental Distilling Company in Philadelphia forms the initials NRA (National Recovery Act) with one of the company's most popular products. After repeal, Continental noted, its "midget" bottles of whiskey were in such demand that the company took on twelve hundred people and kept the distillery open twenty-four hours a day to meet production schedules.

National Archives

sale of beer, wine, and distilled spirits. The brewing industry, for example, spent roughly $113 million on advertising and generated $5.5 billion in gross sales in 1974. Rather than representing a social evil, the traffic has emerged as one of the mainstays of the national economy and a source of economic security to countless Americans.

Yet the beverage alcohol industry did not take its return to prosperity for granted. Always in the background, especially during the 1930s, lurked the temperance movement, and industry leaders did not want any political revival of the wet–dry controversy. Consequently, while distillers, brewers, and vintners worked to expand their markets, they consciously avoided many of the practices that had ruined their public image in an earlier age. Advertising, for example, became highly predictable. In the 1940s and fifties, ads showed drinking as part of a tasteful and sophisticated lifestyle, avoiding any themes that even remotely suggested immoderation. Brewers never went back into the saloon business. That connection had hurt them badly, and they were not about to repeat the mistake. This precluded the recurrence of many of the worst aspects of the old competition between saloons, although this is not to say that ginmills reminiscent of the saloon did not reappear. Some did (and are still with us), but they never came back on a preprohibition scale. As historian Perry Duis has shown, ruinous competition was threatening the economic viability of many of the oldtime saloons even before National Prohibition; but the industry decision was a significant final blow. Alcohol problems spelled trouble, and beverage industry leaders wanted none of the blame.

Legal beer arrives in Cleveland, 1933. When Congress legalized 3.2 beer, Cleveland, like many other cities, was caught short: Local brewers could not meet demand and "imports," in this case from the Renner brewery in Akron, did a booming business.

The pride of Milwaukee in 1935 was Floyd Verette, a city bartender who on July 3 downed two quarts of beer in thirty-seven seconds—and came back the next day to better his record by three seconds. Verette is pictured here in his moment of triumph, his daughter on his knee. Though Milwaukee's champion was a formidable contestant, the 1985 Guinness Book of World Records *listed a British drinker who put away two liters of beer— over two quarts—in a mere six seconds.*

National Archives

Liquor producers also abandoned the bold front that had characterized much of the industry before prohibition. Instead of ignoring or scoffing at public concerns over alcohol abuse, accommodation with efforts to alleviate alcoholism more often became the rule. For instance, the 1970s saw the trade organization of the distillers—the Distilled Spirits Council of the United States (DISCUS)—sponsor an advertising campaign to promote "responsible drinking." Other industry representatives, notably Anheuser-Busch, have provided financial support for the public awareness activities of Mothers Against Drunk Driving (MADD) and Students Against Driving Drunk (SADD). Distillers, brewers, and vintners all have contributed funds to alcohol research or education efforts, and some companies have made more than token gestures: In 1980, Seagrams donated some $5.8 million to Harvard University for medical research on alcoholism.

The new traffic, however, is not without its detractors. There have been a variety of sharp objections to the beverage industry's support of research and education projects. Critics have claimed that such support is insignificant in comparison to huge profits, or that it constitutes merely a public relations ploy calculated to divert popular attention from the manufacturers as sources of drinking problems. More damn-

International beer drinking contest, Los Angeles, 1930s. Drinking for flag and country, the winner downed thirteen quarts of beer in about an hour and a half. The contest organizers assured the public that all competitors would drink only the best beer—and that "without danger."

ing are charges—usually leveled without specific evidence—that industry support leads to research conclusions or other activities favorable to the industry's image. Individual researchers, for example, have been criticized for accepting DISCUS funds, while other groups concerned with alcohol and traffic safety have had harsh words for Anheuser-Busch's connection with MADD.

Liquor advertising also has raised serious concern. In the 1960s, there were charges that advertisements deliberately exploited sexual themes, and the 1970s saw heightened worry over industry attempts to expand markets by directing advertising at younger people. But in general the five decades after repeal have left the manufacturers of beverage alcohol with a reasonably good public image, and they have tried to respond to a number of criticisms. Thus distillers have modified some of their most controversial ad copy and have maintained a long-standing policy of not advertising on television. No longer convulsed by fears of extinction at the hands of reformers, the post-repeal industry has shown itself willing to engage in wide-ranging discussions of drinking-related issues—an involvement unthinkable in an earlier age.

Drinking in Post-Repeal America

The rebirth of the alcohol industry reflected an overwhelming American acceptance of drinking as normal social conduct. Yet there were important legacies of the Noble Experiment, and these clearly exerted an influence on post-repeal drinking behavior. After the battle over preservation of the Eighteenth Amendment subsided, drinking once more assumed an old role as one mirror of the quality of American life. Now, however, the mirror has reflected some of the prohibition experience. Indeed, there are many indications that after repeal great numbers of citizens, actuated by temperance convictions, religious beliefs, or other reasons, never went back to the bottle. (Possibly, many people who grew up during the dry years never started drinking in the first place.) According to post-repeal consumption data, an estimated 30 percent of the adult population—those over eighteen—remained abstainers, about the same proportion as in the 1980s. There was no dramatic increase in annual per capita consumption, which rose only slowly from approximately one gallon of absolute alcohol per capita in 1934 to roughly 1.5 gallons in 1941. The figure then climbed to pre-Volstead levels of about two gallons per capita (1916–1919) by the mid-1940s. Thus, even with prohibition dead and gone, abstinence remained an important posture toward drinking.

But abstinence, while significant, was the exception; undeniably, drinking once again became the American norm. (A drinker is defined as anyone who drinks at all, even if only on special occasions.) By the late 1970s, average annual per capita consumption of absolute alcohol had risen steadily to about 2.8 gallons, the highest level since the pre-prohibition years (the level was 2.6 gallons between 1906 and 1910, and 2.56 from 1911 to 1915). The National Institute on Alcohol Abuse and Alcoholism (NIAAA), however, noted in its 1978 report to Congress that consumption seemed to have peaked, although NIAAA was unsure of the cause of the apparent stabilization. The same report estimated that the United States ranked about fifteenth in per capita absolute alcohol consumption—behind Portugal (6.27 gallons annually for drinkers over fifteen years old), West Germany (3.75), and Canada (2.84), but ahead of countries such as Ireland (2.47), Sweden (1.84), and Israel (.86).

Trends in beverage preferences since repeal reflected a gradual shift toward distilled spirits at the expense of beer. Measuring strictly by total gallons of given beverages consumed each year since 1933, beer has led wine and spirits by healthy margins. In 1934, Americans typically drank 13.58 gallons of beer per capita annually, while spirits and wine trailed with .64 and .36 gallons, respectively. By 1975, these figures had increased to 28.08 gallons for beer, 2.58 for distilled liquor, and 2.24 for wine. However, the picture changes substantially if we measure preference by the proportion of absolute alcohol consumed annually in a given beverage. In 1934, Americans drank about 63 percent of their absolute alcohol in beer, 30 percent in spirits, and 7 percent in wine. By the mid-1960s, beer had slipped to some 47 percent, while spirits and wine had climbed respectively to 43 and 11 percent. These figures remained about the same over the next decade, with 1975 readings at 41 percent for spirits, 12 percent for wine, and 47 percent for beer. Internationally, this ranked Americans third as consumers of hard liquor, while only thirteenth in their thirst for beer (as wine drinkers, they occupied a lowly seventeenth place).

While it is possible to gauge American drinking in these broad terms, it is virtually impossible to describe a "typical" post-repeal drinker. Drinking behavior fluctuates according to too many variables to define any real mean. Data for the mid-1970s, for example, indicated that considerably more middle-class and wealthy Americans drank than did the poor (who perhaps could not afford as much liquor) and that people over fifty more often tended to be abstainers than did younger Americans. Researchers have found that other socioeconomic variables play important roles as well: Family stability, level of education, and even occupation may influence how and what people drink.

Ethnic and religious factors remained important determinants of drinking behavior. Decades after the end of National Prohibition, regions with high Catholic and foreign-born (defined either as immigrants or children of immigrants) populations tended to have higher average levels of absolute alcohol consumption than the national norm. This phenomenon, as a number of surveys demonstrated, was often a continuing reflection of European customs. A detailed study by Don Cahalan, Ira Cisin, and Helen Crossley (1969), for example, reported that Americans of Irish heritage had "the highest proportion of drinkers (93%) and heavy drinkers (31%)" in the nation. They were followed by those from Britain (89 percent drinkers, 27 percent heavy drinkers), Italy (91 percent and 21 percent), and Latin America or the Caribbean (61 percent and 23 percent). On the other hand, this same survey found that areas with high concentrations of native-born Americans, fundamentalist Protestants, or Mormons had lower than average consumption levels. Cahalan, Cisin, and Crossley ranked only 18 percent of native Americans (defined as those with fathers born in the United States) who drank as heavy drinkers; 38 percent were likely to be abstainers. Among theologically conservative Protestants (Methodists and similar denonimations, Baptists, or other such groups), 48 percent were abstainers, as opposed to some 20 percent among more liberal Protestants (Lutherans, Presbyterians, and Episcopalians), 17 percent among American Catholics, and 8 percent among Jews.

The same research, corroborated by a number of other studies, also found gender and race playing differentiating roles in drinking behavior. By a wide margin, women tended to be abstainers more often than men (40 percent versus 23 percent), while among women who drank, proportionately fewer were heavy drinkers (8 percent as compared to 28 percent among men). Yet among both sexes, heavy drinking peaked in the age group running from twenty-nine to forty-five, although no satisfactory explanation has emerged for this trend. Black and white males had similar rates of drinking, but black women had both a higher proportion of abstainers than did white women (51 percent in black women, 39 percent in white women) and a higher rate of heavy drinkers (7 percent of white women against 22 percent of black women drinkers).

Over the late 1960s and early seventies, however, there were indications that the extremes (either very high or very low drinking levels or pronounced variations by gender or ethnicity) were flattening out. Several investigations suggested that ethnically or religiously influenced patterns of alcohol use were slowly receding and that American drinking was moving toward a new norm or at least toward drinking styles with fewer variations than the United States had traditionally known—a form of "Americanization," as it were, that the old temperance movement hardly anticipated. But, for the meantime, drinking in America continued to reflect the nation's cultural diversity. It still does.

The wide post-repeal popularity of beverage alcohol did not signal the return of drinking as an unchallenged positive good. The wet–dry struggles had pretty much destroyed any unified popular attitudes toward drinking, leaving the nation ambivalent on the matter. The years of dry teaching, which emphasized liquor as a demon, had raised doubts about the morality or propriety of lifting too many glasses at one time, even though conscience-bound citizens may have otherwise thoroughly enjoyed their favorite drinks. Opinion surveys conducted in the 1950s, for instance, found that words like "drinker," "drinking," and "alcohol" evoked confused images, many of which were negative. Nor were many drinkers comfortable with their imbibing, although the vast majority of citizens no longer perceived liquor or the traffic as inherently evil and a threat to social order.

Post-Volstead Americans were uncertain about what to teach their children in regard to alcohol use. Scientific temperance instruction, which had always had its opponents, was now largely discredited. Local school districts in which dry influences remained strong did continue instruction in the "enslaving" effects of alcohol and tried to guide the young toward abstinence, but most of the nation's schools gradually abandoned this approach. Educator Gail Gleason Milgram pointed out that by 1935 there was very little in the way of coherent schoolrom teaching about alcohol and related issues: In the absence of temperance instructional methods, no one had alternatives to offer. The end of classroom explication about rum meant not that educators endorsed drink but that they lacked a clear idea of what to do with the subject.

Ambivalence toward liquor was also prevalent among governmental leaders immediately after prohibition. In his repeal proclamation, President Roosevelt warned the nation against going on a spree or allowing the rebirth of the saloon. Some states remained dry for years after the collapse of National Prohibition, while in those that did not, officials attempted to follow FDR's lead. Attempts to institute practical liquor regulatory programs, however, varied dramatically. All of the states eventually created a control agency to oversee liquor distribution and sales, but the authority of these new bodies differed considerably. A number of states, such as Pennsylvania, Vermont, and Ohio, allowed beer (and sometimes wine) sales to return to the hands of private enterprise, but they also established government monopolies on package sales (purchases other than by the drink) of distilled liquor. North Carolina, in contrast, banned hard liquor sales in restaurants, and Utah disallowed all sales by the drink. The effects of these regulatory efforts on overall rates of consumption or on drunkenness have never been fully clear. They did, however, demonstrate that virtually all the states felt compelled to place controls on alcohol distribution after repeal and that they were not willing to risk a recurrence of pre-Volstead conditions.

In some states and regions where neorepublican values lingered (particularly in the South but also in other communities throughout the land), local or state laws attempted to keep the citizens dry. The number of dry islands had decreased dramatically by the 1950s, although Oklahoma did not fall fully into the wet column until 1959 (until then, only so-called 3.2 beer had been legal), and Mississippi prohibited the sale of distilled spirits until the mid-1960s. But dry counties and townships remain, even in such urbanized states as New Jersey, where some forty municipalities still ban liquor sales. Local option is still a possibility, should voters decide to employ it.

Alcoholism treatment also was largely ignored through the 1940s, a clear casualty of the Volstead years. Ambivalence and indifference toward alcohol-related problems—compounded by the focus of national attention on the Depression and the defeat of the Axis powers during World War II—discouraged private or public sector efforts on behalf of the individual alcoholic. Such persons generally went unaided in their struggles with the bottle. Drunkards usually were locked into the judicial system, with regular topers arrested over and over again but provided with no medical or psychological treatment. Ambivalent and preoccupied, post-repeal America lacked programs either to prevent problem drinking or to assist the problem drinker—even after the medical ill effects of alcoholism had been well documented.

Over time, the complications of problem drinking did become increasingly visible. The overwhelming majority of Americans have enjoyed their alcohol without difficulties, but after repeal drinking demonstrated anew its darker side. As of 1978, the National Institute of Alcohol Abuse and Alcoholism estimated that of all Americans who drank, some 36 percent could be "classified as either being problem drinkers or having potential problems with alcohol (10 percent and 26 percent, respectively)." These categories included both alcoholics, people physically or psychologically addicted to alcohol, and drinkers whose social or economic functioning or health were otherwise disrupted by alcohol use. This translated into approximately 9,300,000 to 10,000,000 people (of whom perhaps 5,750,000 were alcoholics), or about 7 percent of the American population over eighteen. The same

NIAAA report also suggested the possibility of 3.3 million additional problem drinkers among fourteen- to nineteen-years-olds. These figures are open to challenge, and different sources have advanced higher and lower estimates. Nevertheless, the existence of a major population of problem drinkers is well documented.

By the 1970s, the impact of problem drinking had again captured serious popular attention. To sketch only the broad outlines of the issue, the 1978 NIAAA statistics cited myriad alcohol-related personal and societal complications. In 1975, cirrhosis of the liver—linked closely with problem drinking—ranked sixth on the list of most common causes of death in the United States. Estimates put the number of drinking-related deaths as high as 205,000 a year. The NIAAA report also placed annual financial losses attributed directly or indirectly to alcoholism and problem drinking at some $43 billion—roughly $13 billion in health care costs, $20 billion in lost production, $5 billion in traffic accidents, $2 billion in social attempts to deal with drinking-related problems, $3 billion in violent crime, and $430 million in fire losses. Such health and financial costs matched the gloomiest projections of the temperance movement.

The Posttemperance Response

If the end of prohibition left government without a coherent alcohol policy, the toll of alcoholism never went totally unchecked. Temperance groups had worked for years before they were able to constrain the traffic effectively by law. And after repeal, with the evident survival of intemperance and its related societal implications—but with the federal government unwilling to move directly against alcohol abuse—national concern over the issue emanated from the private sector.

One of the most notable developments was the advent of Alcoholics Anonymous (AA), an organization with an unlikely beginning. In 1935 in Akron, Ohio, mutual acquaintances introduced two alcoholics, the stock analyst William Wilson and a surgeon, Dr. Robert Smith; both men hoped that they might cope with their own alcoholism by discussing it with another alcoholic. Wilson and Smith concluded that they and other alcoholics suffered from a disease and were powerless alone in the face of the bottle. Resolving to help one another remain sober, "Bill W." and "Dr. Bob" then carried their message of self-help to other alcoholics. Additional groups subsequently formed, and the

William Griffith Wilson (1895–1971). Co-founder of Alcoholics Anonymous in 1935, Wilson arguably has had as much, if not more, influence on modern perceptions of alcoholism as any other single individual. Except for a brief period at the beginning of his involvement with AA, Wilson was known only as "Bill W." During his lifetime, he used neither his name nor allowed his picture to be published in connection with AA.

Alcoholics Anonymous World Services

name Alcoholics Anonymous was adopted in 1939. After receiving a modest financial donation from John D. Rockefeller, Jr., and some favorable national publicity, the organization spread steadily throughout the country.

Membership was open to all on a nonsectarian basis. The only common denominator was a desire to stop drinking and a willingness to help others in the same plight. Wilson, in fact, codified this concern in AA's "Twelve Steps," which continue to guide the fellowship (as AA prefers to be called). Under the steps, members admit they are "powerless over alcohol" and that "their lives [have] become unmanageable" (step 1); they then seek a spiritual rebirth that will enable them to admit their shortcomings and "make amends" to those they have hurt, and to trust in God as the only means of living without alcohol (steps 2 through 11). (In AA usage, God is not necessarily the Almighty; faith in the AA group itself can fulfill this role.) Finally, in Step 12, members try "to carry this message to alcoholics, and to practice these principles in all affairs."

From the beginning, anonymity was the key to upholding the ideals embodied in the Twelve Steps. In AA's view, anonymity subordinated personalities to principles and avoided outside interference in the group's concerns, all of which was essential to establishing and maintaining sobriety. Regular meetings of local fellowships, which featured (and still feature) the personal stories of member alcoholics, served to reinforce AA beliefs and assist participants in the practical application of the Twelve Steps.

The appeal of AA was startling. It attracted thousands of Americans, demonstrating that repeal had by no means ended drinking problems. By the late 1970s, some 500,000 had joined and two spinoff (but independent) groups had formed: Al-Anon, for the families of alcoholics, and Ala-Teen, for teenage children of alcoholics. Despite its numbers, the fellowship has maintained its original principles, remained scrupulously nonpolitical, and avoided all outside controversies. AA even kept its own formal structure to a minimum: There is a national board of directors and a general services office in New York City to make policy decisions, handle publication efforts, and to serve, if needed, as a coordinating body for local groups. But the chief efforts of AA proceed at the local level, with anonymity and service still the keys.

Why AA succeeds has puzzled both lay and scholarly observers ever since the organization first attracted national attention. Various studies have stressed the spiritual rebirth arising from participation, the psychological support derived from group activities and a greater understanding of alcoholism, and the restructuring of the recovering alcoholic's life as determined by AA practices. For many participants, AA has proved to be a beneficial form of group therapy.

A historical perspective can shed some light on AA's effectiveness. The self-help idea was not new. Members of the Washingtonian societies, the Reform Clubs, and (to an extent) the dry fraternal organizations were earlier drinkers trying to stay sober using the mutual assistance formula. Like AA, these groups sought to reconstruct the social stability of the drinker and to establish common standards on alcohol use. They also provided a structured lifestyle, keyed to participation in group activities. These steps would enable an alcoholic not only to stop drinking but also to stay off the bottle over time. If a member began drinking again, another participant would offer aid. Thus, by conforming to group norms on drinking, individuals both strengthened the group and took strength from identity with its standards, drawing on the organization in time of need.

In a sense (at least in terms of controlling drinking behavior, even to the point of abstinence), the functions of these groups can be compared to the old New England towns. Where norms were recognized and accepted, community members maintained them for the good of themselves and for others; from this arrangement came stability, identity, purpose, and security. AA, like the Washingtonians and Reform Clubs in an earlier day, has offered its members just such a community. In fact, modern clinicians have spoken of some self-help groups as "therapeutic communities."

For all its success, however, AA has been subject to criticism. Its strong spiritual emphasis and its insistence on abstinence have drawn fire. Other voices have complained that the group is oriented toward white, middle-class drinkers. In response, AA can justifiably say that it never claimed that its approach could work for everyone; moreover, the organization demonstrated an ability to broaden its popular base. AA now functions well among black, Hispanic, and other minority groups, and it has consistently produced more impressive results than any other alcoholism treatment regimen. By the 1960s, clinicians routinely built AA participation into rehabilitation programs, and many AA volunteers—who worked with the programs as part of their own "Twelfth Step" experience—earned the respect of the clinical community.

As Alcoholics Anonymous began its climb to national prominence, interest in alcohol problems surfaced elsewhere. Throughout the late 1930s, research reports on various aspects of alcoholism appeared with increasing frequency in scientific and medical journals. Usually the studies identified the condition as some kind of psychological disorder that could have medical complications. These efforts were often less than revealing. Research was restricted to a limited number of areas, research standards were not uniform, and old wet–dry animosities sometimes clouded the judgment of researchers. Moreover, some studies, in effect, reinvented the wheel: Work performed by the old Association for the Study of Inebriety was generally overlooked in the 1930s. Many of the new researchers covered much of the same ground under the mistaken impression that they were charting unexplored territory. But whatever the deficiencies, this new work did build a scientific literature as a prerequisite for effective alcohol-related research. It was also another sign that not all of post-repeal America sought to ignore its drinking problems.

The caliber of research gradually improved. In 1938, a group of scientists interested in alcohol-related questions founded the Research

Council on Problems of Alcohol. The council's immediate goal was to generate funding for medical research on alcoholism; but its activities also extended to the prevention of alcoholism through public education, investigations of drinking-related traffic problems, and studies of other health complications of alcohol use. The Research Council was short-lived, but its program stimulated further work at Yale University.

Indeed, the evolution of the Yale Center of Alcohol Studies in the later 1930s and early forties was the breakthrough that reignited significant scientific and academic interest in alcohol use. The center (located at Rutgers University since 1962) was originally a section of the Laboratory of Applied Physiology at Yale (the director of the laboratory, Dr. Yandell Henderson, had been a member of the Research Council). As interest in alcohol studies grew, it took on its own identity. Over the 1940s and fifties, the center faculty and staff conducted a broad range of inquiries in physiology, psychology, sociology, education, law, and other disciplines. The center also established the Yale Plan Clinics in New Haven and Hartford, Connecticut, in order to assess the demand for and the best methods of alcoholism treatment and prevention (and found, as AA had already, that alcoholics came from all walks of life—thus refuting the skid row stereotype). Significantly, in conducting its various projects, the center brought a general vitality and scholarly respectability to an area too long dominated by wet–dry controversies. For the first time since the heyday of the old Association for the Study of Inebriety, science once more had a major claim to the field.

The Yale Center launched important ventures beyond research projects. In 1940, it inaugurated the *Quarterly Journal of Studies on Alcohol* (now the *Journal of Studies on Alcohol*), which quickly became a focal point for international research. Three years later the center began the annual Summer School of Alcohol Studies; it was an immediate success and drew former and active temperance workers, liquor industry representatives, social workers, educators, researchers, clinical personnel, AA participants, and a range of other individuals—professionals and laymen—with an interest in alcohol problems. Perhaps the most important contribution of the center, however, was its popularization of the modern disease conception of alcoholism.

The disease concept came from E. M. Jellinek, affiliated with the center, either in residence as director or through his publications, from the 1940s to the early 1960s. Jellinek (who was familiar with the ideas of the Association for the Study of Inebriety when he framed his own con-

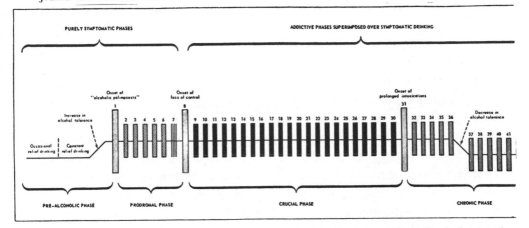

E. M. Jellinek's phases of alcohol addiction, 1952. Jellinek depicted alcoholism as a progressive disease, with increasing health and societal complications as the drinker passes through successive phases. Although explained in modern medical terms, Jellinek's illustration is still readily comparable to such earlier graphic depictions of the addiction process as Rush's "Moral and Physical Thermometer" and Currier's Drunkard's Progress.

cepts) depicted a disease with a symptomatic progression of phases leading eventually from psychological to physical addiction. If not checked, alcoholism could kill either by itself or through medical complications. And Jellinek agreed with AA—whose members provided data for his early studies—that the problem drinker, once addicted, generally could not stop because of a loss of control over drinking and a physiological or psychological craving for alcohol. He cautioned that his theories lacked empirical foundation and that subsequent work would probably lead to modifications. Still, both laymen and professionals in the field (forgetting, or never knowing, that the old association and the temperance movement previously had advanced the same view) saw the disease concept as a breakthrough in dealing with alcohol-related issues.

The implications of Jellinek's ideas were profound. The revived notion of alcoholism as a disease—that alcoholics were not immoral but physically or psychologically sick—began to break down some of the moral stigma traditionally attached to drinking problems. This shift, in turn, prompted increasing numbers of alcoholics to seek help. Equally important, a number of private organizations arose to build public support for alcoholism treatment, popularize the disease conception, and encourage the prevention of problem drinking. The Yale

Center was active in founding the most significant of these, the National Committee for Education on Alcoholism (renamed the National Council on Alcoholism [NCA] in the early 1950s).

Marty Mann, a former alcoholic with experience in advertising and communications, launched the National Committee in 1944 with the organizational help of some of the Yale faculty. She hoped that public education about the disease concept of alcoholism would prove the key to leading Americans away from problem drinking and, for those who needed it, into treatment. The Committee gradually established chapters in dozens of communities. These volunteer organizations worked with churches, governmental agencies, schools, industry—virtually any group interested in alcoholism treatment—to provide assistance to the alcoholic and to spread the committee's educational message.

The activities of the Yale Center also had a profound influence on the views of organized religion toward alcohol. Once bastions of the temperance movement, most of the large denominations gradually dropped their prohibitionist stances in favor of ministries or other outreach efforts directed toward alcoholics. Not infrequently, such change occurred as the various denominations sent representatives to the Yale Summer School or became convinced of the veracity of the disease conception through center publications or contacts with its personnel. In 1951, Episcopal minister David Works, who was also a recovering alcoholic, founded the North Conway Institute (New Hampshire) with the expressed intention of marshalling American churches in support of the ideas coming out of Yale. Churches developing active (and puralist) social orientations—an increasingly prominent aspect of American religion over the 1950s and sixties—were especially receptive to the disease conception and often became prominent advocates of public assistance for the alcoholic. Except in a few and generally very conservative denominations, the new appeal has replaced the old drumfire of temperance.

Indeed, despite concern over alcohol-related issues, none of the sponsors of these post-repeal efforts—Alcoholics Anonymous, the Yale (Rutgers) Center, the National Council on Alcoholism, or the churches—considered (or today considers) itself a temperance organization. The very word "temperance" was charged with emotion and had a horrible public image; consequently, most groups avoided it like the plague. On more than one occasion, for example, members of the Yale Center deliberately insisted that their work was a world apart from the reformers of the previous generation. Yet if those in what has become known as the "alcoholism movement" were not (and are not) prohibitionists, in a sense they remained temperance workers. In the context of their times, they have tried to alleviate drinking problems, to increase public awareness of the alcoholic's plight, and (with the exception of AA, which endorses no political or social programs) to influence the formation of relevant public policy. The old temperance movement did nothing less in its era. With the exceptions of prohibitionist policies and the neorepublican social vision, many of the goals of the modern organizations are similar to those of the earlier dry crusade.

Like temperance advocates, post-repeal activists have tried to spread their views on alcohol problems as widely as possible. In the 1950s and sixties, their message had an appreciable impact on a number of fields. They stimulated interest in alcoholism treatment in the medical community, an interest not extinct but largely dormant since the Volstead Act. In the mid-1950s, for instance, both the American Hospital Association and the American Medical Association passed resolutions urging the treatment of alcoholism as a disease (as Jellinek had defined it). Industry also responded. Beginning with an innovative program started in 1943 by Du Pont, other corporate efforts designed to rehabilitate rather than discharge alcoholic employees gradually evolved. Such employee assistance programs offered high recovery rates and—although a number of studies conducted in the late 1970s have questioned this point—considerable financial savings in the retaining of skilled personnel. By the early 1980s there were some 2,250 of these programs in business and industry. In the public sphere, state governments began funding agencies to supervise a wide variety of alcohol-related activities. In fact, the 1960s saw the emergence of an "alcoholism constituency," fighting political and bureaucratic battles for its share of state and federal dollars and for recognition of its importance in relation to other public health program commitments.

An important part of that recognition came during the 1960s and seventies, as the federal government took an increasingly active interest in drinking-related questions. In 1944, the U.S. Public Health Service labeled alcoholism the nation's fourth largest public health problem, although little governmental action was immediately forthcoming to deal with the area. Subsequently, however, a division in the National Institute of Mental Health addressed itself to alcoholism, pointing the way toward greater direct federal involvement in treatment and research. In the meantime, the courts were also active. In 1966, two federal Appeals Court decisions (*Driver* v. *Hinnant* and *Easter* v. *District of Columbia*) supported the notion of alcoholism as a disease. Two years later, in *Powell* v. *Texas*, the Supreme Court noted the force of the arguments for the disease conception (although it also observed that not all of its proponents were in complete agreement, and that in any case arrests for public intoxication were still legal). These decisions further spurred legislative measures, culminating in the Comprehensive Alcohol Abuse and Alcoholism Prevention, Treatment, and Rehabilitation Act of 1970. With this act, Congress established a separate agency to direct federal efforts against alcohol problems. The new unit—the National Institute on Alcohol Abuse and Alcoholism—gave the alcoholism constituency a seemingly permanent voice in public health program and research planning. And although disputes over specific policies and goals have occurred (and continue to occur), NIAAA enabled alcohol-related treatment, research, educational, and public information activities to proceed on a level not attained since the height of the antiliquor crusade.

In assuming its coordinating role, NIAAA took on many of the old temperance movement's functions (with the important exception, of course, of prohibitionist ventures). In retrospect, this step was not surprising. Since the New Deal and the emergence of the welfare state, government has enlarged its role in social services, particularly in health-related fields. The transfer to government control of many activities that had rested previously in private hands reflected a general approach to handling social problems. In the case of alcohol problems, the transfer came at the urging of a coalition of private voices already convinced of the need for federal intervention.

The creaton of NIAAA stimulated additional governmental as well as private efforts in the field. Following NIAAA's birth, the National Conference of Commissioners on Uniform State Laws recommended a Uniform Alcoholism and Intoxication Act (1971) to all the states. The suggested act would remove many alcohol-related infractions from the criminal justice system, substituting medical treatment for punishment. In the 1970s, the states began active consideration of this legislation, and many of them enacted the measure or variants of it (thus fulfilling, we should recall, one of the suggestions the Association for the Study of Inebriety had advanced a century before). At the same time, neither local and state nor federal authorities tried to monopolize efforts against alcoholism, and a wider variety of private groups than ever before remained active in the field. In fact, the alcoholism movement emerged as a classic example of the mixture of private and public enterprise that has come to characterize so many facets of modern American life.

"The New Temperance" or the Frustration of Consensus

Yet if the rise of the alcoholism movement underscored America's continuing concern with drinking problems, it did not provide a consensus on how society should handle these issues. As it originally evolved, the new movement lacked the legal suasionist focus of the old prohibition drive. Modern efforts to address alcohol problems mirror the diversity of alcoholism itself, the constituencies concerned about it, and the changing nature of drinking practices in the decades after repeal.

Popular ambivalence toward alcohol use has been a root cause of this lack of consensus—and America's ambivalence has been undeniable into the 1980s. By the late 1970s, as many as 30 percent of the nation's citizens did not drink at all, while others tolerated considerable latitude in drinking behavior. It remains common enough to shrug off "getting loaded" at a college party as an instance of adolescent conduct; in some social circles, heavy drinking, even to the point of drunkenness, is still the mark of a "real man." In other cases, drinkers who see nothing wrong with their own imbibing hold doubts about it in others. Adults who routinely attend cocktail parties, for instance, can express deep concern over drinking among their children. And although the nation spent (and spends) huge sums annually on consumer purchases of beverage alcohol and generally has accepted the idea that alcoholism is a disease, Americans still place a severe social stigma on alcoholism.

Into the 1980s, trends in drinking patterns have done little to clarify matters. While available statistics (as of 1986) are insufficient for precise comparisons with prior decades, it is clear that alcohol beverage consumption has leveled off nationally. At least one survey (conducted for *Time* magazine in 1985) has reported that, among Americans eighteen or older, only 67 percent drank alcohol beverages, one of the lowest estimates in some time. A third of those polled indicated that they were drinking less than they had before, while "only 6% said they were drinking more."

Industrial sources seemingly corroborate these findings. Distillers have estimated that annual per capita consumption of spirits dropped some 15 percent between 1974 and 1985. After significant growth over the 1960s and seventies, wine sales slowed considerably by the mid-eighties, and some large vinting firms experienced reduced profits for the first time in years. By 1986, for example, Gallo, America's largest wine company, had to move vigorously into such new product lines as "wine coolers" (a light wine and fruit juice combination) to maintain profits. Traditional wines were no longer the marketing success they were a decade earlier. Brewers have faced similar difficulties as beer sales declined substantially. Per capita annual consumption fell from about 31 gallons in 1980 to some 29 gallons five years later. Many liquor retailers, bars, and restaurants have also reported declining revenues, while distributors of such beverages as low-alcohol or dealcoholized wines and beers, sparkling ciders, and seltzer waters—even specialty teas and coffees—have done increasingly well with their products.

Some traditional bastions of American drinking have felt these changes. The "three Martini lunch," for instance, may not have to be legislated out of existence; it could wither away as American businesses take a dimmer view of drinking on the part of their employees, especially management personnel. This has been the case among many corporate executives who have nothing against drinking *per se* but are well aware that neither they nor their employees would function at peak performance after several drinks. College campuses also have experienced signs of moderating consumption, although they are hardly as pronounced as off-campus developments. Many institutions have promulgated alcohol-use policies after consultation with student groups (aimed not at eliminating drinking, but at controlling excesses), and the 1980s have seen, by at least one scholarly report, a decrease in the number of students who drink and drive. Editorials in campus newspapers calling for responsible drinking practices are not unusual, and groups such as BACCHUS (Boost Alcohol Consciousness Concerning the Health of University Students) and SADD (Students Against Driving Drunk) conduct publicity efforts on the health and safety aspects of drinking.

Yet it is too early to draw conclusions on what these changing drinking patterns signify, or even how deeply they will touch the populace. If business has declined for many liquor dealers, for example, others, particularly neighborhood bars with established clientele, report little or no change in consumption patterns. And while college and university students might share a greater awareness of the various consequences of problem drinking, most of them still drink. Indeed, some have lodged serious objections to official efforts to restrict campus drinking: In late 1984, for instance, angry students at Illinois State University, chanting "We want beer" and engaging in vandalism, dispersed only after police moved in with tear gas. While this is an extreme example, it is indicative of the regard alcohol continues to enjoy among students. As a Rutgers University dean observed, most undergraduates simply cannot imagine "an environment in which alcohol is not readily accessible."

Moreover, authorities can only speculate on why other populations have moderated their alcohol use. There are a number of theories, all with varying degrees of plausibility—although some are less convincing than others: One observer has postulated that, to an extent, the socially conscious generation of the 1960s is feeling guilty over its affluence and loss of activism. To assuage these feelings, some former activists (supposedly) deny themselves indulgences—like drinking. A more reasonable hypothesis centers on the self-image of many upwardly mobile young professionals ("Yuppies"): Concerned with fitness and "looking good," they may be leery of the health complications or calories associated with excessive drinking. "There's no such thing as a fat yuppie," one wag noted in *Time*. Still others offer suggestions to the effect that, even if its decks are awash, neorepublicanism remains afloat for many Americans. Anthropologist Dwight Heath detects a desire to enforce "law and order" in some of the modern voices that would discourage drinking. Columnist George Will has suggested that greater concern over drinking-related issues is a reflection of a return to more conservative social values (a thesis he drew, in part, from an earlier edition of *Drinking in America*). Whatever interpretations Americans place on their drinking behavior, however, it is clear that there is little in the way of agreement. The old antiliquor consensus of the prohibition crusade, or even the earlier view of alcohol as a positive good, has left only a confused legacy.

It is worth noting that recent changes in drinking patterns, no matter what interpretations different observers assign to them, have taken place largely independent of the alcoholism movement. Indeed, one can argue that, rather than shaping events, the alcoholism constituency has become a prime example of the ambivalence and confusion surrounding attitudes toward alcohol and its associated dilemmas. Fundamental cleavages have emerged in the alcoholism field. By the late 1960s, for instance, there was already considerable professional debate over the validity of the conception of alcoholism as a disease. The issue intensified over the 1970s, and Jellinek's original description of the condition as a relatively uniform disease entity, as he warned when he first wrote on the subject, gave way to a more complex view. Researchers and clinicians gradually came to accept that there are various alcoholisms with an unknown range of etiologies—although not without opposition from those we may term "purist Jellinekians," who were (and are) mostly laymen. Public health expert Dan E. Beauchamp has noted that the literature is now replete with challenges to the disease conception. There are some plausible arguments, for example, for considering alcoholism a habit rather than a disease and for thinking that the differences between alcoholics and so-called "normal" drinkers have been exaggerated. If this is the case, the disease model may be a faulty base for effective public policy regarding alcohol use.

All of this has come, it should be stressed, in the face of a rather successful effort on the part of such groups as the National Council on Alcoholism to convince the lay public—and even the courts, as evidenced in the *Easter* and similar cases—of the validity of the disease conception. In any event, no one questions the fact that alcohol problems have severe health implications; but it seems clear that the disease idea, which gave the post-repeal alcoholism movement so much impetus, has lost some of its ability to rally the field. NIAAA, for example, does not emphasize a uniform disease explanation. Rather, much of its work has centered on the "special problems" of such groups as blacks, women, Indians, or Hispanics, only reinforcing doubts about the extent of common sources of alcoholism (and thus approaches to its treatment).

Other differences have centered on the proper balance between treatment and prevention. Prevention involves individual or societal measures designed to stop drinking problems before they start, or at least to keep them within bounds. This idea has been attractive in theory, and certainly prohibitionists thought that their approach to the matter would be prevention at its most effective. Since repeal, however, there has been little agreement on techniques that might demonstrate the practical superiority of prevention over treatment or other means of controlling alcohol problems. Until the 1960s, prevention generally meant alcohol education in the schools and public awareness campaigns, and there has been some speculation that the moderation of drinking in the 1980s owes something to these efforts. Belief in the efficacy of alcohol education, however, at least as a means of bringing about widespread and lasting attitudes toward alcohol use or nonabusive drinking practices, was largely a matter of faith. There was little proof of its effectiveness.

Yet prevention has found articulate champions. Over the 1970s, newer thinking on the subject envisioned a more comprehensive approach to prevention. In *Beyond Alcoholism: Alcohol and Public Health Policy* (1980), Beauchamp has offered an incisive statement of this new position. He has argued that a prevention effort "aimed at controlling exposure [to alcohol] in the first place" would "minimize damage that does occur." Citing historical and statistical evidence from a number of countries, as well as the experience of National Prohibition, he finds a causal relationship between policies that limit the availability of beverage alcohol (and thus consumption) and a reduction of drinking-related problems. It therefore should be possible, Beauchamp holds, to design a policy in which the *"primary message would be minimal or non-use of alcohol and zero growth in per capita alcohol consumption."* This approach would work if supported by such measures as alcohol education, limits on liquor advertising, the taxation of the beverage industry (which would keep beverage prices high, thus also contributing to reduced consumption), highway safety measures such as mandatory passive restraints in automobiles, and stricter legislative and regulatory controls over alcohol beverage sales. Beauchamp is clear on another point: Such a policy is not prohibitionist; it would respect pluralist values and the rights of those who chose to drink. But it would insist that society also has the right to act responsibly on behalf of the common welfare—which would include taking steps to assure that people are not unduly encouraged to drink.

To an extent this view has garnered a following, if an unstructured one. From time to time, NIAAA has discussed tax-based or other measures aimed at limiting per capita annual consumption of alcohol, and both the national government and the states have acted legislatively. Much of this activity has involved the legislation of higher drinking ages. During the early 1970s, many states dropped the minimum legal age for the purchase of alcoholic beverages, usually to eighteen. Later in the decade, the trend reversed as lawmakers considered evidence (much of it hotly disputed) that raising the legal age to twenty-one would prevent an appreciable number of traffic accidents. More states fell into line as statistics (which were also open to various interpretations) indicated that the step indeed was saving lives. Unpersuaded states, such as New York, came around with a federal prompt: In 1984, President Ronald Reagan signed into law a measure that would cut fed-

Don Boring, *Daily Cougar* (University of Houston)

Raising the age limit for the legal purchase of beverage alcohol (the "drinking age") has prompted particular concern among restaurant and tavern owners. Under "dram shop" laws, they can be held responsible for certain of the actions of intoxicated patrons. Such potential liability led to this cartoon in the student newspaper at the University of Houston, where in Texas the 21-year-old limit became effective in September 1986. The jibe at ID checks for an older clientele also reflected something of student discontent over restrictions on campus drinking because of the age change.

eral highway funds to states with legal purchasing ages of under twenty-one. "I'm against it [the effort to raise the drinking age]," said one New York State senator, "but I voted for it. You can't ignore millions of dollars in Federal highway funds."

The higher legal drinking ages have won widespread public support. As of 1986, only seven states and the District of Columbia had failed to adopt the twenty-one-year-old age limit. The reluctance of the District of Columbia to pass such legislation prompted one U.S. senator to state heatedly that "this is the nation's capital, not the national saloon." These sentiments have attracted the enthusiastic applause of such groups as MADD, SADD, RID (Remove Intoxicated Drivers), and NCA.

Other preventative steps also have become law. A number of states have passed dram-shop laws, akin to the old Adair Law of nineteenth-century Ohio, which seek to prevent alcohol sales to intoxicated individuals. Under these laws, courts can hold retailers liable for certain damages deriving from sales to drunken patrons. The full impact of these laws must await future analysis, but victims of drunken drivers already have successfully sued tavern and restaurant owners who sold alcohol to customers who then caused traffic accidents. Some states have taken this idea farther. New Jersey, for example, has framed legislation holding hosts liable for resulting damages should they provide an already intoxicated drinker with more alcohol—including drinks offered in the privacy of a home. Again, full assessment of such laws will have to await the accumulation of evidence; at the same time, however, one can argue that the dram-shop and host-liability initiatives already have yielded some preventative results. In some areas, retail outlets, especially taverns and restaurants, have become more careful about whom they serve (and, in this regard, some state agencies have considered programs to train bartenders to identify intoxicated patrons more accurately). Many colleges, fearful of liability and related costs of litigation and insurance, have moved to control campus drinking more carefully; some have closed their campus pubs. Thus, by the mid-1980s, many Americans saw a direct financial stake in keeping alcohol-related problems to a minimum.

The appearance of groups willing to agitate aggressively for more restrictive alcohol control efforts, and especially for maximum enforcement of toughened drunken driving laws, has offered yet another case study in the popular appeal of prevention. Organizations such as MADD and RID were not first-generation members of the alcoholism movement. MADD, founded by Candy Lightner after her child died as the result of an accident caused by a drunken driver, has attracted considerable public support (including mothers of other children killed in alcohol-related traffic incidents) for its campaign to come down hard on intoxicated drivers. The group's approach is overtly preventative. As one member who lost a child wrote in a fundraising appeal, "MADD is trying to keep a tragedy like mine from happening to you."

Generally unconcerned with treatment, the disease concept, and other issues that captured the attention of the older alcoholism constituency, MADD has proved itself adept at lobbying and organizing public pressure. The same can be said for RID. MADD has taken its case for stronger laws against drunken driving to legislators and judges, launched alcohol education efforts aimed at the public schools, and raised public consciousness regarding the perils of drinking and driv-

MADD
DONOR SURVEY

For Donors in Texas

Survey #: 0233559Z

This survey has been prepared for:

*TELL ME WHAT YOU THINK
MADD SHOULD DO!*

6F3   Norma 23   7CN

D I R E C T I O N S

MADD must establish its action priorities for the remainder of 1986. Please take a minute to share your opinion on the questions listed below and return to MADD by July 30th! Thank you.

1. **Should MADD launch a national advertising campaign against drunk driving?**   YES ☐   NO ☐

2. **Should MADD give high priority to youth education programs about the hazards of drunk driving?**   YES ☐   NO ☐

3. **On which grade levels should MADD youth educational programs focus?**
   - ☐ Grammar School
   - ☐ Middle School
   - ☐ High School

4. **What types of public policies do you want MADD to support?** (Check your *top* priority.)
   - ☐ Stiffer penalties for drunk drivers
   - ☐ Lower legal blood alcohol content limits for drivers
   - ☐ Stricter enforcement of laws
   - ☐ Banning open containers of alcohol in vehicles
   - ☐ Victim rights and assistance

5. **Do you favor use of sobriety check points to catch drunk drivers?**   YES ☐   NO ☐

6. **Are there enough anti-drunk driving messages in the media?**
   - ☐ OK
   - ☐ Too Many
   - ☐ Too Few

And finally, are you still MADD enough to fight?   YES ☐   NO ☐

Thank you.   *PLEASE READ MY MESSAGE ON THE BACK OF THIS SURVEY!*

PLEASE RETURN BY JULY 30TH!

*Fund-raising flier from Mothers Against Drunk Driving (MADD).
While not exactly comparable to the temperance pledges of the nineteenth
and early twentieth centuries, the MADD agenda indicates the group's
''legal suasion'' approach and does ask interested parties to commit themselves to the cause on paper.*

ing. And while MADD seems to have made its peace with the beverage industry, RID has continued to hold the traffic responsible, at least in part, for drinking-related highway problems; liquor advertising, especially when aimed at young people, has drawn the group's particular fire. Both MADD and RID have been much less reticent than the rest of the alcohol constituency about using the law to establish their preventative programs. Indeed, in early 1986, MADD endorsed a Constitutional amendment that would guarantee certain rights to the victims of crimes, including the right to financial compensation for victims of such crimes as drunken driving. While more than time separates MADD and RID from the old temperance movement—neither group is prohibitionist, nor have they (yet) placed their issues within a broader social vision—there is no denying that their militancy has struck a familiar chord.

MADD and RID have not been operating in a vacuum. Public concern over alcohol problems had risen to new levels by the mid-1980s; alcohol consumption had fallen; legislatures had shown a greater willingness to act on alcohol-related issues; there had been concrete proposals to base public policy on the reduction of alcohol use and the stricter control of the alcohol beverage industry. There even had been suggestions that all drinking carries inherent risks, and that society therefore should be concerned with all alcohol use rather than focusing narrowly on alcoholism. Some of this has a neorepublican cast. Such developments have raised serious questions: Had American temperance sentiments revived? Was there a "neoprohibitionist" movement afoot? The media and a variety of voices in and out of the alcohol field were answering these questions with a decided "yes." Moreover, they were not all happy about it.

Opposition to the alleged "new temperance" (as *Time* termed it in 1985) has grown from a number of roots. Representatives of the alcohol beverage industry were among the first to level charges of neoprohibitionism. While the industry's public image, as explained earlier, remains positive, calls for sharply curtailed consumption, stronger regulation of beverage sales, and the like were hardly calculated to please distillers, brewers, and vintners. Such groups as the National Student Association have taken umbrage at the raising of drinking ages and campus sales restrictions; such laws and regulations, they have claimed, are blatantly discriminatory and unenforceable. And in the face of general public acceptance, stricter enforcement of drunken driving laws also have given rise to a number of protests on libertarian grounds (police spot checks of motorists—a practice MADD has earnestly endorsed—have drawn the most criticism in this regard).

Some members of the alcohol studies field have voiced their skepticism as well. A 1985 article by two alcohol researchers who questioned the efficacy of raising drinking ages, for example, drew a stern rebuke from MADD and the Insurance Institute for Highway Safety. Such arguments probably will intensify. Mark Keller, one of the most respected members of the alcoholism field and editor emeritus of the *Journal of Studies on Alcohol*, stated the position of many when he charged control advocates with ignoring "history lessons." Unlike some scholars, Keller has found no useful lessons in the prohibition experience (at least none that would prove positive guides for current policy). If the media have written of a "new temperance," Keller has used the term "alcohol inhibitionism" to describe the calls for a firmer, control-oriented and legally oriented alcohol policy, and its proponents "new inhibitionists." Right or wrong—and advocates of both views have employed the "lessons" of the past—such appeals to history have brought the centuries-old American controversy over alcohol into bold relief for another generation.

Issues beyond the so-called new temperance, however, have added to controversies surrounding alcohol-related questions. For instance, while the alcoholism constituency has scored some notable victories in molding aspects of popular opinion, it also has added to the confusion in American attitudes toward drinking. NIAAA offered a good example: In the mid-1970s, the institute sponsored a public campaign calling on the nation to "drink responsibly," a theme mirrored in the efforts of other groups, including some representatives of the licensed beverage industry. Yet other concerned voices—some of whom favored policies encouraging lower alcohol consumption—dissented. While not professing abstinence, they argued that responsible drinking was only an invitation to problem drinking for many people (shades here of the old dry aversion to moderate drinking?) and that in any case NIAAA should not be in the business of endorsing any drinking. Under pressure, NIAAA dropped its campaign, which, in turn, generated displeasure in other quarters.

Similarly, in 1976, the National Council on Alcoholism and other groups reacted sharply when a Rand Corporation study suggested that some alcoholics apparently could go back to social drinking after recovery, although the Rand report never suggested such a return to drinking as a treatment goal. The report, critics charged, would induce alcoholics to relapse (at least one subsequent study of this possibility found no evidence to sustain the fear). NIAAA, which had financed the Rand study, then virtually repudiated it, as well as a follow-up Rand report (1980) that reached similar conclusions. There was a comparable storm of protest when the *Journal of Studies on Alcohol* published a number of articles in seeming agreement with the Rand findings.

Such disputes were illustrative of others. One thinks here, for example, of the dismay following the news that MADD would accept financial support from a major brewer. Some observers have seen these disputes as cause for alarm. The merits of the Rand report, the responsible drinking campaign, or industry funding for MADD aside—not to mention the debates over "neoprohibitionism" or "inhibitionism"— incidents like these hardly give the impression of an alcoholism movement that knows where it is going or how to get there. America's ambivalence on alcohol-related matters, it is easy to conclude, is amply shared by policymakers in the field.

An Age of Ambivalence?

Ambivalent attitudes have proved a significant source of frustration for those concerned with combating alcohol problems. This is understandable. A number of studies have argued forcefully that more uniform popular views on acceptable drinking behavior would alone (without legal compulsion) reduce alcoholism and related complications. In 1967, for instance, the Cooperative Commission on the Study of Alcoholism, a national panel of experts, released findings (*Alcohol Problems: A Report to the Nation*) that recommended carefully planned modifications in American drinking patterns in order "to reduce rates of alcoholism and other types of problem drinking." In theory, this was a sound approach; in fact, societies sharing common values on alcohol consumption have kept alcohol-related difficulties to a minimum. The experiences of Italians, Jews, other tightly knit ethnic groups, Alcoholics Anonymous, and even the New England towns of colonial America are all testimony to this phenomenon. Converting theory into practice, however, is another story (and to their credit, the commission members harbored no illusions about doing so).

Planning major modifications in American drinking behavior would be a formidable task. That any group of policymakers could ever agree on new standards is itself doubtful; even if they could, building a popular national consensus around these norms would be another affair entirely. In the historical instances in which behavioral norms acted to check drinking excesses, alcohol use was in a healthy balance with other societal mores and traditions. Drinking behavior, in short, was intertwined with a coherent system of generally stable and accepted cultural norms. But America has lacked precisely such a context of uniform values for generations. In fact, the nation's pluralism, which has contributed so immensely to the vitality and quality of life in the United States, frequently also has made consensus on important social issues difficult. Civil rights, the proper role of government in formulating public policy, free speech, and other crucial matters are of a piece with drinking behavior in this regard. None of these great issues has proved amenable to simple solutions in a system of democratic pluralism, and there is little reason to think any official attempts at implementing important changes in drinking patterns will become easier. As one critic of the Cooperative Commission report noted, our cultural diversity could make the effort an exercise in frustration. As a whole, wrote the editor of *Christianity Today*, the country lacks the "commitment to religious or ethical values that exert profound influence on behavior." And if the experience of the past is any guide to future policy, that lack is a stumbling block indeed.

Controversies of this kind have pointed to a related issue, for there is now another dimension to the matter of constructing a national consensus. Such groups as NCA, NIAAA, and even alcohol-related research teams in academe have taken on lives of their own. They have become institutionalized (in the case of NIAAA, as part of the federal bureaucracy), with expenses and payrolls to meet, and the need to justify their activities. These are natural developments in the rise of institutions and are not necessarily bad, but they have led to charges that certain actions reflect self-interest as much as a desire to deal with alcohol problems. A variety of studies, for example, some of them by dispassionate scholars, have implied that a range of NIAAA's findings, including its reports on the number of alcoholics and the impact of drinking on the economy, were designed, in part, to make the institute's work—and budget—look essential. There have been other illustrations of the tendency: In 1981, when the Reagan administration suggested certain funding cuts for NIAAA, the alcoholism movement reacted with consternation. Rather than present a unified opposition, however, many advocates of research, treatment, and prevention programs instead chose to defend their individual turf; wrangling sometimes became bitter as different groups argued for the importance of funding particular efforts. Admittedly, some of these disagreements arose from honest differences over policy or research approaches. But it was also clear that the leading organizations of the alcoholism constituency would (and probably will) defend their vested interests, a fact that will have a significant impact on efforts to mold any consensus on alcohol policy.

Thus, by the late 1980s, the United States lacked recognized standards of acceptable drinking behavior that might serve as guides for an alcohol consumption policy. Whether the energies at work in treatment, prevention, policy debates, research, the liquor industry, and elsewhere can produce any agreement will remain an open question into the foreseeable future. Like others before it, NIAAA, to its credit, has called for "a new national consensus concerning what constitutes responsible use and nonuse of alcoholic beverages." A worthy sentiment—but ambivalence and division remain the standing realities of our time.

Yet there are limits to this ambivalence. In some respects, Americans have moved beyond the conflicts of would-be policymakers and reform groups and reached a number of clear, if tacit, decisions on alcohol use. The United States is a wet country. That decision, at least, seems final; there is no ambivalence on the matter. The more thoughtful advocates of tighter controls on beverage alcohol have fully acknowledged as much. They have no quarrel with pluralist values and they have not used alcohol-related issues to advance a particular, broader sociopolitical vision. Despite cries of "neoprohibitionism," there is little likelihood that a public policy aimed, for example, at minimizing per capita annual consumption of alcohol (should a consensus for such a step ever materialize) would serve to generate a new dry crusade. A prohibition movement on the classic American model is not in the offing in the late twentieth century.

Americans also have accepted a second point: Commitment to a wet culture implies an acceptance of a certain amount of drinking-related difficulties. The one will probably never exist without at least some of the other. Americans may deplore alcohol problems, but they are not surprised by them—and the demise of National Prohibition certainly demonstrated that citizens were not willing to abolish drinking as a means of curing alcoholism and related social ills. Evidently, the only major restrictions the public will tolerate without serious objections are increased minimum drinking ages, which do not limit the ability of most adults to get a drink, and tougher steps against drunk drivers. Certainly the drinking-related mayhem on the highways has become too appalling to ignore. Yet when a Tennessee legislative committee suggested in 1983 that the state force individuals convicted of driving under the influence of alcohol to wear special uniforms with "D-U-I" printed across the back—shades here of the scarlet "D" worn by Robert Cole in Puritan Massachusetts—many Tennesseans, not surprisingly, objected vigorously.

Thus, it is entirely possible that Americans have reached a tacit but important final decision on drinking: If they have accepted alcohol as a normal part of life, they have also decided that dealing with the problems of alcohol—barring any breakthroughs on the treatment or prevention fronts—is an equally normal social function. The alcohol question will be a matter not of eliminating alcoholism but of keeping drinking and any problems it creates within limits society can tolerate. This attitude, no matter how unpalatable to some, may represent the new consensus on drinking in America. In some ways, it may represent a more flexible return to the orderly communal ideals of the past.

Appendix:

Apparent Consumption of Alcoholic Beverages and Absolute Alcohol in Each Class of Beverage, in U.S. Gallons per Capita of the Drinking-age Population, U.S.A. 1790-1985 [a] [b]

	Spirits[b]		Wine[b]		Beer[b]		Total
	Beverage	Absolute Alcohol	Beverage	Absolute Alcohol	Beverage	Absolute Alcohol	Absolute Alcohol
1790	5.10	2.30	0.60	0.10	34.00	3.40	5.80
1800	7.20	3.30	0.60	0.10	32.00	3.20	6.60
1810	8.70	3.90	0.40	0.10	31.30	3.10	7.10
1820	8.70	3.90	0.40	0.10	28.00	2.80	6.80
1830	9.50	4.30	0.50	0.10	27.00	2.70	7.10
1840	5.50	2.50	0.50	0.10	6.30	0.50	3.10
1850	4.17	1.88	0.46	0.08	2.70	0.14	2.10
1860	4.79	2.16	0.57	0.10	5.39	0.27	2.53
1870	3.40	1.53	0.53	0.10	8.73	0.44	2.07
1871–80	2.27	1.02	0.77	0.14	11.26	0.56	1.72
1881–90	2.12	0.95	0.76	0.14	17.94	0.90	1.99
1891–95	2.12	0.95	0.60	0.11	23.42	1.17	2.23
1896–1900	1.72	0.77	0.55	0.10	23.72	1.19	2.06
1901–05	2.11	0.95	0.71	0.13	26.20	1.31	2.39
1906–10	2.14	0.96	0.92	0.17	29.27	1.47	2.60
1911–15	2.09	0.94	0.79	0.14	29.53	1.48	2.56
1916–19	1.68	0.76	0.69	0.12	21.63	1.08	1.96
1920–30[c]	—	—	—	—	—	—	0.90

	Spirits[b]		Wine[b]		Beer[b]		Total
	Beverage	Absolute Alcohol	Beverage	Absolute Alcohol	Beverage	Absolute Alcohol	Absolute Alcohol
1934	0.64	0.29	0.36	0.07	13.58	0.61	0.97
1935	0.96	0.43	0.50	0.09	15.13	0.68	1.20
1936–41	1.40	0.63	0.80	0.14	17.22	0.77	1.54
1942–46	1.84	0.83	1.11	0.18	23.44	1.05	2.06
1947–50	1.63	0.73	1.12	0.20	23.76	1.07	2.00
1951–55	1.69	0.76	1.20	0.21	22.79	1.03	2.00
1956–60	1.82	0.82	1.28	0.22	21.81	0.98	2.02
1961–65	2.03	0.92	1.38	0.23	22.42	1.01	2.16
1966–70	2.42	1.09	1.57	0.26	24.50	1.10	2.45
1971	2.62	1.18	2.08	0.33	25.90	1.17	2.68
1972	2.60	1.12	2.16	0.31	26.62	1.20	2.63
1973	2.61	1.12	2.25	0.33	27.49	1.24	2.69
1974	2.57	1.10	2.13	0.31	27.76	1.25	2.66
1975	2.58	1.11	2.24	0.32	28.08	1.26	2.69
1976	2.54	1.09	2.26	0.33	28.09	1.26	2.68
1977	2.56	1.10	2.37	0.34	29.05	1.31	2.75
1978	2.60	1.12	2.51	0.36	29.78	1.34	2.82
1980	2.51	1.03	2.64	0.34	30.79	1.39	2.76
1985	2.18	0.90	2.99	0.34	29.68	1.34	2.58

[One U.S. gallon = 3.785 liters = 0.833 imperial gallon.]

Source: Except for the prohibition period and 1985, this appendix is reproduced, with permission, from a table in Merton M. Hyman, Marilyn A. Zimmermann, Carol Gurioli, and Alice Helrich, *Drinkers, Drinking, and Alcohol-Related Mortality and Hospitalizations: A Statistical Compendium* (New Brunswick, 1980) (copyright 1980, *Journal of Studies on Alcohol,* Inc.). Figures for 1985 are the authors' estimates, based on data reported from industry sources and in *Jobson's Wine Marketing Handbook, 1985* (New York, 1985) and *Jobson's Liquor Handbook, 1986* (New York, 1986). "Alcoholic Beverage Consumption in the United States," *The Bottom Line,* 7(1986), 15–17.

[a]Through 1973 the drinking-age population was the population aged 15 years and over; data since 1973 . . . are based on a drinking-age population aged 14 and over. [The table does] not show the illegally produced alcohol that enters consumption; [it is] based on "tax-paid withdrawals."

[b]Through 1971 the average absolute alcohol content in distilled spirits was assumed to be 45%; beginning in 1972 that percentage has been changed to 43. Through 1951 the average alcohol content of wine was assumed to be 18%; in 1952–68, 17%; in 1969–71, 16%; beginning in 1972, 14.5%. The beer data through 1840 essentially reflect consumption of cider, the average alcohol content of which was assumed to be 10% by volume; through 1919 the average alcohol content of beer was assumed to be 5% by volume; since 1934, 4.5%.

[c]For the prohibition years, we have adapted the total absolute alcohol figures provided in W. J. Rorabaugh, *The Alcoholic Republic: An American Tradition* (New York, 1979). Between 1930 and 1933, absolute alcohol consumption probably rose slightly, perhaps to just over one gallon per year.

Sources

General

The most helpful single source in researching *Drinking in America* was the library of the Rutgers University Center of Alcohol Studies. The center has perhaps the best collection of alcohol-related literature in the world, and we took particular advantage of the scientific and social science references contained in the vast *Classified Abstract Archive of the Alcohol Literature*. The key to this collection is the *CAAAL Manual: A Guide to the Use of the Classified Abstract Archive of the Alcohol Literature* (New Brunswick, 1965), prepared by Mark Keller, Vera Efron, and E. M. Jellinek. The Raymond G. McCarthy Memorial Collection holds the full-text originals of the works abstracted in CAAAL, including considerable material from the nineteenth and early twentieth centuries. The center also maintains an extensive file of uncatalogued nineteenth- and twentieth-century documents—newspaper clippings, legal briefs, surveys, reports, pamphlets, and manuscripts (notably the "Minute Book of the Sons of Temperance of Milton, N.J., 1871-72"). The files are kept in boxes (there are over eighty) arranged by category ("Temperance," "Prohibition," "Attitudes," "Advertising and Propaganda," etc.), and we mined this wealth of information liberally. In addition, the library also holds a substantial number of early texts on drinking customs, beverage production, and the views of the temperance movement (including a fine collection of temperance fiction).

We also found good collections of temperance fiction—crucial to understanding popular attitudes toward drinking and alcoholism from the antebellum period to the 1900s—in the Alexander Library of Rutgers University, the libraries of Princeton and Northwestern universities, the Willard Library in the national headquarters of the Woman's Christian Temperance Union in Evanston, Illinois, and the New York Public Library. We looked at a great many titles and have cited selected volumes in the chapter references.

The Willard Library was an especially rich source. It has a fine collection of temperance periodicals and, of course, WCTU records on both national and state activities. The Willard Library also offered an excellent opportunity to select graphic materials not available elsewhere.

Although we were interested primarily in illustrated matter, the following yielded valuable materials for our text: Harry T. Peters Collection, Museum of the City of New York; Still Picture Branch, National Archives, Washington, D.C.; and the Picture Collection, Library of Congress, Washington, D.C.

We used the social science and medical literature extensively and cite specific works both in the text and in the chapter sources. We relied on the following works on a general basis: Don Cahalan, Ira Cisin, and Helen Crossley, *American Drinking Practices: A National Study of Drinking Behavior and Attitudes* (New Brunswick, 1969); Don Cahalan and Robin Room, *Problem Drinking among American Men* (New Brunswick, 1974); Mark Keller and Mairi McCormick, *A Dictionary of Words about Alcohol* (New Brunswick, 1968); Benjamin Kissin and Henri Begleiter, eds., *The Biology of Alcoholism*, 5 vols.(New York, 1971–77); Harry Milt, *The Revised Basic Handbook on Alcoholism* (Maplewood, N.J., 1977); M. H. Moore and D. R. Gerstein, eds., *Alcohol and Public Policy: Beyond the Shadow of Prohibition* (Washington, 1981); Jack H. Mendelson and Nancy K. Mello, *Alcohol: Use and Abuse in America* (Boston, 1985); E. M. Jellinek, *The Disease Concept of Alcoholism* (Highland Park, N.J., 1960); Merton M. Hyman, Marilyn A. Zimmermann, Carol Gurioli, and Alice Helrich, *Drinkers, Drinking, and Alcohol-Related Mortality and Hospitalizations: A Statistical Compendium* (New Brunswick, 1980); U.S. National Institute on Alcohol Abuse and Alcoholism, *Alcohol and Health: New Knowledge. Second Special Report to the Congress* (Washington, D.C., 1975); and U.S. National Institute on Alcohol Abuse and Alcoholism, *Third Special Report to the U.S. Congress on Alcohol and Health,* ed. Ernest P. Noble (Washington, D.C., 1978). A convenient and reliable guide to the alcohol literature, especially in the social sciences, is Penny Booth Page, *Alcohol Use & Alcoholism: A Guide to the Literature* (New York, 1986).

Numerous books discuss various aspects of the history of American beverages. Many are of an antiquarian bent, but the following all have something to recommend them: John Hull Brown, *Early American Beverages* (Rutland, Vt., 1966); Gerald Carson, *The Social History of Bourbon: An Unhurried Account of Our Star-Spangled American Drink* (reprint, Lexington, Ky., 1984); Frank Schoonmaker and Tom Marvel, *American Wines* (New York, 1941); Vincent P. Carosso, *The California Wine Industry, 1830–1845: A Study of the Formative Years* (Berkeley, 1951); John Doxat, *Drinks and Drinking* (London, 1971); Harry B. Weiss and Grace M. Weiss, *The Early Breweries of New Jersey* (Trenton, 1963); Morris Weeks, Jr., *Beer and Brewing in America* (New York, 1949); United Brewers Industrial Foundation, *American Beer and Ale: A Handbook of Facts and Figures* (New York, c.1937); Edward R. Emerson, *Beverages, Past and Present: An Historical Sketch . . . ,* 2 vols. (New York, 1908); Stanley Baron, *Brewed in America: A History of Beer and Ale in the United States* (Boston, 1962); Roland Krebs, *Making Friends Is Our Business: 100 Years of Anheuser-Busch* (n.p., 1953); Harry B. Weiss, *The History of Applejack* (Trenton, 1954); and Oscar Getz, *Pictorial History of Whiskey* (n.p., 1975).

The theme of neorepublicanism had its roots in our reading of both primary source materials and the works of other historians. The following studies were among the most helpful in shaping the theme—although we should note that their authors would not necessarily agree with our interpretation: John J. Rumbarger, "The Social Origins and Function of the Political Temperance Movement in the Reconstruction of American Society, 1825–1917" (Ph.D. thesis, University of Pennsylvania, 1968); James R. Turner, "The American Prohibition Movement, 1865–1897" (Ph.D. thesis, University of Wisconsin, 1972); Edna Tutt Frederickson, "John P. St. John: The Father of Constitutional Prohibition" (Ph.D. thesis, University of Kansas, 1930); Jed Dannenbaum, *Drink and Disorder: Temperance Reform in Cincinnati from the Washingtonian Revival to the WCTU* (Urbana, 1984); Clifford S. Griffin, *Their Brothers' Keepers: Moral Stewardship in the United States, 1800–1865* (New Brunswick, 1960); Norman H. Clark, *Deliver Us from Evil: An Interpretation of American*

Prohibition (New York, 1976); Paul A. Carter, *The Twenties in America* (2d ed., New York, 1975); and Robert H. Wiebe, *'The Search for Order, 1877–1920* (New York, 1967).

The struggle over the Eighteenth Amendment has a historical literature of its own. While we cite specific studies in the chapter references, the following titles (in addition to the works cited in the preceding paragraph) were especially useful in framing our overall approach to the issue. Old and unabashedly protemperance, but still a superb source, is Daniel Dorchester's monumental *Liquor Problem in All Ages* (New York, 1888); Ernest H. Cherrington, *The Evolution of Prohibition in the United States of America* (Westerville, Ohio, 1920), is a helpful chronology. Worth reading, but sometimes dominated by overt hostility to the temperance movement, are Andrew Sinclair, *Prohibition: The Era of Excess* (Boston, 1962), and John Kobler, *Ardent Spirits: The Rise and Fall of Prohibition* (New York, 1973). No friend of the drys either, but possessed of a great deal of information and a breezy style, is J. C. Furnas, *The Life and Times of the Late Demon Rum* (New York, 1965). *The Dry Decade* (New York, 1931), by Charles Merz, has stood up very well over time, and still standard is John A. Krout, *The Origins of Prohibition* (New York, 1925). A recent collection of essays—Jack S. Blocker, Jr., ed., *Alcohol, Reform, and Society: The Liquor Issue in Social Context* (Westport, Conn., 1979)—is rewarding and offers fresh points of view on a number of questions, as does David E. Kyvig, ed., *Law, Alcohol, and Order: Perspectives on National Prohibition* (Westport, Conn., 1985). John C. Burnham's "New Perspectives on the Prohibition 'Experiment' of the 1920s," *Journal of Social History II* (1968):51–68, is properly regarded as a minor classic in the field. Additional information on alcohol reform leaders may be found in Mark Edward Lender, *Dictionary of American Temperance Biography: From Temperance Reform to Alcohol Research, the 1600s to the 1980s* (Westport, Conn., 1985). Comprehensive, but biased and marred by some serious inaccuracies, is Ernest Cherrington, ed., *The Standard Encyclopedia of the Alcohol Problem*, 6 vols. (Westerville, Ohio, 1924–28). Even its blatantly Anti-Saloon League stance, however, offers insight into temperance views on any number of matters. Less formal, but still useful, are Donald Barr Chidsey, *On and Off the Wagon: A Sober Analysis of the Temperance Movement from the Pilgrims to Prohibition* (New York, 1969); Thomas M. Coffey, *The Long Thirst: Prohibition in America* (New York, 1975); and Herbert Asbury, *The Great Illusion: An Informal History of Prohibition* (New York, 1950).

We need more studies of the liquor question at the state level, but of those we have, many are of good caliber. In aggregate, they show clearly that most Americans took the wet-dry wars seriously and did not see it, as some authors have alleged, as a peripheral matter "put over" by scheming minorities or dedicated fanatics. We relied on the following works: Earl C. Kaylor, Jr., "The Prohibition Movement in Pennsylvania, 1865–1920" (Ph.D. thesis, Pennsylvania State University, 1963); Larry D. Engelmann, "O Whiskey: The History of Prohibition in Michigan" (Ph.D. thesis, University of Michigan, 1971), revised and published as *Intemperance: The Lost War against Liquor* (New York, 1979); Gilman Ostrander, *The Prohibition Movement in California, 1848–1933* (Berkeley, 1957); Norman H. Clark, *The Dry Years: Prohibition and Social Change in Washington* (Seattle, 1965); Paul E. Isaac, *Prohibition and Politics: Turbulent Decades in Tennessee, 1885–1920* (Knoxville, 1965); Harry Malcolm Chalfant, *Father Penn and John Barleycorn* (Harrisburg, 1920); C. C. Pearson and J. Edwin Hendricks, *Liquor and Anti-Liquor in Virginia, 1619–1919* (Durham, 1967); James B. Sellers, *The Prohibition Movement in Alabama, 1702–1943* (Chapel Hill, 1943); Daniel J. Whitener, *Prohibition in North Carolina, 1715–1945*

(Chapel Hill, 1945); William Elliott West, "Dry Crusade: The Prohibition Movement in Colorado, 1858–1933" (Ph.D. thesis, University of Colorado, 1971); G. K. Kenner, "Prohibition Comes to Missouri, 1910–1919," *Missouri Historical Review LXII* (1968): 363–97; Jimmie Lewis Franklin, *Born Sober: Prohibition in Oklahoma, 1907–1959* (Norman, 1971); Robert S. Bader, *Prohibition in Kansas: A History* (Lawrence, 1986); and Lewis L. Gould, *Progressives and Prohibitionists: Texas Democrats in the Wilson Era* (Austin, 1973).

Periodicals also constituted an important resource. In particular, they were one of the best ways to follow changing opinions—or quick reactions to specific events—on the part of many groups. The most helpful were the *Union Signal* (and the predecessor publications of the WCTU); the *American Issue* (Anti-Saloon League); the *Quarterly Journal of Inebriety* (American Association for the Study and Cure of Inebriety); the *Annual Statistical Review of the Distilled Spirits Industry* (published under various titles by the Distilled Spirits Institute and later by the Distilled Spirits Council of the United States); the *Brewers' Almanac* (United States Brewers' Association); the *Anti-Saloon League Year Book*; the *Journal* (Addiction Research Foundation, Toronto); the *Alcoholism Report* (Washington, D.C.); the *Journal of the American Medical Association;* the *Quarterly Journal of Studies on Alcohol* (in its earlier years, the voice of the Yale—now Rutgers—Center of Alcohol Studies; currently published as the *Journal of Studies on Alcohol*); the *Clipsheet* (Board of Temperance of the Methodist church); and the *Grapevine* (Alcoholics Anonymous).

ONE: The "Good Creature of God": Drinking in Early America

Books: Stanley Baron, *Brewed in America: A History of Beer and Ale in the United States* (Boston, 1962); Daniel Dorchester, *The Liquor Problem in All Ages* (New York, 1888); John C. Furnas, *The Life and Times of the Late Demon Rum* (New York, 1965); C. C. Pearson and J. Edwin Hendricks, *Liquor and Anti-Liquor in Virginia, 1619–1919* (Durham, 1967); Henry A. Scomp, *King Alcohol in the Realm of King Cotton* (n.p., 1888); Carl Bridenbaugh, *Cities in the Wilderness: The First Century of Urban Life in America, 1625–1742* (New York, 1938); G. Thomann, *Liquor Laws of the United States: Their Spirit and Effect* (New York, 1887); George Lee Haskins, *Law and Authority in Early Massachusetts: A Study in Tradition and Design* (New York, 1960); Richard S. Dunn, *Puritans and Yankees: The Winthrop Dynasty of New England, 1630–1717* (New York, 1971); Edmund S. Morgan, *The Puritan Family: Religion and Domestic Relations in Seventeenth-Century New England* (rev.ed., New York, 1966); John A. Krout, *The Origins of Prohibition* (New York, 1925); Thomas J. Wertenbaker, *The Puritan Oligarchy* (New York, 1947); Samuel Eliot Morison, *Builders of the Bay Colony* (rev. ed., Boston, 1964); William Bradford, *Of Plymouth Plantation,* ed. Samuel Eliot Morison (New York, 1952); Cotton Mather, *Diary of Cotton Mather, 1681–1709,* Vol. I (New York, 1911); B. B. James and J. F. Jameson, eds., *Journal of Jasper Danckaerts, 1679–1680* (New York, 1912); J. H. Trumbull, ed., *The Public Records of the Colony of Connecticut,* Vol. I (Hartford, 1850); *Report of the Record Commissioners of the City of Boston: Dorchester Town Records* (3d ed., Boston, 1896); *Report of the Record Commissioners of the City of Boston: Boston Records from 1660 to 1701* (Boston, 1881); *Report of the Record Commissioners Containing the Roxbury Land and Church Records* (2d ed., Boston, 1884); Samuel Sewell, *Diary,* ed. Mark Van Doren (New York, 1927); Nathaniel B. Shurtleff, ed., *Records of the Governor and Company of Massachusetts Bay in New England,* 5 vols. (Boston, 1853–54); Thomas Anburey, *Travels through the Interior Parts of America,* 2 vols. (London, 1789);

Johann D. Schoepf, *Travels in the Confederation*, ed. Andrew J. Morrison, 2 vols. (Philadelphia, 1911); Andrew Burnaby, *Travels through the Middle Settlements in North America in the Years 1759 and 1760* (London, 1798); J. F. D. Smyth, *A Tour in the United States of America* (London, 1784); Philip A. Bruce, *Institutional History of Virginia in the Seventeenth Century*, 2 vols. (New York, 1910); John Stokes Adams, ed., *An Autobiographical Sketch of John Marshall* (Ann Arbor, 1937); W. J. Rorabaugh, *The Alcoholic Republic: An American Tradition* (New York, 1979); Charles S. Sydnor, *Gentlemen Freeholders* (Chapel Hill, 1952); Lorenzo Johnston Greene, *The Negro in Colonial New England* (New York, 1942); John R. Larkins, *Alcohol and the Negro: Explosive Issues* (Zebulon, N.C., 1965); Jerrold E. Levy and Stephen J. Kunitz, *Indian Drinking* (New York, 1974); Craig MacAndrew and Robert B. Edgerton, *Drunken Comportment* (Chicago, 1969); Joy Leland, *The Firewater Myths* (New Brunswick, 1976); Gerald Carson, *The Social History of Bourbon* (reprint, Lexington, Ky., 1984); Harry B. Weiss, *The History of Applejack* (Trenton, 1954); Willard R. Jillson, *Early Kentucky Distillers* (Louisville, 1940); Alice M. Earle, *Home Life in Colonial Days* (New York, 1898); William Byrd, *The Secret Diary . . . , 1709-1712*, ed. Louis B. Wright (Richmond, 1941); William B. Weeden, *Economic and Social History of New England* (Boston, 1891); Hewson L. Peke, *Americana Ebrietatis* (New York, 1917); Elise Lathrop, *Early American Inns and Taverns* (New York, 1937); Edward Field, *The Colonial Tavern* (Providence, 1897); Bernard Bailyn, *The New England Merchants in the Seventeenth Century* (Cambridge, Mass., 1955); Victor S. Clark, *History of Manufactures in the United States* (Washington, D.C., 1916); L. H. Butterfield, ed., *The Diary and Autobiography of John Adams*, 4 vols. (Cambridge, Mass., 1961); Benjamin Rush, *The Autobiography of Benjamin Rush . . . ,* ed. George W. Corner (Princeton, 1948); David Freeman Hawke, *Benjamin Rush: Revolutionary Gadfly* (Indianapolis, 1971).

Articles: Dean Albertson, "Puritan Liquor in the Planting of New England," *New England Quarterly XXIII* (1950):477-90; "John Dane's Narrative, 1682," *New England Historical and Genealogical Register VIII* (1854):147-56; E. G. Baird, "The Alcohol Problem and the Law: III. The Beginnings of Alcohol-Beverage Control Laws in America," *Quarterly Journal of Studies on Alcohol VI* (1945):335-83, *VII* (1946):110-62; Mark Edward Lender, "Drunkenness as an Offense in Early New England: A Study of 'Puritan' Attitudes," *Quarterly Journal of Studies on Alcohol XXXIV* (1973): 353-66; Allyn B. Forbes, ed., "The Autobiography of Thomas Shepard," *Publications of the Colonial Society of Massachusetts XXVII* (1932):321-400; Douglass Adair, ed., "James Madison's Autobiography," *William and Mary Quarterly*, 3d ser., *II* (1945):191-209; "Diary of Colonel Landon Carter," *William and Mary Quarterly*, 1st scr., *XVI* (1908):149-56, 257-69; Fleming Nevin, "The Liquor Question in Colonial and Revolutionary War Periods," *Western Pennsylvania Historical Magazine XIII* (1930):195-201; Timothy G. Coffey, "Beer Street, Gin Lane: Some Views of 18th-Century Drinking," *Quarterly Journal of Studies on Alcohol XXVII* (1966):669-92; Harry G. Levine, "The Discovery of Addiction: Changing Conceptions of Habitual Drunkenness in America," *Journal of Studies on Alcohol XXXIX* (1978):143-74; W. D. Houlette, "Rum-Trading in the American Colonies before 1763," *Journal of American History XXVII* (1934):129-52; Nancy Oestreich Lurie, "The World's Oldest On-going Protest Demonstration: North American Indian Drinking Patterns," *Pacific Historical Review XL* (1971):311-32; Joseph Westermeyer, " 'The Drunken Indian': Myths and Realities," *Psychiatric Annals IV* (1974):29-36; R. C. Dailey, "The Role of Alcohol among North American Indian Tribes as Reported in the *Jesuit Relations*," *Anthropologica X* (1968):45-57; Gilman M. Ostrander, "The Making of the Triangular Trade Myth," *William and Mary Quarterly*, 3d ser., *XXX* (1973): 635–44; Arthur M. Schlesinger, Sr., "A Dietary Interpretation of American History," *Massachusetts Historical Society Proceedings LXVIII* (1944–47):199–227; Henry B. Parkes, "Morals and Law Enforcement in Colonial New England," *New England Quarterly V* (1932):431–52; John May, "Journal of Col. John May . . . Relative to a Journey to the Ohio Country, 1789," *Pennsylvania Magazine of History and Biography XLV* (1929):101–79.

Pamphlets: Increase Mather, *Wo to Drunkards* (Cambridge, Mass., 1673); Cotton Mather, *Sober Considerations, on a Growing Flood of Iniquity: . . . the Woful Consequences [of] the Prevailing Abuse of Rum* (Boston, 1708); Samuel Danforth, *The Woful Effects of Drunkenness* (Boston, 1710); Samuel Willard, *The Peril of the Times Displayed* (Boston, 1700); *The Indictment and Tryal of Sr Richard Rum* (3d ed., Boston, 1724); George Whitefield, *The Heinous Sin of Drunkenness* (Philadelphia, 1740); Anthony Benezet, *The Mighty Destroyer Displayed* (Trenton, 1779 [orig. 1774]); Anthony Benezet, *Remarks on the Nature and Bad Effects of Spiritous Liquors* (Philadelphia, 1774); Benjamin Rush, *An Inquiry into the Effects of Spiritous Liquors on the Human Body* (Boston, 1790); Benjamin Rush, *An Inquiry into the Effects of Ardent Spirits upon the Human Mind and Body, with an Account of the Means of Preventing and of the Remedies for Curing Them* (8th ed., Brookfield, Mass., 1814).

Documents: *Report of the Special Commission to Investigate the Problem of Drunkenness in Massachusetts* (Boston, 1945); U.S. National Institute on Alcohol Abuse and Alcoholism, *Third Special Report to the U.S. Congress on Alcohol and Health,* ed. Ernest P. Noble (Washington, D.C., 1978).

Other: John J. McCusker, Jr., "The Rum Trade and the Balance of Payments of the Thirteen Continental Colonies" (Ph.D. thesis, University of Pittsburgh, 1970); Karen R. Stubaus, " 'The Good Creatures': Drinking Law and Custom in Seventeenth-Century Massachusetts and Virginia" (Ph.D. thesis, Rutgers University, 1984); David Joel Mishkin, "The American Colonial Wine Industry: An Economic Interpretation" (Ph.D. thesis, University of Illinois, 1967); Ann Pinson, "The New England Rum Era: Drinking Styles and Social Change in Newport, R.I., 1720–1770" (Working Papers on Alcohol and Human Behavior, no. 8, Department of Anthropology, Brown University, 1980).

TWO: Metamorphosis: From "Good Creature" to "Demon Rum," 1790–1860

Books: Clifford S. Griffin, *Their Brothers' Keepers: Moral Stewardship in the United States* (New Brunswick, 1960); Alice Felt Tyler, *Freedom's Ferment: Phases of American Social History from the Colonial Period to the Outbreak of the Civil War* (New York, 1962 [orig. 1944]); Ian R. Tyrrell, *Sobering Up: From Temperance to Prohibition in Antebellum America, 1800–1860* (Westport, Conn., 1979); Jed Dannenbaum, *Drink and Disorder: Temperance Reform in Cincinnati from the Washingtonian Revival to the WCTU* (Urbana, 1984); John Kobler, *Ardent Spirits: The Rise and Fall of Prohibition* (New York, 1973); Frank L. Byrne, *Prophet of Prohibition: Neal Dow and His Crusade* (Madison, 1961); W. J. Rorabaugh, *The Alcoholic Republic: An American Tradition* (New York, 1979); Merton M. Hyman, Marilyn A. Zimmermann, Carol Gurioli, and Alice Helrich, *Drinkers, Drinking, and Alcohol-Related Mortality and Hospitalizations: A Statistical Compen-*

dium (New Brunswick, 1980); Daniel Dorchester, *The Liquor Problem in All Ages* (New York, 1888); Frederick Marryat, *A Diary in America,* 3 vols. (London, 1839); Charles J. Latrobe, *The Rambler in North America, 1832-1833,* 2 vols. (London, 1835); Basil Hall, *Travels in North America in the Years 1827 and 1828,* 3 vols. (Edinburgh, 1829); A. T. Jackson, *The Diary of a Forty-niner* (New York, 1906); Thomas D. Clark, *The Rampaging Frontier* (Indianapolis, 1939); R. G. Cleland, *This Reckless Breed of Men: The Trapper and Fur Traders of the Southwest* (New York, 1950); E. C. Abbott and H. H. Smith, *We Pointed Them North: Recollections of a Cowpuncher* (Norman, 1939); Elliott West, *The Saloon on the Rocky Mountain Mining Frontier* (Lincoln, Neb., 1979); Leland D. Baldwin, *Whiskey Rebels: The Story of a Frontier Uprising* (Pittsburgh, 1939); Steven R. Boyd, ed., *The Whiskey Rebellion: Past and Present Perspectives* (Westport, Conn., 1985); Norman H. Clark, *Deliver Us from Evil: An Interpretation of American Prohibition* (New York, 1976); Sister Joan Bland, *Hibernian Crusade: The Story of the Catholic Total Abstinence Union of America* (Washington, D.C., 1951); Richard Stivers, *A Hair of the Dog: Irish Drinking and American Stereotype* (University Park, Pa., 1977); Ray A. Billington, *The Protestant Crusade, 1800-1860: A Study of the Origins of American Nativism* (New York, 1938); Paul E. Johnson, *A Shopkeeper's Millennium: Society and Revivals in Rochester, New York, 1815-1837* (New York, 1978); Lyman Beecher, *Autobiography, Correspondence . . . ,* ed. Charles Beecher (New York, 1865); Lyman Beecher, *Six Sermons on the Nature, Occasions, Sins, Evils, and Remedy of Intemperance* (New York, 1827); *Permanent Temperance Documents of the American Temperance Society* (Boston, 1836); *Temperance Manual of the American Temperance Society* (Boston, 1836); *Centennial Temperance Volume: A Memorial of the International Temperance Conference . . .1876* (New York, 1877); John B. Gough, *An Autobiography* (Boston, 1845); John B. Gough, *Platform Echoes* (Hartford, 1886); Charles Jewett, *Speeches, Poems, and Miscellaneous Writings . . . on Temperance and the Liquor Traffic* (Boston, 1849); Patrick Rodgers, *Father Theobald Mathew: Apostle of Temperance* (New York, 1935); W. A. Hallock, *Light and Love: A Sketch of the Life and Labors of the Rev. Justin Edwards, D.D.* (New York, 1855); Timothy Shay Arthur, *Ten Nights in a Bar-Room, and What I Saw There* (Boston, 1854); Timothy Shay Arthur, *Temperance Tales: Or, Six Nights with the Washingtonians* (Philadelphia, 1848); Lucius Manlices Sargent, *Temperance Tales,* 6 vols. (New York, 1848); Sons of Temperance, *The Fountain and the Bottle: Comprising Thrilling Examples of the Opposite Effects of Temperance and Intemperance* (Hartford, 1850).

Articles: George F. Talbot, "Temperance and the Drink Question in the Old Time," *Maine Historical Society Collections,* 2d ser., *VI* (1895):357-92; William Breitenbach, "Sons of the Fathers: Temperance Reformers and the Legacy of the American Revolution," *Journal of the Early Republic III* (1983):69-82; John Q. Anderson, "Drinking, Fighting, and Fooling: Sidelights of the Social History of Antebellum Louisiana," *Louisiana History V* (1965):29-40; "Moderate Drinking: Its Results," *American Temperance Magazine II* (1851):261-66; "What Is to Be Done?" *American Temperance Magazine II* (1851):307-11; "John B. Gough," *American Temperance Magazine I* (1851):387-91; Allan M. Winkler, "Drinking on the American Frontier," *Quarterly Journal of Studies on Alcohol XXIX* (1968):413-45; Mark Keller, "The Evils of Drunkenness as Sketched by George Cruikshank," *Quarterly Journal of Studies on Alcohol V* (1944):483-504; Mark Edward Lender and Karen R. Karnchanapee, " 'Temperance Tales': Antiliquor Fiction and American Attitudes toward Alcoholics in the Late 19th and Early 20th Centuries," *Journal of Studies on Alcohol XXXVIII* (1977):1347-70; "The Cause in Ireland," *Prohibitionist II* (1855):54; Frank L. Byrne, "Maine Law Versus Lager Beer: A Dilemma of Wisconsin's Young Republican Party," *Wisconsin Magazine of History XLII* (1958–59):115–20; Milton A. Maxwell, "The Washingtonian Movement," *Quarterly Journal of Studies on Alcohol XI* (1950):410–51; Leonard U. Blumberg, "The Significance of the Alcohol Prohibitionists for the Washington Temperance Societies: With Special Reference to Paterson and Newark, New Jersey," *Journal of Studies on Alcohol XLI* (1980):37–77.

Pamphlets: Leonard Bacon, *Total Abstinence from Ardent Spirits* (New Haven, 1829); Leonard Bacon, *A Discourse on the Traffic in Spiritous Liquors . . .* (New Haven, 1838); [Evesham, N.J., Association for Discouraging the Unnecessary Use of Ardent Spirits], *Extracts and Observatons on the Customary Use of Ardent Spirits . . .* (Philadelphia, 1823); H. D. Kitchel, *An Appeal to the People for the Suppression of the Spirit Traffic* (Hartford, 1845); Abiel Abbot, *An Address, Delivered before the Massachusetts Society for Suppressing Intemperance . . .* (Cambridge, Mass., 1815); William E. Channing, *An Address on Temperance* (Boston, 1837); Daniel Drake, *A Discourse on Intemperance* (Cincinnati, 1828); Justin Edwards, *The Well-Conducted Farm*, American Tract Society, no. 176 (New York, c. 1835); *Proceedings of the Fourth National Temperance Convention, Saratoga, N.Y., 1851* (New York, 1851).

Periodicals: *Congressional Globe* (Washington, D.C.); *New York Times; Brooklyn Daily Eagle; New York Herald; New York Independent; New York Tribune; American Museum* (Philadelphia); *Temperance Recorder* (Albany); *Enquirer* (Albany); *American Temperance Magazine* (New York).

Documents: Historical Files, "Temperance" (uncatalogued materials), Boxes 1–3, "Prohibition" (uncatalogued materials), Box 1, Rutgers Center of Alcohol Studies Library, Rutgers University; Harry T. Peters Collection (graphic materials), Museum of the City of New York.

Other: Donald Weldon Beattie, "Sons of Temperance: Pioneers in Total Abstinence and 'Constitutional Prohibition'" (Ph.D. thesis, Boston University, 1966); Jean R. Kirkpatrick, "The Temperance Movement and Temperance Fiction, 1820–1860" (Ph.D. thesis, University of Pennsylvania, 1970); John J. Rumbarger, "The Social Origins and Function of the Political Temperance Movement in the Reconstruction of American Society, 1825–1917" (Ph.D. thesis, University of Pennsylvania, 1968).

THREE: Search for Consensus: Drinking and the War Against Pluralism, 1860–1920

Books: Robert H. Wiebe, *The Search for Order, 1877–1920* (New York, 1967); Ernest H. Cherrington, *The Evolution of Prohibition in the United States* (Westerville, Ohio, 1920); Leigh D. Colvin, *Prohibition in the United States* (New York, 1926); Eliza Stewart, *Memories of the Crusade* (Chicago, 1890); James Black, *Brief History of Prohibition and the Prohibition Reform Party* (New York, 1880); Henry Blair, *The Temperance Movement* (Boston, 1888); Daniel Dorchester, *The Liquor Problem in All Ages* (New York, 1888); *The Woman's Dictionary and Encyclopedia* (Akron, 1909); George M. Hammell, ed., *The Passing of the Saloon . . .* (Cincinnati, 1908); Perry R. Duis, *The Saloon: Public Drinking in Chicago and Boston, 1880–1920* (Urbana, 1983); George Howell, *The Case of Whiskey* (Altadena, Calif., 1928); James Timberlake, *Prohibition and the Progressive Movement, 1900–1920* (Cambridge, Mass., 1963); Robert Hunter, *Poverty* (New

York, 1904); John Koren, *Economic Aspects of the Liquor Problem* (Boston, 1899); Robert H. Bremner, *From the Depths: The Discovery of Poverty in the United States* (New York, 1956); Leonard U. Blumberg, Thomas E. Shipley, Jr., and Stephen F. Barsky, *Liquor and Poverty: Skid Row as a Human Condition* (New Brunswick, 1979); Annie Wittenmeyer, *History of the Woman's Temperance Crusade* (Philadelphia, 1878); Frances Willard, *Glimpses of Fifty Years* (Columbus, 1889); Frances Willard, *Woman and Temperance* (Hartford, 1883); Mary R. Melendy, *The Ideal Woman* (n.p., 1915); *The 1914 Year Book of the United States Brewers' Association. Containing the Reports . . . on the Alcohol Question and Saloon-Reform* (New York, 1914); John D. Venable, *Out of the Shadow: The Story of Charles Edison* (East Orange, N.J., 1978); G. Thomann, *Real and Imaginary Effects of Intemperance: A Statistical Sketch* (New York, 1884); Archbishop John Ireland, *The Church and Modern Society* (Chicago, 1896); Barbara L. Epstein, *The Politics of Domesticity: Women, Evangelism, and Temperance in Nineteenth-Century America* (Middletown, Conn., 1981); Ruth Bordin, *Women and Temperance: The Quest for Power and Liberty, 1873–1900* (Philadelphia, 1981); Jack S. Blocker, Jr., *'Give to the Wind Thy Fears': The Women's Temperance Crusade, 1873–1874* (Westport, Conn., 1985); Timothy Shay Arthur, *Strong Drink: The Curse and the Cure* (Philadelphia, 1877); Albert Day, *Methomania: A Treatise on Alcoholic Poisoning* (Boston, 1867); *Centennial Temperance Volume: A Memorial of the International Temperance Conference . . . 1876* (New York, 1877); J. E. Turner, *The History of the First Inebriate Asylum in the World . . .* (New York, 1888); John King, *The American Family Physician: Or, Domestic Guide to Health* (Indianapolis, 1864); Thomas D. Crothers, ed., *The Disease of Inebriety* (New York, 1893); Thomas D. Crothers, *Inebriety: A Clinical Treatise . . .* (Cincinnati, 1911); George M. Beard, *Stimulants and Narcotics* (New York, 1871); Leslie Keeley, *The Nonheredity of Inebriety* (Chicago, 1896); C. S. Clark, *The Perfect Keeley Cure: Incidents at Dwight . . .* (Milwaukee, 1893); Ernest H. Cherrington, *History of the Anti-Saloon League* (Westerville, Ohio, 1913); K. Austin Kerr, *Organized for Reform: A New History of the Anti-Saloon League* (New Haven, 1985); Edward H. McKinley, *Marching to Glory: The History of the Salvation Army in the United States of America, 1880–1980* (San Francisco, 1980); Jack London, *John Barleycorn* (New York, 1913); Carry A. Nation, *The Use and Need of the Life of Carry A. Nation* (Topeka, 1909); Peter Odegard, *Pressure Politics: The Story of the Anti-Saloon League* (New York, 1928); Andrew Sinclair, *Prohibition: The Era of Excess* (Boston, 1962); Joseph R. Gusfield, *Symbolic Crusade: Status Politics and the American Temperance Movement* (Urbana, 1963); William Rufus Scott, *Revolt on Mount Sinai: The Puritan Retreat from Prohibition* (Pasadena, 1944).

Articles: Robert F. Bales, "Cultural Differences in the Rate of Alcoholism," *Quarterly Journal of Studies on Alcohol VI* (1946):482–98; Charles R. Snyder, "Culture and Jewish Sobriety: The Ingroup-Outgroup Factor," in David J. Pittman and Charles R. Snyder, eds., *Society, Culture, and Drinking Patterns* (New York, 1962), pp. 188–225; Albert P. Ullman, "Sociocultural Backgrounds of Alcoholism," *Annals of the American Academy of Political and Social Science: Understanding Alcoholism CCCXV* (1958): 48–59; A. J. Grover, "A Respectable Saloon," *Union Signal III* (1882):4; "Abolitionists and Prohibitionists: Or Moral Reform Embarrassed by Ultraism," *New Englander and Yale Review CCLXII* (1892):1–25; "Where Do They Come From?" *American Issue VIII* (1900):13; Archbishop John Ireland, "The Catholic Church and the Saloon," *North American Review CLIX* (1894):498–505; J. V. Tracy, "Prohibition and Catholics," *Catholic World LI* (1890):669–74; John G. Woolley, "Has the Prohibition Party Outlived Its Usefulness?" *Leslie's Weekly CX* (1910):488–95; Sarah E. Williams, "The Use of Beverage Alcohol as Medicine, 1790–1860," *Journal of Stud-*

ies on Alcohol XLI (1980):453–66; Thomas D. Crothers, "Are Inebriates Curable?" *Journal of the American Medical Association XVII* (1891):923–27; N. S. Davis, "Inebriate Asylums . . . ," *Quarterly Journal of Inebriety III* (1877):80–88; T. L. Mason, "Opening Address," *Quarterly Journal of Inebriety III* (1878):19–37; Leonard U. Blumberg, "The American Association for the Study and Cure of Inebriety," *Alcoholism: Clinical and Experimental Research II* (1978):234–40; Mark Edward Lender, "Jellinek's Typology of Alcoholism: Some Historical Antecedents," *Journal of Studies on Alcohol XL* (1979):361–75; Horatio M. Pollock, "A Statistical Study of 1,739 Patients with Alcoholic Psychoses," *State Hospital Bulletin* (New York) *VII* (1914):204–68; Mark Edward Lender, "Women Alcoholics: Prevalence Estimates and Their Problems as Reflected in Turn-of-the-Century Institutional Data," *International Journal of the Addictions XVI* (1981):443–48.

Pamphlets: G. Brown, *Lecture on Temperance, with Numerous Conundrums* (Paterson, N.J., 1873); Luther Benson, *Fifteen Years in Hell: An Autobiography* (Indianapolis, 1879); Thomas N. Doutney, *The Life-Struggle, Fall, and Reformation of Thomas N. Doutney* (Battle Creek, 1890); G. Thomann, *The Effects of Beer upon Those Who Make and Drink It* (New York, 1886); J. M. Van Buren, *Gospel Temperance: A New Principle* (New York, 1883); A. A. Miner, *Argument on the Right and Duty of Prohibition* (Boston, 1867); *Dr. Haines' Golden Specific for the Cure of Drunkenness* (Cincinnati, c.1887).

Periodicals: *Harper's Weekly; Atlantic Monthly; Liquor Man's Advocate; New York Times; North American Review; Quarterly Journal of Inebriety; Journal of the American Medical Association; American Journal of Insanity; Union Signal; American Issue; Boston Medical and Surgical Journal; Anti-Saloon League Year Book.*

Other: A. E. Wilkerson, "A History of the Concept of Alcoholism as a Disease" (D.S.W. thesis, University of Pennsylvania, 1967); Bartlett Campbell Jones, "The Debate over National Prohibition, 1920–1933" (Ph.D. thesis, Emory University, 1961); Norman H. Dohn, "The History of the Anti-Saloon League" (Ph.D. thesis, Ohio State University, 1959); Samuel Unger, "A History of the National Woman's Christian Temperance Union" (Ph.D. thesis, Ohio State University, 1933).

FOUR: Drier and Drier, and Wetter and Wetter: Drinking and the Pluralist Renaissance

Books: Jack S. Blocker, Jr., *Retreat from Reform: The Prohibition Movement in the United States, 1890–1913* (Westport, Conn., 1976); Jack S. Blocker, Jr., ed., *Alcohol, Reform, and Society: The Liquor Issue in Social Context* (Westport, Conn., 1979); David E. Kyvig, ed., *Law, Alcohol, and Order: Perspectives on National Prohibition* (Westport, Conn., 1985); Larry Engelmann, *Intemperance: The Lost War against Liquor* (New York, 1979); Louis Albert Banks, *The Lincoln Legion: The Story of Its Founder and Forerunners* (New York, 1903); Forrest E. Linder and Robert D. Grove, *Vital Statistics Rates in the United States, 1900–1940* (Washington, D.C., 1943); William E. Leuchtenburg, *Franklin D. Roosevelt and the New Deal, 1932–1940* (New York, 1963); Clarence Darrow and Victor S. Yarros, *The Prohibition Mania* (New York, 1927); Irving Fisher, *The "Noble Experiment"* (New York, 1930); Irving Fisher, *Prohibition at Its Worst* (rev. ed., New York, 1927); Clarence Darrow, *The Story of My Life* (New York, 1932); Upton Sinclair, *The Cup of Fury* (New York, 1956); Robert Lewis Taylor, *Vessel of Wrath: The Life and Times of Carry Nation* (New York, 1966); John Kobler, *Capone*

(New York, 1971); Frederic F. Van de Water, *The Real McCoy* (Garden City, 1931); Thomas M. Coffey, *The Long Thirst: Prohibition in America* (New York, 1975); Frederick Lewis Allen, *Only Yesterday: An Informal History of the 1920s* (New York, 1931); Martha Bensley Bruere, *Does Prohibition Work?* (New York, 1927); Clark Warburton, *The Economic Results of Prohibition* (New York, 1932); Donald Barr Chidsey, *On and Off the Wagon: A Sober Analysis of the Temperance Movement from the Pilgrims to Prohibition* (New York, 1969); Ella Boole, *Give Prohibtion Its Chance* (Evanston, 1929); Roland Krebs, *Making Friends Is Our Business: 100 Years of Anheuser-Busch* (n.p., 1953); Roy Asa Haynes, *Prohibition Inside and Out* (New York, 1923); Mabel Walker Willebrandt, *The Inside of Prohibition* (Indianapolis, 1929); Ernest Gordon, *When the Brewer Had the Stranglehold* (New York, 1930); Norman H. Clark, *Deliver Us from Evil: An Interpretation of American Prohibition* (New York, 1976); Harry S. Warner, *An Evolution in Understanding of the Problem of Alcohol: A History of Collegiate Idealism* (Boston, 1966); Paul A. Carter, *The Twenties in America* (2d ed., New York, 1975); David E. Kyvig, *Repealing National Prohibition* (Chicago, 1979); William C. Durant, ed., *Law Observance* (New York, 1929); Peter Odegard, *Pressure Politics: The Story of the Anti-Saloon League* (New York, 1928); Andrew Sinclair, *Prohibition: The Era of Excess* (Boston, 1962); Grace C. Root, *Women and Repeal: The Story of the Women's Organization for National Prohibition Reform* (New York, 1934); Ernest Gordon, *The Wrecking of the Eighteenth Amendment* (Francestown, N.H., 1943).

Articles: John C. Burnham, "New Perspectives on the Prohibition 'Experiment' of the 1920s," *Journal of Social History II* (1968):51–68; Samuel Crowther, "Prohibition or Poverty: An Interview with Henry Ford," *Ladies' Home Journal XLVII* (1930):56; "Temperance Reformers Whom Whiskey Advocates Eulogize," *American Issue VIII* (1900):4; "Prediction of a Kansas Editor," *American Issue XXXI* (1924):4; Ira Landrith, "Opposition to Prohibition Bolshevistic," *Union Signal XLIV* (1923):6; Walter F. Wilcox, "An Attempt to Measure Public Opinion about Repealing the Eighteenth Amendment," *Journal of the American Statistical Association XXVI* (1931):243–61; Paul A. Carter, "Prohibition and Democracy: The Noble Experiment Reassessed," *Wisconsin Magazine of History LVI* (1973):189–201.

Pamphlets: Evangeline Booth, *Some Have Stopped Drinking* (Westerville, Ohio, 1928); [Anti-Saloon League], *Fundamental Facts for Patriots: The Eighteenth Amendment, How Adopted . . .* (Westerville, Ohio, c.1927); Earl Godwin, *What Is Prohibition?* (Evanston, 1929).

Periodicals: *Union Signal; American Issue; New York Times.*

Documents: National Commission on Law Observance and Enforcement, *Enforcement of Prohibition Laws of the United States* (summary and 5 vols.), 71st Cong., 3d sess. (1930); U.S. Congress, Senate, Senate Subcommittee on the Committee on the Judiciary, "Modification or Repeal of National Prohibition," 72d Cong., 1st sess. (1932); Historical Files, "Prohibition" (uncatalogued materials), Box 1, Rutgers Center of Alcohol Studies Library, Rutgers University.

Other: Ronald Morris Benson, "American Workers and Temperance Reform, 1866–1933" (Ph.D. thesis, Notre Dame University, 1974); William Stuart Forth, "Wesley L. Jones: A Political Biography" (Ph.D. thesis, University of Washington, 1962); Dayton E. Heckman, "Prohibition Passes: The Story of the Association Against the Prohibition Amendment" (Ph.D. thesis, Ohio State University, 1939).

FIVE: The Age of Ambivalence: Drinking in
Modern America

Books: *Alcoholics Anonymous: The Story of How Many Thousands of Men and Women Have Recovered from Alcoholism* (3d ed., New York, 1976); Ernest Kurtz, *Not-God: A History of Alcoholics Anonymous* (Center City, Minn., 1979); Robert Thomsen, *Bill W.* (New York, 1975); [William Griffith Wilson et al.], *Alcoholics Anonymous Comes of Age* (New York, 1957); Charles Jackson, *The Lost Weekend* (New York, 1944); E. M. Jellinek, *The Disease Concept of Alcoholism* (Highland Park, N.J., 1960); Cooperative Commission on the Study of Alcoholism, *Alcohol Problems: A Report to the Nation*, ed. Thomas F. A. Plaut (New York, 1967); Yale University Center of Alcohol Studies, *Alcohol, Science, and Society: Twenty-nine Lectures with Discussions as Given at the Yale Summer School of Alcohol Studies* (New Haven, 1945); Paul C. Conley and Andrew A. Sorenson, *The Staggering Steeple: The Story of Alcoholism and the Churches* (Philadelphia, 1971); David J. Armor, J. Michael Polich, and Harriet B. Stambul, *Alcoholism and Treatment* [Rand Report] (Santa Monica, 1976); Don Cahalan, Ira Cisin, and Helen Crossley, *American Drinking Practices: A National Study of Drinking Behavior and Attitudes* (New Brunswick, 1969); Merton M. Hyman, Marilyn A. Zimmermann, Carol Gurioli, and Alice Helrich, *Drinkers, Drinking, and Alcohol-Related Mortality and Hospitalizations: A Statistical Compendium* (New Brunswick, 1980); Carolyn L. Wiener, *The Politics of Alcoholism: Building an Arena Around a Social Problem* (New Brunswick, 1981); Henry Saffer and Michael Grossman, *Beer Taxes, the Legal Drinking Age, and Youth Motor Fatalities*. National Bureau of Economic Research Working Paper Series, No. 1914 (Cambridge, Mass., 1986). Dan E. Beauchamp, *Beyond Alcoholism: Alcohol and Public Health Policy* (Philadelphia, 1980).

Articles: Virgil W. Peterson, "Vitalizing Liquor Control," *Journal of Criminal Law and Criminology XL* (1949):119–34; Gail Gleason Milgram, "A Historical Review of Alcohol Education: Research and Comments," *Journal of Alcohol and Drug Education XXI* (1976):1–16; Jay L. Rubin, "The Wet War: American Liquor Control, 1941–1945," in Jack S. Blocker, Jr., ed., *Alcohol, Reform, and Society: The Liquor Issue in Social Context* (Westport, Conn., 1979), pp.235–58; Marvin A. Block, "The Progress of Community Action against Alcoholism in the United States of America," *International Journal on Alcohol and Alcoholism II* (1957):1–16; Mark Edward Lender, "Jellinek's Typology of Alcoholism: Some Historical Antecedents," *Journal of Studies on Alcohol XL* (1979):361–75; Mark Keller, "Mark Keller's History of the Alcohol Problems Field," *Drinking and Drug Practices Surveyor XIV* (1979):1–28; Jay L. Rubin, "Shifting Perspectives on the Alcoholism Treatment Movement, 1940–1955," *Journal of Studies on Alcohol XL* (1979):376–86; Seldon D. Bacon, "The Classic Temperance Movement of the U.S.A.: Impact Today on Attitudes, Action, and Research," *British Journal of Addiction LXII* (1967):5–18; Don Cahalan, "Why Does the Alcoholism Field Act Like a Ship of Fools?" *British Journal of Addiction LXXIV* (1974):235–38; Harvey McConnell, "The Back Page," *Journal* (Toronto) *VIII* (1979):16; Stanton Peele, "The New Prohibitionists," *The Sciences* XXIV (1984):14–19.

Periodicals: *Union Signal; American Issue; New York Times; Wall Street Journal; Time* Magazine; *Quarterly Journal of Studies on Alcohol; Journal* (Toronto); *Clipsheet; Grapevine.*

Documents: *Driver v. Hinnant*, 356 F.2d 761 (4th Cir. 1966); *Easter v. District of Columbia*, 361 F.2d 50 (D.C. Cir. 1966); *Powell v. Texas*, 392 U.S. 514 (1968); National Conference of Commissioners on Uniform State Laws, "Uniform Alcoholism and

Intoxication Treatment Act," U.S. Congress, Senate, Committee on Labor and Public Welfare, Subcommittee on Alcoholism and Narcotics, 92d Cong., 1st sess. (1971); U.S. Congress, Senate, Committee on Labor and Public Welfare, "Comprehensive Alcohol Abuse and Alcoholism Prevention, Treatment, and Rehabilitation Act," 91st Cong., 2d sess. (1970); Historical Files, "Alcoholism" (unnumbered), "Advertising and Propaganda," "Attitudes," Rutgers Center of Alcohol Studies Library, Rutgers University; U.S. National Institute on Alcohol Abuse and Alcoholism, *Alcohol and Health: New Knowledge. Second Special Report to the Congress* (Washington, D.C., 1975); U.S. National Institute on Alcohol Abuse and Alcoholism, *Third Special Report to the U.S. Congress on Alcohol and Health,* ed. Ernest P. Noble (Washington, D.C., 1978).

Index